WORLD CUP

RUGBY'S BATTLE OF THE GIANTS

WORLD CUP

RUGBY'S BATTLE OF THE GIANTS

GERALD DAVIES

In memory of my parents, Tudor and Mary

– GERALD DAVIES –

Edited by Phil McNeill

Designed by Robert Kelland

With thanks to
Eve Cossins, Mark Crossland, Joseph Crowe, Lyn Evans, Pauline Evans, Ailsa Jensen, Mike Richards, Ray Setterfield, Catherine McNeill, Deanne Pearson, John Scott, Ken Vaughan, and to Chris Dighton at Hayters for the statistics

Special thanks to Paul Ackford, Rob Andrew, Serge Blanco, Jonathan Davies, Colin Deans, John Gallagher, Simon Geoghegan, Pat Lam, Michael Lynagh, Gareth Rees, Philippe Saint-André and Joel Stransky

Published by David Crowe and Mark Peacock

First published in Great Britain in 1999 by Generation Publications
11-12 Tottenham Mews, London W1P 9PJ

generationgroup@btconnect.com

A catalogue record for this title is available from the British Library

ISBN 1 903009 12X

Production by Mike Powell & Associates (01494 676891)
Origination by Colour Systems Ltd, London
Printed and bound in Italy by Giunti Industrie Grafiche

All photographs by Allsport, with thanks to Justin Davies and Neil Loft

Page 2: David Campese of Australia, the biggest star of the 1991 World Cup

Page 3: Nemesis in the shape of All Black Jonah Lomu for Tony Clement of Wales

Above: The unmistakable kicking boot of Neil Jenkins of Wales

CONTENTS

FOREWORD

DAVIES THE PEN TAKES WING

JPR Williams and TGR Davies go back a long way, having first played together for Wales in 1969. Their record-breaking careers ended before the Rugby World Cup began – but, as JPR observes, that has given Gerald the chance to watch it all at close quarters

Thomas Gerald Reames Davies was the epitome of what the Welsh admired in a rugby player – flair! Whenever he had the ball in his hand there was an air of expectation. He played a lot of his rugby as a centre threequarter, but it was as a wing threequarter that he became world-famous.

He is a small man in stature, but was a brilliant rugby player. I can vouch for this, having played alongside him on many occasions for the famous Welsh side in the Seventies, and the successful British Lions tour to New Zealand in 1971.

He was brought up in the Carmarthenshire village of Llansaint, where he went to school. He then went on to Queen Elizabeth Grammar School, Carmarthen, Loughborough and Cambridge University.

He first came to national prominence playing for Loughborough college in the Middlesex Sevens. I first played against him for Bridgend against Cardiff at the beginning of my career in the late Sixties. At this time he was playing in the centre.

Gerald attained a teaching position at Christ's Hospital, Sussex and at this time joined the London Welsh club, who were on the crest of a wave, eventually supplying seven players to the 1971 British Lions tour to New Zealand.

I never saw Gerald die with the ball. He either scored a try or got the ball back inside to myself or another supporting player. It was on the 1969 Welsh tour to New Zealand that Gerald was converted from a centre into a wing by the coach Clive Rowlands. He scored many tries for Cardiff, Loughborough, London Welsh, Wales and the

British Lions. I remember his four tries against Hawke's Bay in New Zealand, the last of which resulted in the opposing full back and wing colliding as Gerald was putting the ball down between the posts! He also scored four tries for Cardiff against Pontypool, all of which were completely against the run of play. Pontypool dominated the game totally, but Gerald received the ball on four occasions and the result was four scintillating tries.

Gerald Davies played 46 matches for Wales and scored 20 tries

I shared a room at the Angel Hotel, Cardiff, for ten years with Gerald and formed a great friendship. I was the excitable one, whereas he was the calming influence.

Gerald is now a well-respected writer with *The Times*. He has covered every World Cup for the newspaper, and the fruits of his knowledge are here in this book. He will, of course, be remembered as an exciting and brilliant rugby player. But above all this, he is genuinely a really nice guy.

INTRODUCTION

RUGBY ENTERS THE FUTURE

In the space of three World Cup tournaments, the world of rugby has changed beyond recognition. For better or worse is a matter of debate, but one thing is certain: every player of the past would have loved the chance to take part in rugby's supreme challenge

BY GERALD DAVIES

In 1987 the world of rugby changed. From that moment on, men of a certain age, nodding dreamily by the fire or holding forth with a pint of smooth bitter beer in hand at the club bar, could assert without fear of contradiction that rugby was not what it used to be.

Such reminiscences could no longer be dismissed as nostalgic ramblings about a rosy-hued Corinthian past, its devil-may-care mood contrasting with what they saw as an increasingly humourless present. Whether the past was quite as full of high spirits as they recalled it did not matter – the advent of the Rugby World Cup made change a matter of irrevocable fact. The month of May 1987 was a watershed. From then on, rugby authorities would have to reconsider their conceptions of the sport and the entire future of the game.

On the afternoon of Friday May 22 at Eden Park in Auckland, New Zealand, the inaugural World Cup was launched to the portentous kettledrum start of Richard Strauss's sunrise from *Thus Sprach Zarathustra* and Holst's *Planets*, climaxing with the thundering theme of machismo from the Hollywood movie *Rambo*. A new dawn was breaking for rugby union which would, in a short time, thrust the game from the familiar backyard of the eight countries of the International Rugby Board into the stratosphere. Nations unknown to us hitherto were brought officially within rugby's orbit.

This all came as a result of one of those routine meetings held annually by the International Rugby Football Board to discuss and pronounce upon changes to the labyrinthine laws of the game and fixtures for overseas tours. In 1985, there had been something significantly more. At its meeting in Paris the IRFB made the startling announcement of a Rugby World Cup. This was startling because if they had contemplated such an idea in the past, they had refrained from committing themselves to anything remotely like a formal competition of any kind.

Indeed, to begin with the IRFB refrained from calling it the World Cup. It was rather 'The International Rugby Football Board competition for the Webb Ellis Cup'. There was a discreet reticence to go any further. This was true to

The most famous moment in the brief history of the Rugby World Cup, as South Africa's President Nelson Mandela presents the Webb Ellis trophy to South Africa's captain François Pienaar in 1995

form. To put this surprising announcement in its context, the home unions of England, Ireland, Scotland and Wales had refused for many years to recognise that the Five Nations Championship existed. What had evolved into the most cherished midwinter festival of rugby played between the five European countries was, in the administrators' eyes, merely a series of independent and unrelated games.

That there should be a league table positioning the separate nations in order of superiority depending on their wins and losses, with points awarded accordingly; that there should be a declared Champion; a Triple Crown winner or a team which accomplished a Grand Slam of victories; and that someone should be the dismayed possessor of a Wooden Spoon – all this was, according to the official line, nothing more than a gimmick dreamed up by the base opportunism of newspapers and the rest of the unscrupulous media.

Of course, this did not stop a union, when the time came, from celebrating a triumph. They just did not wish to acknowledge its formal existence, because it was not deemed appropriate to the amateur spirit of rugby union, and not at all conducive to the survival of amateurism. Rugby union was to be played for fun, in a gentlemanly spirit. A proper tournament, blessed by the authorities, smacked of professionalism.

In this they would be proved to be quite right, of course. In another meeting ten years later, again in Paris – a city famed for its revolutionary zeal – the game of rugby union football, after a century of amateurism, would be declared "open". Persistently assaulted on many flanks, not least by outsiders who wanted to hijack the game – rich moguls with television interests were threatening to contract players on professional terms – the administrators of the International Rugby Board, as it had now been modified, could no longer defend the crumbling barricades of cherished amateurism.

So that after the third World Cup in South Africa in 1995, the game was up. Players henceforth could expect to be compensated for their efforts, not with a jug of beer, gratefully received, but with a well-renumerated sponsorship contract from the beer-makers themselves. They could now be paid to drink their brew. Rugby players, like any other sportsman, could make their livelihood out of their favourite pastime.

It is true, in any case, that rugby would have felt it necessary to jettison the amateur ethos in time, and to abandon a way of life which had served so well to sustain the game over the generations. Sport, aided and abetted by television, had already been transformed into a commercial enterpise. Amateurism in rugby union was a lovable old relic that had seen better days, and the Rugby World Cup simply hastened its end.

But in losing part of its culture, rugby would gain another. Every four years, the world's best rugby nations would gather together to compete in a clash of the titans for the title of World Champion.

Hitherto, we could only speculate as to which was the best rugby team in the world. No nation played all the others, or even a portion of them, in any one period of twelve months. Who deserved the accolade was a matter of animated debate. One man's point of view was as valid as another. It could not be settled.

From now on, in six games played over a span of five weeks, the point would be determined for us. The best team would come out on top. Of course, this would not necessarily stop the debate…

In 1987, the World Cup was new. We looked forward to the jamboree not only with fascination but also, dare I say, with trepidation, too. We were exhilarated by the prospects and yet we feared that rugby union might lose its roguish camaraderie and its Corinthian mood. We longed to believe that, despite the inevitable intrusion of commercial imperatives and the fiercely combative nature of the game which the tournament would reinforce, rugby was not about to lose the sunshine in its soul.

In the event, the 1987 tournament established itself immediately as a great success. The four-year cycle became the fervent focus of every nation's attention. Thankfully, for all the changes that have been wrought in the intervening years, we eagerly look forward to the fourth in the series – for, as the Millennium beckons, rugby union still has the talent to amuse.

But how do we feel – those of us, that is, who look back with nostalgia to our own playing days, before the

World Cup began? There is a lot of joy in the memories; many a tall tale to be embellished, many a friendship to cherish. It was a good time to be a part of rugby.

But I would guess that each player of a certain vintage, if asked, would have wished to have the good fortune of playing in the World Cup. To reach the Final of the tournament would have to be thought of as the ultimate challenge; every nerve and sinew put to the test in a single game. On a tour – whether with the Lions, the Springboks, the Wallabies or the All Blacks – there is a series of international matches. There is always tomorrow; another bite of the cherry. This does not diminish the toughness of the games, but the reassuring fact is that after the first Test there is another. There is time to make amends, for wrongs to be righted, or for a triumph to be disputed. Few players get to return to a second World Cup Final. To win must be the sweetest and keenest of treasures.

Each sportsman needs to pit his wits against the best his day has to offer. Each competitor, however much he may yearn for peace and solitude in a distant dressing room when the heat of combat is about to begin and that strange nervous fatigue engulfs him, knows that he needs to be where he is. He has to be there. He needs the chance to prove how good he is; or to find out amid the turmoil where in the rankings he truly rests. He will not lie easily until he does.

The World Cup is such a testing arena; the final rugby frontier which is inescapable and has to be pursued. There is no turning back. I would like to have had a go.

Neil Jenkins of Wales kicks a penalty against world champions South Africa at the Millennium Stadium, built on the site of Cardiff Arms Park, where the 1999 World Cup Final will take place

1987

THE WEBB ELLIS TROPHY

In New Zealand and Australia

THE SOUTHERN HEMISPHERE TEAMS HAD BEEN THE DRIVING FORCE BEHIND THE DECISION TO STAGE A WORLD CUP – AND NOW IT WAS BEING PLAYED ON THEIR HOME TURF, THEY RATHER FANCIED THEIR CHANCES OF WINNING IT...

Right: Australia find a place in the sun against England

STARTING A DUST-UP DOWN UNDER

The first Rugby World Cup seemed to take even its participants by surprise. A World Cup? Wasn't that the kind of thing that went on in professional sports? But by the time the tournament ended, all of rugby knew the only way was up...

"Japan and Fiji are world champions for their style, but that is not winning rugby. New Zealand and Australia are those who win games. Their pressure game is so well organised that they fool the opposition into making mistakes. It is not New Zealand and Australia who win the games, it is the opposition who lose them."

FRANCE COACH JACQUES FOUROUX

Modesty of ambition was still the key to rugby in 1987, World Cup or no World Cup. There was uncertainty, too. This was only be to be expected. After all, this was uncharted territory upon which rugby was suspiciously embarking. With the exception of France, who had proposed such a tournament a couple of decades earlier, the four Home Unions seemed staid and reluctant about the idea. The southern hemisphere, bullish about initiating the Cup, nevertheless remained guarded. The competition was split across the Tasman Sea, the responsibility to be shared between Australia and New Zealand.

The opening ceremony took place in New Zealand, where three of the four pools were played and where three of the home unions were resident for the period of their group matches. England in Pool 1 were away from it all in Australia. For if there was an unassuming, discreet quality about the Rugby World Cup in Auckland, then the tournament was almost unnoticed in Sydney and Brisbane.

There was, I remember, hardly anything to celebrate or even to announce in Queen Street, the main thoroughfare of New Zealand's capital city, that the inaugural World Cup was about to lift off. Taking a taxi to downtown Auckland, the driver was simply looking forward to the live broadcast at 1 am of the FA Cup Final between Tottenham Hotspur and Coventry from Wembley. There was certainly no fever of anticipation. The most eye-catching piece of bunting across the main street advertised a forthcoming Gilbert and Sullivan's *Mikado*.

The late Lew Pryme, then executive director of Auckland RFU, who was asked to mastermind the opening ceremony at Eden Park, concluded that "the World Cup is in people's minds but it is not in the streets". He had been given three weeks to prepare the ceremony which, clearly, was not expected to outshine the tinsel-town

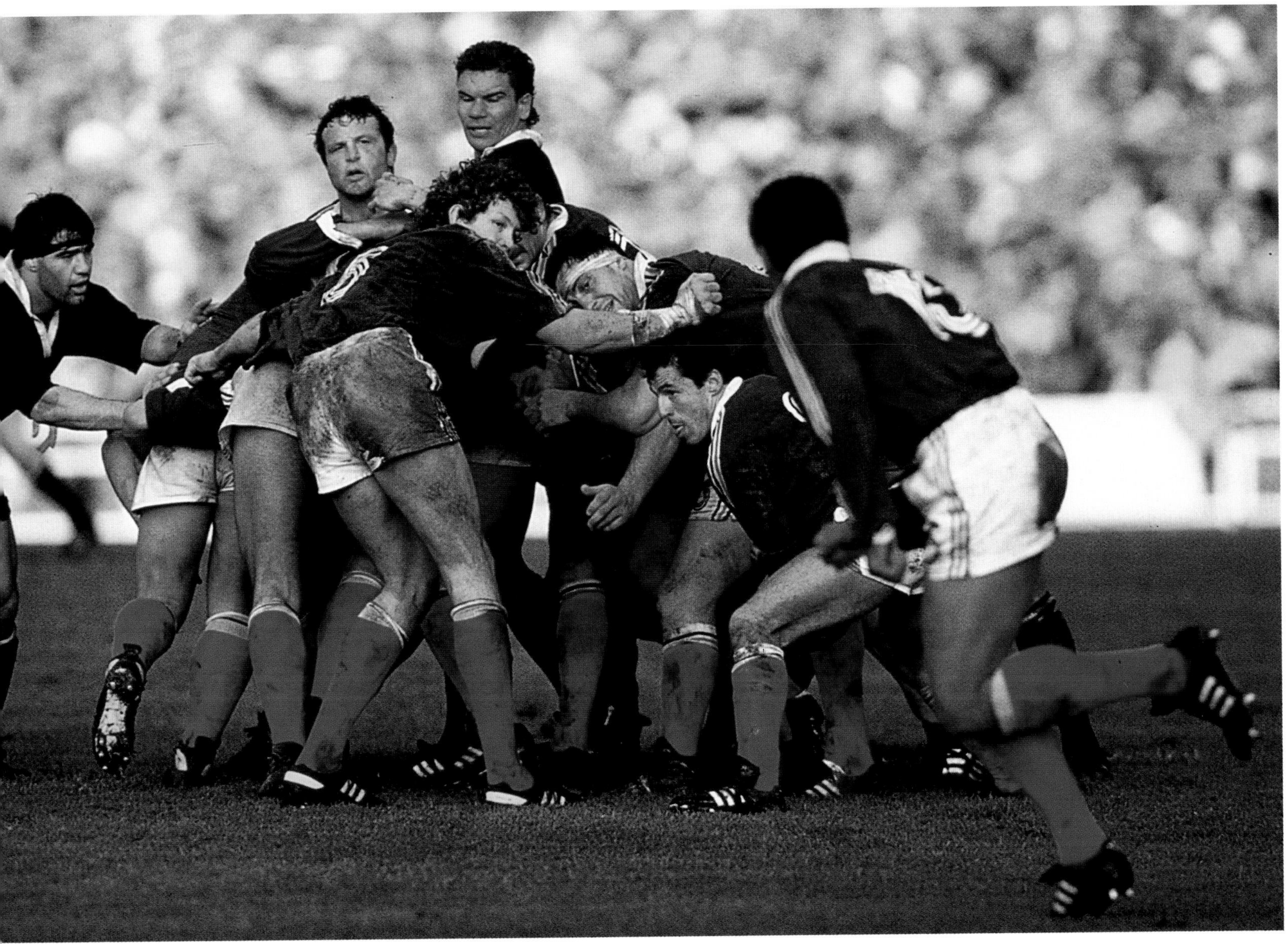

extravaganza of the Los Angeles Olympics three years earlier. It was a humble beginning – which was no bad thing for a fledgling tournament. Expectations were finger-crossing-hopeful rather than high, and any hint of razzmatazz would have been inappropriate.

There was hardly a sponsor in sight. It was a beer-and-sandwiches sort of event of surprising innocence; a rugby club fête, a roll-up-your-sleeves, muck-in, we're-all-part-of-this-together kind of event. Refreshingly, it was free of humbug and conceit.

Decades of festering iniquity caused by South Africa's apartheid policy ensured that the republic had not been invited to the party. This meant, in some minds, that the eventual winner would regret that the Springboks could not be present. Without South Africa, no country could legitimately claim to be the world champions, the

France's Pierre Berbizier feeds out from a scrum during the World Cup Final against New Zealand. Opposite: Japan get a rare feel of the ball in their 60-7 defeat by England

"A few days before the World Cup was due to start, a military coup took place in Fiji. Russ Thomas, chairman of the New Zealand Rugby Union, assured everyone that the Fijian team would still turn up for the tournament, but, regrettably, a little later than planned. The coup was led by Colonel Rambuko, a former Fijian player who had toured Britain. After Western Samoa were advised to stand by, Fiji hastily made a point of turning up, whatever the upheavals at home. Such is south Pacific rivalry. Having arrived, they were later to make a flamboyant mark on the competition. Eventually, everything was in place for the tournament to begin."

argument ran. (Their absence from the international rugby arena, however, had emasculated their potency, as was demonstrated when, after the dismantling of apartheid, they emerged in 1992 to embark on a series of international fixtures. They then realised that the world had moved on and new standards had been set.)

It is doubtful whether the Springboks would have lasted the course in 1987. They had won a series against England in 1984 but the English were seriously under-strength. Eighteen were unable to travel because of injuries or unavailability. In addition, for what it was worth, the rebel tour by the New Zealand Cavaliers in 1986 also lost a series. But only South Africa, with their infinite capacity for self-praise, would have imbued these games with anything other than hapless gestures by the visitors to keep the republic within the rugby community. Any rugby contact was better than nothing.

Nevertheless, the contest for the World Cup was incomplete without South Africa. They left an obvious gap. The tournament, however, was not free of politics.

A few days before the start, a military coup took place in Fiji. Russ Thomas, chairman of the New Zealand Rugby Union, assured everyone that the Fijian team would still turn up for the tournament but, regrettably, a little later than planned. The coup was led by Colonel Rambuko, a former Fijian player who had toured Britain in 1970. After Western Samoa were advised to stand by, Fiji hastily made a point of turning up, whatever the upheavals at home. Such is south Pacific rivalry. They were later to make a flamboyant mark on the competition.

Eventually, everything was in place for the tournament to begin. In tune with rugby's tradition of wining and dining, a banquet was held in Auckland to welcome the 12 teams who would play in New Zealand. There was another in Brisbane for the four teams in Australia.

On Eden Park, thin rain fell through the faint and reluctant sun as schoolgirl go-go dancers strutted their stuff and young gymnasts twirled. Then came the entrance of Waka Nathan, the legendary Maori player of the Sixties, who ran a lap of honour round the field before delivering the match ball.

England's John Kendall-Carpenter, chairman of the Rugby World Cup committee, opened the first tournament for the first William Webb Ellis Cup.

Some felt there were several weaknesses that day. The organisers had erred in choosing Friday for the opening ceremony. It is a working day. No matches had ever been played on a Friday. In addition, the fact that the fixture was between New Zealand and Italy hardly seemed a worthy enough event to seek a doctor's paper for a day off work. Thus the ground, with 46,000 capacity, was only half full.

But the organisers had other well-intentioned considerations to take into account. They were those of the benign amateur, born of a voluntary ethos. The first game was meant to reflect what the World Cup was partly to represent and to which, in years to come, it might aspire. It was a symbol of rugby's future. New Zealand, one of the eight founder-members of the International Rugby Football Board, the game's governing body, were playing Italy, who hitherto had no seat at rugby's high table, and who might be seen as representing the new order. Competing for the Webb Ellis Cup gave rugby the chance to embrace the wider world.

For the moment, Italy knew their place well enough. They were not about to join the hierarchy just yet. In the first match of the new tournament, they held their mighty opponents to 17-6 before the interval. But by the game's end New Zealand, captained by David Kirk in the absence through a hamstring injury of Andy Dalton, had gone on to establish a record international score. They were to accumulate another 53 points in the second half without further reply from Italy.

Not only had the All Blacks established a benchmark for other teams to follow, but John Kirwan, their tall, powerfully-built right wing, had scored a magnificent solo try to set a standard for individual players to emulate. This try also gave a hint of what riches might lie ahead over the next month.

The movement began straight from the kick-off after the first New Zealand score. Kirk passed to Grant Fox and the outside half handed the ball to the right wing very near his own line. With his aggressive, high knee-lift action and pumping arms, Kirwan began his run. Stepping this way and that, slipping a tackle or two, feinting to pass and then holding on, he left half a dozen players sprawled in his wake. He just kept on going until, presumably to his immense surprise, he emerged from a throng of defending players and found himself in the clear field. A truly magnificent try.

In another respect, too, this could be seen as a pleasing start for the All Blacks. Their previous outings, prior to the World Cup, would have left them shamefaced and flawed. In August and September 1986, under the captaincy of David Kirk, they had lost the Bledisloe Cup in a three-match series at home against Australia. Subsequently, in the winter of the same year, after winning the first Test, they lost the second and final Test against France in a brutal match in Nantes under the captaincy of Jock Hobbs. By their standards, these were unsatisfactory results and reflected, or were the legacy of, the unhappy times suffered by the rugby fraternity in New Zealand. In April 1986, a rebel team, the New Zealand Cavaliers, against widespread public disapproval and government censure, had departed like a thief in the night for racist South Africa. The move had splintered New Zealand even more than the South African tour there in 1981.

John Kirwan, scorer of a magnificent solo try against Italy in the opening match

'My selection for last year's tour of France came as a bit of a surprise. I was the dark horse then. This year I feel the pressure even more. The full back position was one of the very few up for grabs in the trial so I could not afford to play badly.'

JOHN GALLAGHER
before the All Blacks' opening 70-6 victory against Italy

Rugby, which normally acts as a unifying force in New Zealand, had deeply divided the nation on this occasion. Without exaggeration, family was set against family, sons against fathers. Friends since schooldays became foes overnight. There was hatred in the air which left many scars.

This strong sense of disgust may have found expression in the low turn-out of spectators to see the opening game. They wanted to make a point. But with this victory, against however modest opposition, and the recognition of the game's thrills personified in Kirwan's great 80-metre run, the old loyalties began to stir afresh.

David Kirk's smile, his youthfulness, his enthusiasm, his clean-cut figure, his vulnerability was not of NZ's traditional muscular and taciturn mould. Where he would boldly go, others would surely wish to follow. Let us say, he went a long way to melt the hard hearts. In him, New Zealand found a figure they would forgive for past misconduct. As the days passed and Andy Dalton, still the nominated captain, failed to recover from his injury, Kirk became the very acceptable face of All Black rugby; a public relations man's dream.

"The World Cup has had a tremendous effect. It is the most exciting thing to happen since I entered the game. The television exposure will be good and if we could make the quarter-finals the interest would be tremendous."
USA COACH RON MAYES (a New Zealander), on the eve of the Americans' 21-18 victory against Japan

The Australian forwards out-jump their English rivals during their 19-6 win in the opening fixture

If the beginning had been somewhat low key, in terms of imbalance between the opening-day combatants, the fixtures from Saturday through to Monday belonged to traditional adversaries; duels which seemed to stem from time immemorial. They brought with them a vast baggage of old scores. Australia and England were opening Pool 1 at the Concord Oval and not at the Sydney Cricket Ground where internationals had been played in the past. Wrangling over financial issues such as sponsorship and the division of the gate money had forced the Australian Rugby Union to build their own ground in Sydney's suburbs. There were no such problems the other side of the Tasman Sea. France would play Scotland in Christchurch on the same day while, come Monday in Wellington, Ireland would face Wales. Yet, the Sunday in between reflected the ambitions the rugby World Cup had for the game: USA against Japan, Fiji against Argentina and Canada against Tonga. This was the embodiment of what was referred to as "the brotherhood of rugby".

Strangely, the fact that there was a World Cup match in

Sydney scarcely touched the Australian imagination, despite a widespread belief within the game that their team were possible finalist contenders. Such potential glory should have aroused keen interest in a nation which basks lovingly in sporting success. But at that stage the tournament was largely ignored.

In Alan Jones, their coach, Australia had the most flamboyant promoter of rugby; rugby as show-business. As if prompted by a director's commands of *Sound! Lights! Action!*, Alan Jones would put on a performance for his audience, captivating the media with a string of graphic images.

"One day you're a cockerel," he said, about winning and losing, "next day you're a feather-duster." Another of his sayings, relating to his aspirations for the team, was: "It's the Gucci Factor: long after you've paid the price, the style remains." Or, as he was to say of a particularly stilted game by his side: "We've been reading from the music sheet for a while. It's time we threw it away." All this made marvellous newspaper copy and led Mick Doyle, the Irish coach, to remark: "In all my rugby life I've not heard anybody talk such a good game."

"In Alan Jones, their coach, Australia had the most flamboyant promoter of rugby; rugby as showbusiness. 'One day you're a cockerel,' he said, about winning and losing, 'next day you're a feather duster'. Another of his sayings, relating to his aspirations for the team, was: 'It's the Gucci Factor: long after you've paid the price, the style remains.' Or, as he was to say after a particularly stilted game by his side: 'We've been reading from the music sheet for a while. It's time we threw it away.' All this made marvellous newspaper copy and led Mick Doyle, the Irish coach, to remark: 'In all my rugby life I've not heard anybody talk such a good game'."

If anyone could persuade the Australian public that there was something worthy in rugby union which should draw them away from rugby league, Australian Rules and the rest, then it was Jones. He had inspired his team to win the grand slam of victories in Britain and Ireland in 1984 and a successful Bledisloe Cup series in New Zealand during 1986, a year in which they also beat France in Sydney. He had a record of 16 wins in 20 matches, with four defeats against New Zealand.

He was in fine fettle as the tournament began. So was his team. They were certainly favourites to beat England. They duly did so but, controversially, not without the help of the referee, Keith Lawrence from New Zealand. He misjudged a moment and clearly unsettled an England team which had, in an enterprising, attacking fashion, played far better than expected and had created many scoring chances. The incident occurred 11 minutes into the second half, immediately after a scintillating try by Harrison had drawn the match level against Michael Lynagh's two first-half penalties.

Rory Underwood had a terrific match on the wing. Australia had no one to match his sprinter's pace. But for some desperate tackling by the Wallabies, Underwood would have been on the scoresheet. Mike Harrison, the captain, had his moments, too. Indeed, both England wings could have scored tries in the first 20 minutes but were brought down short of the line, as were Peter Winterbottom, the pack leader, and Kevin Simms in the centre.

The two wingers were prominent in England's try; the one inspiring the move, the other crowning it. Underwood ran daringly out of defence, linking up with Simms and Jamie Salmon, who sent a long pass to Jon Webb. He put Harrison away to score. This indicated England's true potential to play with élan which, sadly, they were rarely to fulfil. They just needed the courage, it was felt, to cast aside their rigid adherence to conformity.

The score, with Webb's wonderful conversion, stood at 6-6. Webb had come on as replacement to win his first cap after Marcus Rose was taken off concussed on a stretcher. Then Keith Lawrence's error occurred.

The England forwards, among whom Dean Richards was magnificent, were enjoying a powerful afternoon against probably the tallest pack they had ever come against. Four of them – Campbell, Cutler (both locks), Coker (No 8 but usually a lock) and Tuynman (wing

'There is too much desire in the Mon Désir.'

FRANCE MANAGER YVES NOE
after moving his players from Auckland's Mon Désir Hotel because the piano bar was full of attractive young women

forward) – were over 6ft 5ins. This was at a time when England were without John Hall, the wing forward, and Steve Bainbridge, their lock, both on the sidelines injured.

England had the ball, only for Salmon's pass to Simms to go astray on their own 22-metre line. Campese kicked on the loose ball. In attempting to pick up the ball near England's line the winger knocked it forward as Peter Williams, the English outside half, put in a tremendous tackle. While Campese looked forlorn, thinking the chance had gone, the referee awarded the score. England never properly recovered from this and soon after, Simon Poidevin scored another try. Lynagh kicked another penalty to add to his conversion, making the final score 19-6.

England were to suffer in another way from the referee's whistle. The penalty count went against them by 18 to 6, which is a substantial discrepancy. There was misfortune for England. Because international regulations stipulate that a concussed player cannot play for three weeks, Marcus Rose was ruled out from any further participation in the tournament. He was sent home along with John Hall, who had to have treatment for a knee injury. The team having played so well against Australia, Michael Weston, the manager, and Martin Green, the coach, would wonder why it went so awry for them later.

"It was my fault. I shouted at the referee to find out what was happening, but didn't hear the whistle. We are bitterly disappointed, because that is the second soft try we have given the French in matches against them this year. From a lead of 16-6 we should have won the game."

SCOTLAND CAPTAIN COLIN DEANS after Serge Blanco's match-saving try for France

France flanker Dominique Erbani shows his scrum half skills during the thrilling 20-20 draw with Scotland

"The opportunity was there for us to do it, and we failed. But France are such an aggressive side, and they never stopped working."

SCOTLAND SCRUM HALF ROY LAIDLAW

There was pleasure in knowing that England could more than match a team from the southern hemisphere whose players had a collective reputation, in the imaginations of Europeans, reaching the realms of fearsome but self-defeating hyperbole.

If there was satisfaction in this, there was admiration in the heroic struggle of the France versus Scotland match

Sensational starter with a surprise ending

1987 GROUP MATCH IN CHRISTCHURCH • SCOTLAND v FRANCE

Scotland captain Colin Deans was expecting fireworks in the first match against Grand Slam champions France. But no one could have predicted the twists and turns of a game that began the World Cup with a bang

BY COLIN DEANS

The 1987 inaugural World Cup was an exciting yet daunting prospect – the first competition of its kind and no one had any experience of playing three internationals in 10 days. Scotland's preparation could not have been better. We had played five internationals that season, won three and lost two.

The most memorable loss was the defeat by France in Paris, a 28-22 spectacular, which was to set the scene for our first game in the 87 World Cup: that memorable day in Paris we clawed back from 22-7 down at half-time to push the French to the final whistle and narrowly lose the game.

Although downhearted in the dressing room, we all knew we were good enough to beat the French, especially on a neutral ground in New Zealand.

But the preparation for our 1987 encounter against the French was not as we would have planned. The journey from Edinburgh to Auckland via Gatwick, Los Angeles and Honolulu took about 40 hours because runway fog at Auckland caused us to be diverted to Christchurch .

After a day in Auckland training, we had to attend the official World Cup dinner, which was a boring affair for the "alakadues". We were presented with our World Cup caps, which were a terrible colour purple but nevertheless, something to cherish for years to come. The next day saw us travel down to Christchurch where our first game was being played. Imagine our astonishment when our opponents – France – arrived for the same flight.

"Iain Milne and I were surprised to have the pleasure of Jean-Pierre Garuet as company for the flight to Christchurch. As is usual in front row confrontations, little was said but a few grunts..."

We were fortunate to have been at the airport first, so most of us were sitting together, but there were exceptions, namely myself and Iain Milne. We had the pleasure of Jean-Pierre Garuet's company for the flight. As is usual in front-row confrontations, very little was said but a few grunts. It made it a very difficult flight for both parties.

The preparation for the game went as well as we could expect. In trying to find some privacy, we even trained in the grounds of a prison! The day of the game arrived and we all felt that this was the most important date so far in Scottish rugby history. The feeling in the camp was that if we beat France in Chistchurch we had a chance of going all the way.

There was a meeting in Derrick Grant's room to have a last-minute discussion. A light lunch of omelette, chips and the then traditional Mars bar. There were telegrams of good wishes from various bodies, including the Scottish Sports Council.

Arriving at the ground we found it in absolutely perfect condition – like a bowling green. The local province, Canterbury, had been having a great run in the Ranfurly Shield and had ploughed their gate-money into a £90,000 drainage system. The sun was shining and as we changed in the dressing room we could hear a pipe band playing on the pitch. To hear the pipes so far from home really did bring a lump to our throats.

I went out to toss a coin with Daniel Dubroca to decide the direction we would play. There was a roar of delight when I came back to tell the boys I'd won the toss and had elected to play with the very low sun at our back. Even before a ball was kicked I felt we would do well. There was a tremendous atmosphere among the team.

It was only minutes before we had four points on the board, but to tell the truth, I'm still puzzled about the way it came about. There was a lineout inside the French half. As I went to throw in I saw we only had two men in the line. Now I'm the only one who can decide when a shortened lineout is required and I hadn't asked for that. No one has admitted calling for it on the Scottish side so it may well have been that a Frenchman called and in the noise the boys took up their position for the two-man line.

I threw a long one over the tail and Finlay Calder, who had already been in action with a great run, caught the ball, ripped through the French defence and sent out a perfect scoring pass to Derek White. Unfortunately, Gavin Hastings missed the conversion, although we didn't know then how vital an extra couple of points would have been.

Just after this we had a disaster. John Rutherford, who seemed to have completely recovered from a knee injury he had picked up in a no-account game in Bermuda, had to compete for a high ball from the lineout and in a crushing tackle Sella put him down. That ended John's appearance in the World Cup and after being stretchered off, he was soon on his way home to Scotland. Fortunately, an exploratory operation revealed that the damage wasn't as bad as first feared. It was a blow. But full marks to Doug Wylie, who moved to stand off, with Alan Tait of Kelso coming in for his first cap in Doug's place at centre. Alan is a strong, very gifted lad whom I thought might make the team anyway on sheer ability.

Serge Blanco took the Scots by surprise with his cheeky try, but Scotland battled back to finish a pulsating match at 20-20

We got over our shock at losing John and proceeded to take the game to the French again. Our scrummaging was first-class, mainly due to Iain 'The Bear' Milne, and we took three strikes against the head. In addition, those daily lineout sessions were paying dividends and we did well in that department.

But it was our tackling which really got to the opposition. We put down everything that moved, without any ceremony. The French were getting rattled, throwing punches in the front row of the scrum and in the rucks. But we took all that and it made us knit closer as a team. By half-time we led 13-6, with Gavin adding three penalty goals to the try, while the French had a couple of penalties.

An advertising break for the great god television meant that the half-time split was five minutes, double the normal time. My team talk to the boys was simple – keep playing this way and keep tackling. When play resumed, the desperate French threw everything at us and eventually from a two-man line in our territory, Berbizier gave to Champ, who in turn sent Sella over for an unconverted try.

"Hey, what's he up to?" Deans couldn't believe his eyes when Blanco scored

Then Berbizier himself touched down a similar score from a five-metre scrum. However, Gavin had landed another penalty so we led 16-14 with ten minutes to go.

Winger Matt Duncan had a nasty head gash, caused by a stray French boot, but stayed on. Then disaster struck again when Matt, following a typical bulldozing run, was judged to have failed to release the ball when tackled. It seemed to us that he had not really been held but had somersaulted out of the so-called tackle.

Berbizier had rolled off the field to get medical attention. Matt was suffering from his head and face injury and looking light-headed. Our physio, Dave McLean, was waiting to treat him and I shouted to the referee to allow Dave on, but evidently he didn't hear me. Then there was a chorus of shouts from our lads and I turned to see Blanco touching down between the posts. The ball had been lying handy for the penalty to be taken and he had taken advantage to tap it and run while all the medical aid was being administered. What you might call a controversial try.

When we lined up waiting for Blanco's successful conversion kick I had to ask the lads for yet more effort. But I thought: "God knows how they'll produce it. They've given their all."

So there we were with time running out and suddenly down by 20-16. With typical guts, the boys refused to give up. It was wee Roy Laidlaw with a deft kick who took play into the French 22. Then Roy fed White who put Matt in at the corner with a beautiful pass – a magical try.

Now it was all down to Gavin to win the game with his conversion kick. It was a difficult one, from the touchline, and with a ball that none of the kickers were happy about. He struck it well, only to see it go off target by about a foot. But he had played magnificently throughout and no one was going to blame him. The referee whistled no side with scores tied at 20-20.

In the dressing room there was joy and sadness. Joy particularly for Tait's first cap and sadness to hear that John was going home. At the official dinner, Dubroca, my opposite number and captain, made a nice gesture when he took off his own personal player's tie to give to John.

That evening I reflected on how proud I was of the team which had once again run the Five Nations champions off their feet in a pulsating match full of movement and drama. But I now felt certain that because of the tournament ruling regarding tries scored in a drawn match we were fated to meet the All Blacks in two weeks' time.

WELSH TACTICS THAT BLEW IRELAND AWAY

Wales coach Tony Gray on the 13-6 victory in windy Wellington

'There was a distinct improvement in the scrummaging, for which the team had been heavily criticised. We won a major share of the loose possession, too, from which the bigger players were able to make a lot of yardage with the ball. If there was any sense of disappointment, it was the way the players lost their legs, as it were, in the final 10 minutes. That had something to do with the amount of travelling we had done as well as the lack of match practice. It also had something to do with the wind. In wanting to take full advantage of the elements, there was a good deal of kicking for position from both sides. A lot of chasing had to be done in going after our own kicks ahead and to recover those which came from the opposition. In a lot of instances this was unproductive.'

"Hey lads, we'll have the wind in the second half." The Welsh pack savour the sweet smell of success

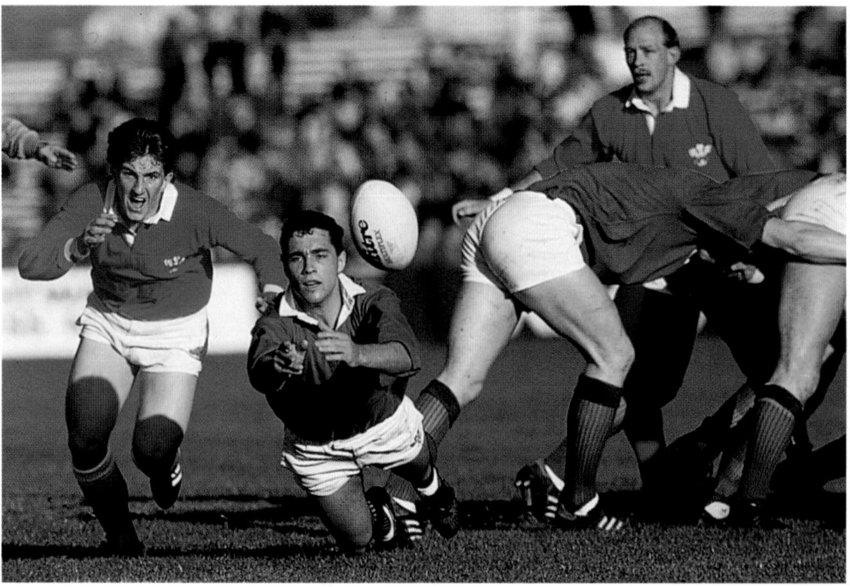

Ireland scrum half Michael Bradley evades his opposite number Robert Jones

which was played in Christchurch. There were disputes over tries at the heart of this match, too. Patrice Lagisquet felt he had scored but was turned down, while Serge Blanco was awarded a score when opinion suggests that perhaps he should not have been. Referee Fred Howard of England was contrary in both cases.

What did affect the play was the injury to John Rutherford who, soon after Derek White had put Scotland in the lead after two minutes, was taken off on a stretcher having damaged his knee cartilage and ligaments. This marvellous and influential outside half, with a fine nose for a break and an instinctive flair for rugby's movement, is of a kind that Scotland produce only in scarce numbers. He was not to play any further part in the tournament.

The match built to a frenzied climax. After holding the lead from the second minute, Scotland went 16-6 up at one stage, then 16-10 with a quarter of an hour left. Then Pierre Berbizier, the French scrum half, scored a try to close the gap to 16-14. And, in a controversial 79th minute incident, Scotland saw victory slip through their fingers. Matt Duncan, the Scottish right-wing, had a good run but he was tackled so hard that he needed treatment, as did Berbizier.

Colin Deans, Scotland's captain, was expecting a stoppage. The referee did not oblige and while Scotland hesitated and turned their backs, Blanco took a quick penalty and ran half the length of the field to score a try which he also converted. The score stood at 20-16.

Finally and dramatically, with only a minute left of injury time, Matt Duncan crossed the line for Scotland. Gavin Hastings' conversion from the touchline missed by a whisker to end a breathless encounter at 20 points each.

Of the three fixtures to include the International Board countries, Ireland and Wales proved the least inspiring. Ireland experienced a scare before a ball was kicked. Mick Doyle was rushed to hospital in Auckland with a suspected heart attack but, thankfully, medical tests cleared him.

Tranquil is not a word that belongs in Wellington's vocabulary when contemplating an international match. Think of Wellington, New Zealand's centre of government, and you think of wind. Plenty of it – and not just in the debating chamber! This Monday proved to be no exception. Inevitably, it emerged as one of those games of two halves.

Donal Lenihan won the toss for Ireland and chose to play with the wind at his back in the first half, which is precisely what Richard Moriarty, Wales' captain, would have wished had he been given the choice. This would give his side the time, Moriarty reasoned, to adjust to the pace of the game after the six-week lay-off since the Five Nations Championship. The wind could be used to better advantage after the interval.

Captain Mike Harrison scored three tries as England beat Japan 60-7

The loss of Phil Matthews did not help the Irish cause, so that after the first 40 minutes Ireland had only two penalties by Michael Kiernan to show for their efforts. Mark Ring scored Wales' solitary try, with Paul Thorburn kicking a penalty. But it was Jonathan Davies, making judicious use of the wind – low and measured in the first half, high and long in the second – who masterminded the victory. He dropped a couple of goals into the bargain. His was a mature game and this victory by 13-6 avenged the defeat in Cardiff in the Five Nations Championship in April.

The likelihood of becoming runners-up in Pool 2 meant that Ireland would face Australia in the quarter-finals. This failed to daunt Syd Millar, the Irish manager, who pointed out that Ireland had won the three previous games they had played in Australia: the first in 1967, and twice in 1979.

By this stage the International Board countries had played what might have been expected to be their toughest matches. They had played the games against each other

> "The high level of injuries could have the effect of devaluing the competition. So far 11 people have gone home. It could end up with two countries in the Final represented by players some of whom did nothing to help them get there."
>
> ENGLAND MANAGER MICHAEL WESTON already facing an injury crisis after the second round of pool matches

Rees's pieces

BY

GARETH REES

The only man to play in all four Rugby World Cups

People now take the Rugby World Cup for granted and we forget about all the uncertainties that were around when it first started, particularly for a team like Canada where there was no Five Nations or Bledisloe Cup. We didn't have any concept of what it would be like.

For me, the overriding memory of all the World Cups is the opening dinner, because you get all the greatest players in the world in one room. I think that in 1987 the teams who were playing in Australia weren't there, but Jonathan Davies was, and he was probably the best individual in the world.

Then seeing the opening game. For us Canadians it was a chance to watch a lot of rugby for the first time. That was almost as much fun, sitting in the hotel rooms and watching the games. In that first game New Zealand absolutely hammered Italy. John Kirwan was immense and scored that 80-yard solo try.

Our first game was against Tonga. We'd never even seen a video tape of them. We knew they were an island side and that's about it. I remember that Tonga's prop, who I think was one of their chiefs, wouldn't bind properly. His head wasn't interlocked with the other front row and he was standing up all the time. That kind of thing is unheard of now. We tackled like demons, which we've always been known for. We had a hard taskmaster for a coach and a lot of us had been injured in our training, so there was great relief for the guys who were fit and had been selected. We went out there and scored some great tries against Tonga, who really ran the ball.

I didn't start the game as kicker and I don't even remember my first kick in the World Cup. Such was the arrogance of youth that I just expected it to go over. I do remember that there was a lot of interest in my age: I had just turned 19. It was the first time I had had that sort of press attention.

Our coach, Gary Johnston, had banned drinking until after the match. This was a group of guys who had come up through club rugby in Canada, where rugby is a very social sport, so basically, we just lost our minds. That sort of thing doesn't go on these days.

"When the group table went up on the screen, we were leading the group above Wales and Ireland. It was the stuff of dreams"

Against Ireland we were 19-16 up with 15 minutes to go but ended up losing 19-46. We played brilliantly for 60 minutes, but the last 20 were a nightmare. The game in those days was much more static, which suited us well. But they had a great back line with guys like Hugo MacNeill and Tony Ward and they went a try up. That's where our inexperience told, because we tried to catch up playing too expansive a game for us and the floodgates opened.

That was frustrating, but for guys in Canada who had thought of the Five Nations as a different league, it was uncharted territory. I remember watching Ireland play Wales on TV the day after the Tonga game and it was abysmal rugby. That was the first time we got a sniff that maybe we could do something here. And because we had put so many points on Tonga, when the group table went up on screen, we were leading the group above Wales and Ireland. That was a wonderful feeling – it was the stuff of dreams.

I had no right to consider myself in the same league as Jonathan Davies, but that's what Canada has had throughout all the World Cups: we believe in ourselves. Jonathan was brilliant at the time; his pace was so pure. I was really fired up to play against him but he played really well and got the best of me. He captained Wales for the first time that day. We were 9-6 up at half-time, and we used a 10-man scrum as our attacking weapon. We had three pushovers that collapsed under their posts and the referee refused to give a penalty try because we had 10 men in the scrum and he felt we were destabilising it. Wales won 40-9 and that was the end of our World Cup.

I stayed on to see the Final and New Zealand were always going to win it. it was easy for the Northern Hemisphere sides to say: "Well, they wanted the first World Cup, they put it on and they won it." The next World Cup would show if that attitude was correct.

within the pool system and would from now on embark against those nations which it was hoped would emerge, in due course, as new challengers. Rugby union aspired to a more a global flavour; to move beyond what once had been the old colonies.

Fiji, who had surprised everyone in their defeat of Argentina, fell easy prey to New Zealand 74-13, thereby creating another high-scoring record. The Fijians were thought to have taken this match easy in order to be in better fettle to beat Italy, thereby ensuring they went through to the next round.

Against Argentina, Fiji had been full of enterprise and commitment, qualities which were absent in their game against the All Blacks. Thus with Italy ahead of them, Fiji felt that by holding back their energies they stood a better chance of progress into the quarter-finals. In the event they actually lost 18-15 to Italy, but went through because of their better try count.

There were big scores in other games, too. England notched up 60 points against Japan, as did Scotland against Zimbabwe. France would get close to these scores with 55 against Romania in another windy day at Wellington. It raised doubts as to whether the capital city is a suitable place to hold international matches.

Anxious not to be humiliatingly thrust from the World Cup before the cut for the quarter-final stage, Ireland, who had lost their first match, were desperate to salvage their reputation against Canada.

Before they played them, Ireland had seen Canada impressively dispose of Tonga (37-4) in a match which, much to the Pacific islanders' dislike, was played on a Sunday. It is a day they observe religiously and strictly as a day of rest.

That Canada were able to reverse the defeat of 1974 (40-14) was in large measure due to Gareth Rees at outside half. At 19 years of age, he played brilliantly both as a kicker and a runner. This was the start of a long and distinguished career for him. Indeed, he was to become the main reason for elevating Canada as a competitive,

Mark Cardinal celebrates the try that put Canada 19-16 ahead against Ireland. They eventually lost 46-19.

Left: Hugo Porta's Argentina beat Italy but were edged out of the quarter-finals line-up by Fiji

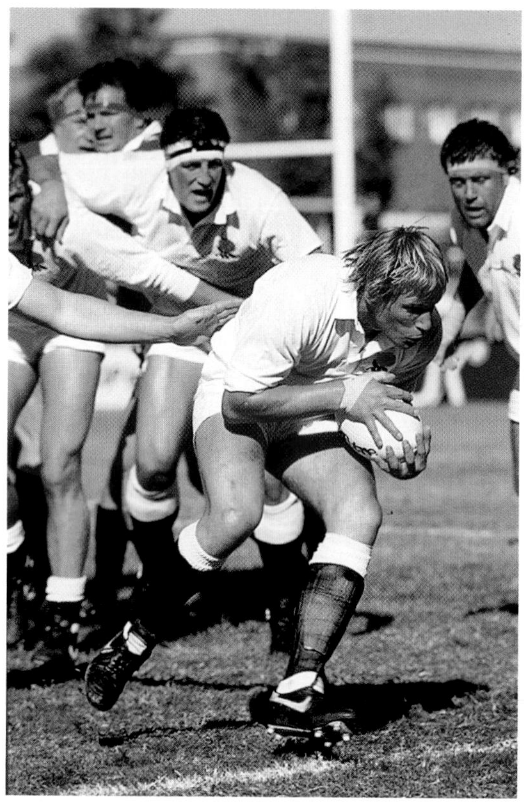

England's rampaging flank forward Peter Winterbottom scored two tries against the USA

if stubborn, force within world rugby over the next dozen years. According to Hans de Goede, their long-serving captain, this victory against Tonga was the most significant moment in Canada's rugby history.

In the event, Ireland won convincingly but not without the Canadians emphasising their progress by playing brilliantly for an hour. Typically, Rees was to put his country into the lead after two minutes with a penalty. Ireland soon gained the upper hand with a penalty by Kiernan and his conversion of Michael Bradley's try. But after the interval Rees played a crucial role in laying the foundation with a couple of penalties and a drop goal, which saw his team regain the lead at 19-16. This was a nervous time for Ireland.

But then Canada fell away. Four tries in the final ten minutes gave Ireland a comfortable win by 46-19.

Argentina, originally thought to be prime candidates to interrupt the progress of the established nations, were ultimately to prove a disappointment. Fiji beat them, while Italy gave them a worrying time. The 46 points the All Blacks were to score against Argentina's 15 gave Hugo Porta's team a try differential deficit to put them in third position in Pool 3. This was a pool where, apart from New Zealand, the three other countries had won a game each. This New Zealand score put the South Americans out of the tournament.

Italy, who had performed with credit after the opening game, defeated Fiji. But it was the Fijians, because of the try difference, who would be the second team from Pool 3 to reach the knockout stage.

But the old order was not to be shaken out of its place just yet. On the 12th day of the tournament, but at different kick-off times in Pool 4, Scotland scored 55 points against Romania, France 70 against Zimbabwe.

Surely, no world record could have stood for so brief a period as that created by Gavin Hastings, who scored 27 points against Romania in Dunedin. At 2.30pm he held the world record for individual points scorer in a match, overtaking Alan Hewson of New Zealand who had scored 26 points in Australia in 1982. An hour later Didier Cambérabéro, the French full back, overhauled Hastings by scoring 30 points against Zimbabwe in Auckland. France and Scotland went through to the quarter-finals.

If it had been a memorable game for Gavin Hastings, it did not prove quite such a happy one for his brother, Scott. A damaged hamstring early in the game against Romania meant that he would not take any further part in the tournament.

After a mistake-strewn match against a very physical Tonga which cost Wales two players – Stuart Evans, prop, and Glen Webbe the winger – as well as losing the immediate services due to injuries of others, the Welsh beat Canada comfortably (40-9). Ieuan Evans equalled the Welsh record of four tries in a single game which he shared with three others (W Llewellyn, 1899; R A Gibbs, 1908; M Richards, 1969).

Yet there was nothing very convincing about their form. Rees, as he was to do on so many other occasions for Canada, put his country into an early lead and was to accumulate all their points. All the game's tries went Wales' way, with eight. Pool 2, with Ireland also lacking conviction, was the least inspiring of all four pools.

England, on the other side of the Tasman Sea, had experienced some difficulties in Pool 1 but with a 70-pointer against Japan and another 34 against the USA, there was no one to halt their progress to the next round. Yet they had failed to recapture the form of their first match.

The most fascinating game in their pool was Australia versus Japan, for whom Hayashi, their captain and lock, and Hirao, their outstanding fly half, were the key figures. Indeed, with speed, commitment and many surprises, they destabilised Australia. Japan were victims of a disputed try when Peter Grigg, the Australian wing, tackled a player without the ball and Matt Burke grabbed the loose ball to score. Japan could well have gone into the lead at the interval but instead, Australia led 16-13.

Two of Australia's eight tries came in injury time to give them the respectable margin. In scoring his 24th try for his country, David Campese, playing at full back, equalled the world record set by Ian Smith of Scotland.

Thus the quarter-finals included the teams expected to be there: the seven nations of the International Board, with Fiji leap-frogging Argentina to be the eighth team.

"So far it's been bows and arrows," commented Alan Jones, never short of the colourful metaphor, as he reviewed the pool stage and prepared for the quarter-finals. "Now it's hand-grenades time."

By this stage, from the mêlée of 24 fixtures played in the 13 days between May 22 to June 3, one fact was perfectly clear. New Zealand were already making a purposeful and unambiguous statement, explicit to all who had seen them play in Auckland, Christchurch and Wellington. They had made an eloquent case, graphically illustrated by scoring 70 against Italy, 74 against Fiji. If they did not continue this progression it was because they made eight changes in the team, including a completely new back row for the game against Argentina when they managed a mere – by their standards – 46 points.

Australia, who had been expected by this stage to sit alongside New Zealand as likely contenders, had adopted a different policy and swapped and changed their personnel a good deal. They had suffered several injuries to key players such as Nick Farr-Jones (scrum half), Brett Papworth (centre) and Roger Gould (full back). By the end of the pool matches they had blooded all their squad players to the demands of the new tournament.

This was the new territory that Alan Jones talked about: of playing three international matches in eight days. Jones experimented with players. Tony Coker, Matthew Burke, David Campese and Steven Tuynman had to adjust to playing in different positions.

The Tongan synchronised sprinting team finished bottom in Pool 2

It was clear that New Zealand had already found their feet. They had, as they say, hit the ground running. While other teams were exhibiting doubts about personnel, or about the fitness of their players, or expressing concern about the uncertain quality of upcoming opposition, the All Blacks were simply getting on with the job. They went on the field, did the business and came off, leaving behind them a scoreline which emphatically demonstrated their superiority over opponents.

Teams often find it hard to lift their game against the lesser teams. Not New Zealand. The score reflected their strength and left no one in any doubt. They were fitter, more powerful and were imbued with the skill which denied fickleness or irresponsible error. In these essential aspects, they were setting new standards. Because of this they were able to keep their distance from their opponents and the scores showed it.

They worried about the sterner contests to come after the round-robin pool games were over and for which, they felt, they were not fully prepared. They were not battle-hardened enough; their matches not having been sufficiently competitive, they believed. The point was that

"The regulations are quite specific in this area and I studied them closely before I did the advertisement."

NEW ZEALAND CAPTAIN AND FARMER ANDY DALTON
after the uproar about his TV advert for a Japanese tractor

POOL 1 FINAL TABLE

	P	W	D	L	F	A	Pts
Australia	3	3	0	0	108	41	6
England	3	2	0	1	100	32	4
USA	3	1	0	2	39	99	2
Japan	3	0	0	3	48	123	0

POOL 2 FINAL TABLE

	P	W	D	L	F	A	Pts
Wales	3	3	0	0	82	31	6
Ireland	3	2	0	1	84	41	4
Canada	3	1	0	2	65	90	2
Tonga	3	0	0	3	29	98	0

POOL 3 FINAL TABLE

	P	W	D	L	F	A	Pts
New Zealand	3	3	0	0	190	34	6
Fiji	3	1	0	2	56	101	2
Argentina	3	1	0	2	49	90	2
Italy	3	1	0	2	40	110	2

POOL 4 FINAL TABLE

	P	W	D	L	F	A	Pts
France	3	2	1	0	145	44	5
Scotland	3	2	1	0	135	69	5
Romania	3	1	0	2	61	130	2
Zimbabwe	3	0	0	3	53	151	0

they were so far ahead of everyone else that not even they were of aware of the fact.

England, Scotland and Ireland had suffered a defeat each while Fiji had lost twice, to reach the knock-out stage. Wales had won all their matches but without engendering any sense of real confidence, nor showing any authority at forward. France were still a long way short of demonstrating the smoothly effective style which had brought them to the World Cup as European champions and Grand Slam winners. It had not all been plain sailing for any of them.

The referees and their interpretation of the laws had, as ever in rugby, caused a few heartaches. In addition, each of the countries, apart from New Zealand, had suffered heavy injuries. These are perennial problems for the game. They were more acute in the World Cup since matches were played at more frequent intervals. There was one other little difficulty…

The many objections that hard-core traditionalists had raised against a World Cup were born of the fear that a tournament of this kind might erode the principle upon which rugby union had existed, indeed upon which it had been sustained: the amateur principle. To begin with, this principle only affected players actually being paid to play the game. But the increased commercialisation of sport in the second half of the 20th century, especially in its final two decades, meant that the principle encroached upon ancillary and off-the-field activities, such as public appearances, journalism, TV interviews, writing books, and so on. These activities, if paid for, were also to be off-limits for the amateur. This was a grey area where hard lines could not properly be drawn.

Feathers were ruffled during the World Cup when Andy Dalton, New Zealand's captain – non-playing as yet – appeared on television promoting a Japanese tractor. The All Blacks' hooker was a farmer. There was no mention of him being an All Black, although Eden Park, Auckland's rugby ground, was mentioned. The Scottish Rugby Union complained. Behind closed doors, the minutiae of the relevant clauses of the amateur regulations were scrutinised. There was a case, apparently, to be made on behalf of Dalton. However, it was thought wiser not to

Argentina managed to restrict John Kirwan and the All Blacks to 'only' 46 points. Opposite: The Italians prepare for their Group 3 showdown with Argentina. Italy lost 25-16, and picked up the wooden spoon

pursue the issue any further. The offending advertisement was taken off the air. If it were to continue, it was concluded, this kind of thing would represent the first steps towards professionalism.

Amateurism was already not only a deeply wounded animal but could be counted as a seriously endangered species. This admirable but ultimately flawed idea, depending as it did on gentlemanly conduct, the kindnesses of men with time on their hands to enjoy some fun and the occasional high jinks, was entering its final stages. The whiff of money was moving inexorably into this humble sporting neighbourhood. Rugby could not ignore it. A growing ambition to be more than it had been in the past was forcing perspectives of the future to change. Andy Dalton's example provided an unmistakable signpost. If he had to withdraw from what appeared to be a lucrative commercial deal off the field, he had finally to accept, too, that, after an injury before the World Cup began, he was probably going to have to pull out from playing any part on the field.

Of these two disappointments for the All Blacks skipper, the sporting one was undoubtedly the more painful.

David Kirk was proving to be a magnificent general of the team and the maturing of the new man in the middle of the front row, Sean Fitzpatrick, meant the All Blacks had already found a successor to Dalton as hooker. This, for Fitzpatrick, was to be the beginning of one of the greatest-ever All Black rugby careers.

· POOL 1 RESULTS ·

AUSTRALIA 19 ENGLAND 6
23 May • Concord Oval, Sydney
Australia: Gould (James 78); Grigg, *Slack, Papworth, Campese; Lynagh, Farr-Jones; Rodriguez, Lawton, McIntyre, Cutler, Campbell, Poidevin, Coker, Tuynman
SCORERS: *Tries:* Campese, Poidevin; *Con:* Lynagh. *Pens:* Lynagh (3).
England: Rose (Webb 2); *Harrison, Simms, Salmon, Underwood; Williams, Harding; Rendall, Moore, Pearce, Dooley, Redman, Winterbottom, Rees, Richards
SCORERS: *Try:* Harrison. *Con:* Webb.
Referee: Keith Lawrence (NZ)

USA 21 JAPAN 18
24 May • Ballymore Oval, Brisbane
USA: Nelson; Purcell, Higgins, Helu, Lambert; Clarkson, Saunders; Bailey, Everett, Paoli, Lambert, Swords; Burlingham (capt), Warhurst, Vizard.
SCORERS: *Tries:* Purcell, Nelson, Lambert. *Cons:* Nelson (3). *Pen:* Nelson.
Japan: Mukai; Taumoefolau, Yoshinaga, Onuki, Kutsuki; Hirao, Ikuta; Yasumi, Fujita, Horaguchi, Miyamoto, Hayashi (capt), Oyagi, Latu, Chida.
SCORERS: *Tries:* Taumoefolau (2), Yoshinaga. *Pens:* Yoshinaga, Kutsuki.
Referee: G Maurette (France)

ENGLAND 60 JAPAN 7
30 May • Concord Oval, Sydney
England: Webb; *Harrison, Simms (Clough 68), Salmon, Underwood; Williams (Andrew 77), Harding; Rendall, Moore, Chilcott, Bainbridge, Redman, Rees, Winterbottom, Richards.
SCORERS: *Tries:* Underwood (2), Rees, Salmon, Richards, Simms, Harrison (3), Redman. *Cons:* Webb (7). *Pens:* Webb (2)
Japan: Mukai; Taumoefolau, Kutsuki, Matsuo, Onuki; Hirao, Hagimoto; Kimura, Fujita, Horaguchi, Oyagi, Kurihara, Miyamoto, Chida, *Hayashi.
SCORERS: *Try:* Miyamoto. *Pen:* Matsuo.
Referee: René Horquet (France)

AUSTRALIA 47 USA 12
31 May • Ballymore Oval, Brisbane
Australia: Leeds; Campese, *Slack, Papworth, Burke; Lynagh, Smith; Lillicrap, Lawton, McIntyre, Coker, Campbell, Miller, Tuynman, Codey.
SCORERS: *Tries:* PT, Smith, Slack, Leeds (2), Papworth, Campese, Codey. *Cons:* Lynagh (6). *Pen:* Lynagh.
USA: Nelson; Higgins, Helu, Vinick, Hein; Horton, Dickson (Saunders 35); Horvath, Johnson, Paoli, Swords, Shiflet (Lambert 24), Finkel, Vizard, Ridnell.
SCORERS: *Try:* Nelson. *Con:* Nelson. *Pen:* Nelson. DG: Horton.
Referee: Brian Anderson (Scotland)

ENGLAND 34 USA 6
3 June • Concord Oval, Sydney
England: Webb; *Harrison, Clough, Salmon, Bailey; Andrew, Hill; Chilcott, Dawe, Pearce, Bainbridge, Dooley, Rees, Winterbottom, Richards.
SCORERS: *Tries:* Winterbottom (2), Harrison, Dooley. *Cons:* Webb (3). *Pens:* Webb (4).
USA: Nelson; Purcell, Higgins, Vinick, Hein; Clarkson, Saunders; Brendel, Everett, Bailey, Causey, *Burlingham, Finkel, Vizard, Lambert.
SCORERS: *Try:* Purcell. *Con:* Nelson.
Referee: Kerry Fitzgerald (Australia)

AUSTRALIA 42 JAPAN 23
3 June • Concord Oval, Sydney
Australia: Campese; Grigg, *Slack, Cook, Burke; Lynagh, Smith; Rodriguez, McBail, Hartill, Cutler, Reynolds, Poidevin (capt), Tuynman, Codey.
SCORERS: *Tries:* Slack (2) Tuynman, Burke (2), Grigg, Hartill, Campese. *Cons:* Lynagh (5).
Japan: Mukai; Taumoefolau, Yoshinaga, Kutsuki, Okidoi; Hirao, Ikuta; Kimura, Fujita, Aizawa, Sakuraba, *Hayashi, Miyamoto, Latu, Kawese.
SCORERS: *Tries:* Kutsuki (2), Fujita. *Con:* Okidoi. *Pens:* Okidoi (2). *DG:* Okidoi.
Referee: Jim Fleming (Scotland)

England lock Steve Bainbridge was a force in open play against the USA. He also dominated the lineouts with his partner Wade Dooley in a game which England won 34-6 to clinch second place in Pool 1 and go on to the quarter-finals

Trevor Ringland of Ireland scores a try in their runaway victory over Canada.
Below: Kevin Phillips takes on the Irish guard in Wales' 13-6 victory.
With both teams beating Canada and Tonga, Wales claimed top spot in Pool 2

· POOL 2 RESULTS ·

CANADA 37 TONGA 4
24 May • Napier
Canada: Wyatt; Palmer, Vaesen, McTavish, Woods; Rees, Stuart; Evans, Cardinal, Handson, van der Brink, de *Goode, Frame, Radu, Robertson.
SCORERS: *Tries:* Stuart, Frame, penalty try, Vaesen (2), Palmer (2).
Cons: Wyatt (2), Rees. *Pens:* Rees.
Tonga: Etaiki; A'Si (Vaipulu 22), Kuteki'Aho, Mohi, Fiela; Liava'A, Fifita; Moto'Apauaka, Afu, Tupou, Fine, Tu'lahalamaka Tahaafe 28), Tu'uta, Fotu, *Valu
SCORERS: *Try:* Valu.
Referee: Clive Norling (Wales)

WALES 13 IRELAND 6
25 May • Athletic Park, Wellington
Wales: Thorburn; I Evans, Devereux, Ring, Hadley; J Davies, Jones; Whitefoot, K Phillips, S Evans, Norster, *R Moriarty, Collins, P Moriarty, Roberts.
SCORERS: *Tries:* Ring. *Pen:* Thorburn.
DGs: Davies (2).
Ireland: MacNeill; Ringland, Mullin, Kiernan, Crossnan; Dean, Bradley; Orr, Kingston, Fitzgerald, Anderson, *Lenihan, McGrath, Matthews (Glennon 35), Spillane.
SCORERS: *Pens*: Kiernan (2).
Referee: Kerry Fitzgerald (Australia)

WALES 29 TONGA 16
29 May • Showgrounds Oval, Palmerston North
Wales: Thorburn; Webbe, Ring, Hopkins, Hadley; Dacey (J Davies 58), Jones; Buchanan, K Phillips, S Evans (Blackmore 40), Richards, *R Moriarty, P Moriarty, P Davies, Roberts.
SCORERS: *Tries:* Webbe (3), Hadley.
Con: Thorburn (2). *Pens:* Thorburn (2).
DG: J Davies.
Tonga: Etaiki; Vunipola, Mohi, Kuteki'Aho, Fiela; Amone (Liava'a 67), Fifita; Tupou (Va'eno 44), Afu, Lutua, Fine, Tu'ungafasi, Tu'uta, Filese, *Valu.
SCORERS: *Tries:* Fiela, Fifita.
Con: Liava'a. *Pens:* Amone, Liava'a.
Referee: David Bishop (New Zealand)

IRELAND 46 CANADA 19
30 May • Carisbrook, Dunedin
Ireland: MacNeill; Ringland, Mullin, Kiernan, Crossnan; Ward, Bradley; Orr, McDonald (Kingston 65), Fitzgerald, *Lenihan, Anderson, McGrath, Collins, Spillane.
SCORERS: *Tries:* Bradley, Crossnan (2), Spillane, Ringland, MacNeill.
Cons: Kiernan (5). *Pens:* Kiernan (2).
DGs: Kiernan, Ward.
Canada: Wyatt; Palmer, Lecky, McTavish, Woods; Rees, Stuart; Evans, Cardinal, Handson, *de Goode, Hindson, Frame, Radu, Ennis.
SCORERS: *Try:* Cardinal.
Pens: Rees (3), Wyatt. *DG:* Rees.
Referee: Fred Howard (England)

WALES 40 CANADA 9
3 June • Invercargill
Wales: Thorburn; I Evans, Devereux, Bowen (Hopkins 72), Hadley; *J Davies, Giles; Whitefoot, A Phillips, Blackmore, Norster, Sutton, P Moriarty (R Moriarty 77), P Davies, Roberts.
SCORERS: *Tries:* I Evans (4), Bowen, Devereux, Hadley, A Phillips.
Cons: Thorburn (4).
Canada: Wyatt; Palmer, Lecky, Woods, Gray; Rees, Stuart (Tucker 52); McKellar, Svoboda, Handson, *de Goode, Hindson, Frame, Breen, Ennis.
SCORERS: *Pens:* Rees (3)
Referee: David Bishop (New Zealand)

IRELAND 32 TONGA 9
3 June • Ballymore Oval, Brisbane
Ireland: MacNeill; Ringland, Mullin, Irwin, Crossnan; Ward, Bradley; Langbroek, Kingston, McCoy, *Lenihan, Anderson, Matthews, Francis, McGrath.
SCORERS: *Tries:* MacNeill (2), Mullin (3).
Cons: Ward (3). *Pens:* Ward (2).
Tonga: Etaiki; Fiela, Mohi, Kuteki'Aho, Liava'a; Amone, Fifita; Tupou, Fungaraka, Lutua, Fine, Tu'ungafasi, Valu (capt), Filese, Kakoto.
SCORERS: *Pens:* Amone (3)
Referee: G Maurette (France)

Grant Fox of New Zealand kicked 10 penalties and 20 conversions in Pool 3.
Below: Classic scrum half play by Martin Yanguela of Argentina against Italy

· POOL 3 RESULTS ·

NEW ZEALAND 70 ITALY 6
22 May • Eden Park , Auckland
New Zealand: Gallagher; Kirwan, Stanley, Taylor, Green; Fox, *Kirk; McDowell, Fitzpatrick, Loe, Pierce, G Whetton, A Whetton, Jones, Shelford.
SCORERS: Penalty try, Jones, Kirk (2), Taylor, Green (2), McDowell, Kirwan (2), Stanley, A Whetton.
Cons: Fox (8). *Pens:* Fox (2).
Italy: Ghizzoni; Mascioletti, Collodo, Gaetenillo, Cuttita; Ambrosio, Lorigiola; Rossi, Morelli, Lupini, Berni, Gardin, Farina, *Innocenti, Artuso.
SCORERS: *Pen:* Collodo. *DG:* Collodo.
Referee: R Fordham (Australia)

FIJI 28 ARGENTINA 9
24 May • Rugby Park, Hamilton
Fiji: Koroduadua; Nalaga, T Cama, Tuvula, E Naituku; Rokowailoa, Tabulutu (Nawalus 25); Namoro, Naiviliwasa, S Naituku, *Rakoroi, Savai, Gale (Vunivalu 58), Qoro, Sanday.
SCORERS: *Tries:* Gale, Rakoroi, Nalaga, Savai. *Cons:* Koroduadua (2), Rokowailoa. *Pens:* Koroduadua (2).
Argentina: Salvat; Campo, Cuesta Silva, Turnes, J Lanza; *Porta, Gomez; Morel, Cash, Molina, Branca, Milano (Schiavio 53), Mostany, Allen, Travaglini.
SCORERS: *Try:* Travaglini. *Con:* Porta. *Pen:* Porta.
Referee: Jim Fleming (Scotland)

NEW ZEALAND 74 FIJI 13
27 May • Lancaster Park, Christchurch
New Zealand: Gallagher; Kirwan, Stanley, Taylor, Green; Fox, *Kirk; McDowell, Fitzpatrick, Drake, Anderson, G Whetton, A Whetton, Jones, Shelford.
SCORERS: *Tries:* Green (4), Gallagher (4), Kirk, Kirwan, PT, A Whetton.
Cons: Fox (10). *Pens:* Fox (2)
Fiji: Koroduadua; Tuvula, Lovokulu, Kubu, T Cama; Rakowailoa, Nawalu, Taga, Rakai, Volavola; J Cama, Savai; Kididromo, Vunivalu, *Rakoroi.
SCORERS: *Try:* J Cama.
Pens: Koroduadua (3).
Referee: Derek Bevan (Wales)

ARGENTINA 25 ITALY 16
28 May • Lancaster Park, Christchurch
Argentina: Salvat; J Lanza, Cuesta Silva, Madero, P Lanza; *Porta, Yanguela (Gomez 65); Dengra, Cash, Molina, Branca, Carrosio, Schiavio, Allen, Travaglini.
SCORERS: *Tries:* J Lanza, Gomez.
Con: Porta. *Pens:* Porta (5).
Italy: Tebaldi; Mascioletti, Gaetenillo, Barba, Cuttita; Collodo, Lorigiola; Rossi, Galeazzo, Lupini, Gardin, Gollela, Pavin, Innocenti (capt), Zanon.
SCORERS: *Tries:* Innocenti, Cuttita.
Con: Collodo. *Pens:* Collodo (2).
Referee: Roger Quittenden (England)

ITALY 18 FIJI 15
31 May • Carisbrook, Dunedin
Italy: Tebaldi; Mascioletti, Gaeteniello, Barba, Cuttita; Colllodo, Ghini; Cucchiella, Romagnoli, Lupini, Gardin, Colella, Dolfato, *Innocenti, Farina.
SCORERS: *Tries:* Cuttita, Cucchiella, Mascioletti. *Pen:* Collodo. *DG:* Collodo.
Fiji: Koroduadua; T Cama, Salusalu, Mitchell, Tuvula; Rakowailoa, Nawalu; Volavola, Naiviliwasa, Naituku, Nadolo, Sanday, Savai, Qoro, *Rakoroi.
SCORERS: *Try:* Naiviliwasa.
Con: Koroduadua. *Pens:* Koroduadua (2). *DG:* Qoro.
Referee: Keith Lawrence (NZ)

NEW ZEALAND 46 ARGENTINA 15
1 June • Athletic Park, Wellington
New Zealand: Crowley; Kirwan, Stanley, McCahill, Wright; Fox, *Kirk; Loe, Fitzpatrick, Drake, Pierce, G Whetton, A Whetton, Brooke, Earl.
SCORERS: *Tries:* Kirk, Brooke, Stanley, Earl, Crowley, A Whetton.
Con: Fox (2). *Pen:* Fox (6).
Argentina: Angaut; Campo, Madero, Turnes (P Lanza 65), J Lanza; *Porta, Gomez; Dengra, Cash, Molina, Branca, Carrosio, Schiavio, Allen, Travaglini (Mostany 44).
SCORERS: *Try:* J Lanza. *Con:* Porta.
Pens: Porta (3).
Referee: Roger Quittenden (England)

· POOL 4 RESULTS ·

FRANCE 20 SCOTLAND 20
23 May • Concord Oval, Sydney
France: Blanco; Lagisquet, Sella, Charvet, Estève; Mesnel, Berbizier; Garuet, *Dubroca, Ondarts, Condom, Lorieux, Erbani, Champ, Rodriguez.
SCORERS: *Tries:* Sella, Berbizier, Blanco. *Con:* Blanco. *Pens:* Blanco (2).
Scotland: G Hastings; Duncan, Robertson, Wyllie, Tukalo; Rutherford (Tait 17), Laidlaw; Milne, *Deans, Sole; White, Tomes, F Calder, Jeffrey, Paxton.
SCORERS: *Tries:* White, Duncan. *Pens:* G Hastings (4).
Referee: Fred Howard (England)

ROMANIA 21 ZIMBABWE 20
23 May • Eden Park , Auckland
Romania: Toader; Marin (Hodorca 5), David, Tofan, Lungu; Alexandru (Ion 60), *Paraschiv, Bucan, Grigore, Leonte, Dumitras, L Constantin, S Constantin, Raducanu, Mariaru.
SCORERS: *Tries:* Paraschiv, Toader, Hodorca. *Pens:* Alexandru (3)
Zimbabwe: Ferreira; Kaulbach, K. Graham, Tsimba (A Buitendag 67) Barrett; Brown, *Jellicoe, Elcombe, Bray, Tucker, D Buitendag, Martin, Sawyer, Gray, Neill.
SCORERS: *Tries:* Tsimba (2), Neill. *Con:* Brown. *Pens:* Ferreira (2)
Referee: Steve Hilditch (Ireland)

FRANCE 55 ROMANIA 12
28 May • Athletic Park, Wellington
R Fordham (Australia)
France: Blanco (Camberabero 14); Lagisquet, Sella, Charvet, Andrieu; Laporte, Berbizier; Garuet, *Dubroca, Armary, Haget, Condom, Erbani, Champ, Carminati.
SCORERS: *Tries:* Charvet (2), Sella, Andrieu, Cambérabéro, Erbani, Laporte, Lagisquet (2). *Con:* Laporte (8). *Pen:* Laporte.
Romania: Ion; Toader, Tofan, David, Lungu; Bezuscu, *Paraschiv, Opris, Ilca (Grigore 12), Pascu, L Constantin, Veres, Necula, Raducanu, Dimitru.
SCORERS: *Pens:* Bezuscu (4).

SCOTLAND 60 ZIMBABWE 21
30 May • Athletic Park, Wellington
Scotland: G Hastings; Duncan, Tait, Robertson, Tukalo; Wyllie, Oliver; Sole, *Deans, Milne, Tomes, Campbell-Lamerton, F Calder, Jeffrey, Paxton.
SCORERS: *Tries:* Tait (2), Duncan (2), Oliver, G Hastings, Paxton (2), Jeffrey, Tukalo (2). *Cons:* G Hastings (8).
Zimbabwe: Ferreira; S Graham, A Buitendag, K. Graham, Barrett; Grobler, *Jellicoe; Elcombe, Bray, Tucker, Martin, Sawyer, Gray, D Buitendag, Neill.
SCORERS: *Try:* D Buitendag. *Con:* Grobler. *Pens:* Grobler (5).
Referee: David Burnett (Ireland)

FRANCE 70 ZIMBABWE 12
2 June • Eden Park , Auckland
France: Cambérabéro; Andrieu, Bonneval (Sella 20), Charvet, Estève; Mesnel, Modin; Tolot, *Dubroca, Ondarts, Lorieux, Condom, Carminati, Joinel, Rodriguez.
Laporte for Sella (43)
SCORERS: *Tries:* Modin (3), Dubroca, Rodriguez (2), Charvet (2), Cambérabéro (3), Laporte, Estève. *Cons:* Cambérabéro (9).
Zimbabwe: Ferreira; Kaulbach, Tsimba, K Graham, Barrett; Grobler, *Jellicoe; Elcombe (Nicholls 27), Bray, Tucker, Martin (Kloppers 37), Sawyer, Gray, D Buitendag, Neill.
SCORERS: *Try:* Kaulbach. *Con:* Grobler. *Pens:* Grobler (2)
Referee: Derek Bevan (Wales)

SCOTLAND 55 ROMANIA 28
2 June • Carisbrook, Dunedin
Referee: Steve Hilditch (Ireland)
Scotland: G Hastings; Duncan, Tait, S Hastings (Cramb 1), Tukalo; Wyllie, Laidlaw; Sole, *Deans, Rowan, White, Tomes (Campbell-Lamerton 42), Jeffrey, F Calder, Paxton.
SCORERS: *Tries:* Tait (2), Jeffrey (3), Duncan, G Hastings (2), Tukalo. *Cons:* G Hastings (8). *Pen:* G Hastings.
Romania: Ion; Pilotschi, Lungu, Tofan; Alexandru, *Paraschiv; Bucan, Grigore, Leonte, S Constantin, L Constantin, Murariui, Dumitras, Raducanu (Dumitri 20).
SCORERS: *Tries:* Murariu (2), Toader. *Cons:* Alexandru, Ion. *Pens:* Alex'du (4).

Serge Blanco kicked two penalties and a conversion for France against Scotland, before handing the job to Guy Laporte, who did the honours against Romania. Didier Cambérabéro took over against Zimbabwe, scoring a world record 30 points

1987 THE ·QUARTER-FINALS·

The luck of the quarter-final draw – or misfortune, perhaps, in this case – saw England facing Wales at Ballymore in Brisbane. The fixture was unblessed. Four months earlier the two countries had played a contest of such intimidation and attrition in the Five Nations Championship that the whole sport seemed to have been betrayed. In the gloom of Cardiff Arms Park, an air of deepening melancholy prevailed. Visions of dull-witted débâcle and Neanderthal recklessness returned.

Wales emerged from Invercargill to join England, who were moving up from Rushcutters Bay in Sydney where they had stayed since arriving in Australia. There were scores to settle. Would rugby be tarnished once more?

At least the fixture ensured that Europe would not be without a representative in the semi-finals. It was the last of the quarter-finals. It would be played on Monday.

The first was between Scotland and New Zealand. Scotland, shorn of influential players such as John Rutherford and Scott Hastings, were not going to stop the All Black juggernaut. "When the death-or-glory time arrives," said Brian Lochore, their coach, "you don't mess around." They did not.

If they had shown rare glimpses of adventure in the earlier rounds, the All Blacks were to find their inspiration for this match in their long history. They might have peered towards the distant horizon to find something different; to play a wider game, perhaps. But, in Christchurch, in the first of the quarter-finals, they returned to the roots of their traditional style.

Physical presence, the power and the speed of their forwards – that was where they found their inspiration. Wayne Shelford, Alan Whetton and Michael Jones personified these qualities. Possession they wanted, possession they found. And possession they kept. They smothered and finally suffocated Scotland into submission. The Scots

Scotland scrum half Roy Laidlaw feeds out from the scrum. Right: Wayne Shelford is hauled down but there was no holding the rampant All Blacks

"The All Blacks have a ruthless, relentless purpose behind them, stemming from their total concentration during the course of the match. That is what we lack. We will make mistakes or take the wrong action. They almost never do, and punish the opposition mercilessly every time they do."

IRELAND LEGEND WILLIE JOHN McBRIDE
Member of the 1971 British Lions – the first visiting team to win a series in New Zealand

found compensation in the firmness of their defence which, for most of the afternoon, held true. They tackled and tackled; then got up to tackle some more. Thrice they picked themselves off the floor to see their line crossed. Of these, John Kirwan's try was disallowed for obstruction. Alan Whetton and John Gallagher both succeeded untrammelled. For all the admirable qualities of New Zealand, the sheer practicality of their approach, shorn of of any delicate finery, but utterly in tune with their ambitions, the game was monotone and played to a predictable and repetitive rhythm: a *Bolero* without the dramatic climax. The only answer to New Zealand's 30 points was a solitary Hastings penalty (30-3).

The following day in Auckland, in contrast, it was time for, shall we say, a bit of rock 'n' roll. Fiji abandoned any sense at all of a classic structure. Extravagantly, they let their hair down. France were a little circumspect to begin with, but soon found that they were on the receiving end of the kind of running brilliance of which they themselves are usually the masters. They responded in parts.

Fiji decided that since they were just far enough from home, where the quiet revolution was taking place, they might as well play and have a bit of fun. The serious side of life can come later, they must have felt, when they would arrive home to what might be an uncertain future.

They played with the same joyous abandon that mesmerised the people of Wales in 1964. The Welsh, ignoring sniffiness, were then the first of the International Board members to invite Fiji, a non-member, to come and play. They provided a vision of another style of rugby; refreshing in its unorthodoxy and its spontaneity.

It was with the same youthful, invigorating spirit that

"We may not have the luck to win on tries like we did against Scotland and a reliable kicker is essential, especially with Koroduadua in such great form for Fiji."

FRANCE COACH JACQUES FOUROUX before the 31-16 quarter-final victory over Fiji, in which Guy Laporte kicked the precise winning margin of 15 points

"Hands up who thinks Fiji can beat France." The Pacific islanders gave *les Bleus* a scare by playing rugby that was more French than the French

they approached the quarter-final. Playing to their instincts, they were not always successful, but who would have wished it otherwise? Kaiava Salusalu and Tomasi Cama tore through the midfield. Manasa Qoro scored a try of extravagance. But France's response to the agile gymnastics of the Pacific islanders was untypically pragmatic. Severo were forced to resort to tactics with which teams are familiar when playing them. Not that they gave up entirely – no French team can deny their rich heritage completely – and demonstrated many a fine touch themselves. But on this day they had, in style, to be content with second best. France won the game but the abiding memory is of Fiji

"Hands up who thinks France can beat Fiji..."

Koroduadua had proved a player of star quality. He was to make a superb break in this game but, with his penchant for holding the ball with one hand, saw it squirt out of his grasp once he was in the open field.

France, in contrast, rolled and pushed their way at close quarters to score two tries from scrummages and another from the lineout. Laurent Rodriguez played a crucial role in all three.

Daniel Dubroca, France's captain, insisted that they dared not try to match the Fijians. The way to victory was by exercising control. For once they were tasting the kind of medicine that they liked to dish out to others. France closing the encounter by scoring the best try of the match. Mocking the instructions that every teacher has given to every schoolboy through the ages, and dismissive of Koroduadua's blooper, Jone Kubu strode blithely in open space and, holding the ball in one hand, gave Damu the chance to score a try of breathtaking – there is no other word for it – panache.

On the day, though, superior French control defeated risk-taking Fijian improvisation with a score of 31-16. Victory was not without its cost. Blanco pulled a leg muscle and would be doubtful for the semi-final.

The referee was Clive Norling. Universally recognised

"We go back home a better side. Ireland will be a better team next year as a result of the World Cup."

IRELAND CAPTAIN DONAL LENIHAN after the 33-15 quarter-final defeat by Australia

Australia climbed all over Ireland to reach the semi-finals, thus forestalling the intervention of the local Ned Kelly impersonator (left)

as one of the world's most accomplished and authoritative referees, he was told by the chairman of the tournament referees appointments committee, Dr Roger Vanderfield of Australia, that he would not be required for the remainder of the tournament. This was a puzzling decision. Referees were chosen on their performance during the competition and some of those still on the panel had committed glaring errors of the kind missing on Norling's report.

Ireland, in the third game to be played, were no match for Australia at the Concord Oval, Sydney. Despite the loss after three minutes of Nick Farr-Jones, the Aussies played purposeful, controlled rugby, designed and largely executed by Michael Lynagh at outside half. His team mustered 24 points in as many minutes with tries by McIntyre, Burke and Smith (who had come on for the injured Farr-Jones), all converted by Lynagh who also added two penalties. Burke scored a second try and a third penalty by the outside half made up Australia's full score.

Hugo MacNeill and Michael Kiernan scored Ireland's tries. Kiernan converted both, as well as kicking a penalty to make it 33-15.

While the three matches had so far gone according to all the pre-match forecasts, each providing rugby of a standard worthy of the late stages of a World Cup, the fourth, played on the Monday in Brisbane, proved, by general consent, to be the worst game of the tournament.

England, who had been thought favourites beforehand, lost. There was no violence as there had been four months earlier in Cardiff, but the quality of the rugby was quite simply abysmal.

The fates were no friendly companions to England. They had not been at their side against Australia in the opening game, nor were they evident at Ballymore either. Indeed, with the rain and the cloying pitch and the shallowness of their own performance, which was far below what had been expected, fortune seemed to have abandoned England. Against a stubborn and spoiling Welsh team, the English were numbingly ineffective. The penalty count went against Wales by 25-9 and England should have profited from that.

Both Martin Green, the England coach, and Mike Harrison, their captain, failed to understand why they had performed so poorly. Nothing beforehand should have led them to expect such a poor performance. All the indications in the build-up suggested that England were bringing their game together more confidently and in a

"I have no idea why England performed so poorly. We were very buoyant and confident beforehand yet we didn't produce it on the field. All the Welsh points were given them: they didn't create, they seized on our mistakes and that was the most disappointing feature."

ENGLAND CAPTAIN MIKE HARRISON
after the 16-3 quarter-final defeat by Wales

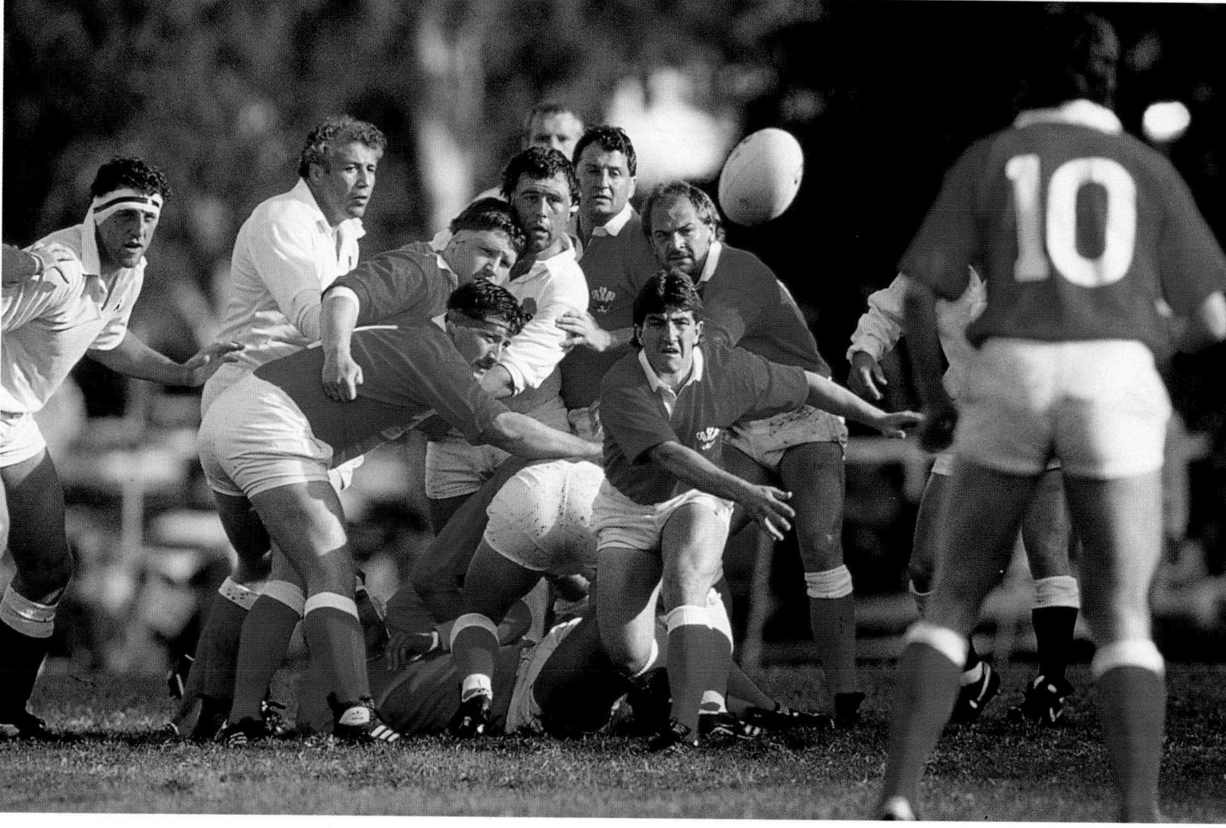

Wales scrum half Robert Jones fires a pass to the waiting Jonathan Davies while, right, centre John Devereux celebrates his try

more structured fashion than Wales. That England should have failed could only be explained by the spell that the spectre of Wales seemed to cast over them.

This psychological barrier, if such it is, would lead to the next generation of players being distributed with cassette recordings of the Arms Park crowd singing the national anthem, *Hen Wlad Fy Nhadau*. This was one means, along with the presence of a resident psychologist, of overcoming their inhibitions about Welsh rugby and its myths. Considering what was to follow in the Nineties, the plan would appear to have worked.

Largely through English errors, Wales contrived to score three tries by Gareth Roberts, Robert Jones and John Devereux, with a couple of conversions by Paul Thorburn, against which Jonathan Webb kicked a solitary penalty for England in a final scoreline of 16-3. Apart from those who gain a one-track and obsessive pleasure in gloating once more over Wales beating England, this was a game of distressingly low standards.

Looking through the wrong end of a telescope, pointed in the wrong direction, Welshmen could observe complacently that England had not beaten Wales outside Twickenham since 1963. This seemed to be enough justification for Welsh pride. Yet, were they to survey the world scene accurately, Wales would recognise that the standards to which they should be aspiring were being set elsewhere. But this hardly seemed to matter.

Robert Jones at scrum half was the only player in the game who showed, by his class, that he deserved the right to exhibit his art on the world stage.

If Wales won the battle, it was England who would ultimately win the war. Lessons learnt, embarrassment

· QUARTER FINALS ·

NEW ZEALAND 30 SCOTLAND 3
6 June • Lancaster Park, Christchurch
NEW ZEALAND: Gallagher; Kirwan, Stanley, Taylor (McCahill 17), Green; Fox, *Kirk; McDowell, Fitzpatrick, Drake, Pierce, G Whetton, A Whetton, Jones, Shelford.
SCORERS: *Tries:* A Whetton, Gallagher. *Cons:* Fox (2). *Pens:* Fox (6).
SCOTLAND: G Hastings; Duncan, Tait, Robertson, Tukalo; Wyllie, Laidlaw; Sole, *Deans, Milne, White, Tomes, Turnbull, F Calder, Paxton.
SCORER: *Pen:* G Hastings.
Referee: David Burnett (Ireland)

FRANCE 31 FIJI 16
7 June • Eden Park, Auckland
FRANCE: Blanco (Cambérabéro 79); Charvet, Sella, Mesnel, Lagisquet; Laport, Berbizier; Ondarts, *Dubroca, Garuet, Haget, Lorieux, Champ, Erbani, Rodriguez.
SCORERS: *Tries:* Lorieux, Rodriguez (2), Laguiquet. *Cons:* Laporte (3). *Pens:* Laporte 2. *DG:* Laporte.
FIJI: Kubu; Damu, Salusalu, T Cama, Mitchell; Koroduadua, Nawalu; Namoro, Rakai, Naituku, *Rakaroi, Savai (Rokiowailoa 45), Sanday, Qoro (Lovoruku 53), Naiviliwasa.
SCORERS: *Tries:* Qoro, Damu. *Con:* Koroduadua. *Pens:* Koraduadua (2).
Referee: Clive Norling (Wales)

AUSTRALIA 33 IRELAND 15
7 June • Concord Oval, Sydney, Australia
AUSTRALIA: Campese; Grigg, *Slack, Papworth, Burke; Lynagh, Farr-Jones (Smith 5); Lillicrap, Lawton, McIntyre, Cutler, Campbell, Poidevin, Miller, Tuynman.
SCORERS: *Tries:* McIntyre, Smith, Burke (2). *Cons:* Lynagh (4). *Pens:* Lynagh (3).
IRELAND: MacNeill; Ringland, Mullin (Irwin 67), Kiernan, Crossan; Dean, Bradley; Orr, Kingston, Fitzpatrick, *Lenihan, Anderson, Mathews, McGrath, Spillane (Francis 59).
SCORERS: *Tries:* MacNeill, Kiernan. *Cons:* Kiernan (2). *Pens:* Kiernan.
Referee: Brian Anderson (Scotland)

WALES 16 ENGLAND 3
8 June • Ballymore Oval, Brisbane
WALES: Thorburn; I Evans, Devereux, Bowen, Hadley; J Davies, Jones; Buchanan, A Phillips, Young, *R Moriarty, Norster (Richards 73), Collins, Roberts, P Moriarty.
SCORERS: *Tries:* Roberts, Jones, Devereux. *Cons:* Thorburn (2)
ENGLAND: Webb; *Harrison, Simms, Salmon, Underwood; Williams, Harding; Rendall (Chilcott 24), Moore, Pearce, Dooley, Redman, Winterbottom, Rees, Richards.
SCORERS: *Pen:* Webb.
Referee: René Hourquet (France)

suffered, England returned home not only to put their house in order but to rebuild it. Stung by this defeat, Twickenham's response was to ring the changes which would usher in the Geoff Cooke and Will Carling era. Within 12 months, Wales were to win the Triple Crown, but the triumph was followed by years of disappointment and depression.

For the moment, though, Tony Gray, the Welsh coach, and Derek Quinnell, his assistant, were left with a few headaches. The injury list was a long one. Jonathan Davies (leg), Bob Norster (hamstring) – both of whom were notable and, at this stage, irreplaceable members of the team – Anthony Buchanan (back) and Gareth Roberts (broken nose). It was a testing time.

The England pack hang their heads in dejection after the crushing defeat by Wales. But many of these men would take a fierce hold over the Red Dragon in the next few years

1987 THE · SEMI-FINALS ·

"The All Blacks put their whole soul as well as body into their play. I'm sure that all 15 players will emigrate if they lose to Wales on Sunday."

FORMER WALES CAPTAIN JEFF SQUIRE

Above: Gary Whetton of New Zealand takes the field for the semi-final against Wales

In both semi-final fixtures there was the element of a northern versus southern hemisphere contest, with most experts believing that the Final would exclude both European teams.

David Hands of *The Times* opened his preview of the New Zealand versus Wales match with a prediction echoing everyone's melancholy foreboding that Wales were facing a day of reckoning. "The lights twinkle brightly over Sydney Harbour as dusk falls," he wrote, "but I fear that the lights are about to go out on Wales when they meet New Zealand in the semi-final of the World Cup in Brisbane."

The All Blacks would be without Michael Jones, 22, who was soon to be considered the world's best flanker. He had not played for his country before the World Cup and he was not going to play in this match either because his religious beliefs would not allow him to play on a Sunday.

Both Australia and France had suffered from injury problems. But France had played in fits and starts with less than we had hoped of their fluid movement. In addition, they were, in Jacques Fouroux's words, "saturated with rugby". With tours to Argentina, Australia and New Zealand, a visit to their own country from New Zealand, and the recently completed Five Nations Championship, France had played consistently for close on two years. They had been looking jaded. Seeking one more effort from their war-weary warriors, their pack of forwards was to be the same that had played, fought and, against the odds, won the infamous battle of Nantes with the All Blacks the previous November.

For this game in Sydney, both Brett Papworth and Nick Farr-Jones were back in the Australian team. The Aussies, even without Steve Tuynman, were strong favourites.

Wales were left as the sole representatives of the British Isles. There was a sense of pride in this, but the prospect of what lay ahead could hardly be viewed with joy. Had they looked through the right end of the telescope, they might have better appreciated that they were about to encounter a team who were playing in a different league.

Bob Norster's hamstring injury finally proved too much and his place in the line-up was taken by Huw Richards. They were also to lose Gareth Roberts and so allow Phil Davies to play.

The All Blacks were, in every sense, a superior breed and would prove the case over the next few years under the changed leadership of Wayne Shelford. David Kirk was to play one more international after the World Cup, against Australia, before going to Oxford University and then embarking on a full-time career. Between 1987 and 1990, the All Blacks would create, under 'Buck' Shelford, a record of 12 consecutive Test wins.

Both semi-finals would be played in Australia. By this stage the authorities were hoping that there would be better support than there had been for the quarter-finals. The attendance at the Concord Oval, Sydney, for the Australia-Ireland game was 14,356. Ballymore in Brisbane had barely 10,000 for England-Wales. Both grounds could hold 20,000.

In different ways, each semi-final match exemplified the exhilarating majesty of rugby as a game. The Australia-France encounter was a thriller in which there were many

"The All Blacks laid Wales on a slab. Coldly and dispassionately, they dissected the battered and bruised body. Emotionless and calculating, they left New Zealand for the first and only time during the tournament. They returned just as impassively. Job done, they went home."

John Devereux of Wales finds that you can't out-run the All Blacks

exits and entrances, heroes and villains. The whole guessing game was not resolved until the final kick with the players, strewn about the field, having given of their last gasp. If it was not a game of great beauty, it was certainly a contest of immense and unrelieved drama. This match provided the World Cup with the glamour that had been so lacking.

The other game was quite the opposite. New Zealand demonstrated the special requirements of power, discipline and efficiency. There was no imaginative adventure here. Yet, in raw strength, disciplined rhythm and in the simplicity of execution there was a kind of beauty. This was no contest between two equally matched teams. As had been suggested, a Grand Canyon separated them. The All Blacks laid Wales on a slab. Coldly and dispassionately, they dissected the battered and bruised body. Emotionless and calculating, they left New Zealand for the first and only time during the tournament. They returned just as impassively. Job done, they went home.

The match in Sydney between Australia and France on Saturday was one of the great games of all time. Some believe it was *the* greatest game. David Hands, asking if there had ever been a game like it, wrote: "It was a French colleague, en route to Concord Oval, who referred to the 'superb ambience' of a Sydney jazz club he had discovered. Five hours later his countrymen, blowing their own brand of hot music, had created an ambience all their own as they made their way into the Final of the inaugural World

Michael Lynagh collars Laurent Rodriguez in a magnificent semi-final that neither team deserved to lose

"I said all along it would be difficult. But I do get disappointed about what this team has achieved and how difficult it is to do the job it seeks to do in Australia. If we want to have in Australia the best side in the world, which we can have and some think we might have, we've got to be much more constructive in the way we treat that side. Hardly anyone knows the World Cup is on here, in Australia, and yet it dominates attention in New Zealand and in Europe. It's very difficult to succeed in that sort of environment."

AUSTRALIA COACH ALAN JONES preparing to raise his troops to play Wales for third place after the semi-final defeat by France

Cup." David Campese, with his 25th try, became the highest try-scorer in international rugby. Michael Lynagh, with 16 points in the match, overtook the Australian Test record of 162 set by his fellow Queenslander Paul Maclean. Three times Australia were in the lead, three times France recovered.

Three minutes were left of normal time and the score stood at 21-21. Serge Blanco wanted to run in his own 22. He erred. To get out of trouble he passed the problem on to Didier Cambérabéro. The wing, usually a fly half, was engulfed. The referee spotted an infringement. Lynagh kicked the penalty. 24-21.

The excitement was pulsating. The French winger made amends by kicking the pressure penalty kick of all time – or so it seemed. Cambérabéro, villain one moment, was a hero once more. 24-24.

Then it was left to Lynagh and Campese to miscalculate and to run and to err. There followed a nail-biting passage of play which involved Patrice Lagisquet, Alain Lorieux, who had had a magnificent game, Denis Charvet and Laurent Rodriguez. Unbelievable to begin with, but as the action unfolded and one pass found another surprising pair of safe hands, momentum grew and the realisation dawned: there is something on here.

"We're going to hide. We are preparing a trick. We are going to play like the Fijians."

FRANCE COACH JACQUES FOUROUX as his team trained behind closed doors for the semi-final against Australia

The ball arrived in Blanco's hands. The full back began his 25-metre journey. Although the cover defence converged on the corner, Blanco, in what must have seemed an eternity to him, reached the line to touch down. It was a closing sequence worthy of a dream. Cambérabéro kicked from the touchline. The whistle went. The victor, at last, could be crowned. Thirty points to 24.

In the wake of Blanco's intoxicating movement, bodies

were scattered, prostrate on the ground. It was literally a breath-taking finale, luminous in its bright colours. Without doubt, it provided the inaugural World Cup with its finest moment.

The following day's semi-final in Brisbane could not possibly match this. What we had was a match of inequality and imbalance. Within the half-hour, with 24 points on the board, the contest was effectively over. Wales, as Tony Gray said afterwards, were systematically dismantled. The All Blacks rucked and drove. Rucked again and drove. Wales, like Scotland, were left to tackle, respite coming only when – because of the intensity of the physical confrontation – a player needed medical attention.

Eight tries were scored, Grant Fox accumulating more than 100 points for the tournament and Allan Whetton maintaining his personal record of scoring a try in every match.

One of the finds of the World Cup for the All Blacks was their 23-year-old full back, John Gallagher. He had made no impression in England's club rugby but emigrated to New Zealand, joined Wellington, and made his way up the ladder in his adopted country. After playing as a utility back for the All Blacks in France in 1986, he won his place at full back for the World Cup. By the time of the tour to Britain and Ireland in 1989, he had become an immensely influential player. With him, the All Blacks became an outstanding attacking force.

The 49 points New Zealand scored were the highest number ever conceded by a home union team, although eight tries had been scored by Scotland against Wales in 1924. John Devereux who, with Robert Jones and Jonathan Davies, had been among Wales' best players, scored the try which Paul Thorburn converted.

Wales suffered the ignominy of having the only player – Huw Richards – sent off in the 30 matches to date. Had Kerry Fitzgerald, the referee, any sense of fairness he would also have sent off Wayne Shelford for his delivery of an outrageous punch on Richards. Fitzgerald was chosen to officiate at the World Cup Final.

Blanco's moment of magic – scoring the try against Australia that put France into the World Cup Final

· SEMI-FINALS ·

FRANCE 30 AUSTRALIA 24
13 June • Concord Oval, Sydney, Australia
FRANCE: Blanco; Cambérabéro, Sella, Charvet, Lagisquet; Mesnel, Berbizier; Ondarts, *Dubroca, Garuet, Lorieux, Condom, Champ, Erbani, Rodriguez.
SCORERS: *Tries:* Lorieux, Sella, Laguisquet, Blanco.
Cons: Cambérabéro (4). *Pens:* Cambérabéro (2).
AUSTRALIA: Campese; Grigg, *Slack, Papworth (Herbert 8), Burke; Lynagh, Farr-Jones; Lillicrap, Lawton, McIntyre, Cutler, Campbell (Codey 20), Poidevin, Miller, Coker.
SCORERS: *Tries:* Campese, Codey. Cons: Lynagh (2).
Pens: Lynagh (3). *DG:* Lynagh.
Referee: Brian Anderson (Scotland)

NEW ZEALAND 49 WALES 6
14 June • Balleymore Oval, Brisbane, Australia
NEW ZEALAND: Gallagher; Kirwan, Stanley (McCahill 73), Taylor, Green; Fox, *Kirk; Drake, Fitzpatrick, McDowell, Pierce, G Whetton, A Whetton, Brooke-Cowden, Shelford.
SCORERS: *Tries:* Shelford (2), Drake, Kirwan (2), A Whetton, Stanley, Brooke-Cowden. *Cons:* Fox (7). *Pen:* Fox.
WALES: Thorburn; I Evans, Devereux, Bowen, Hadley; J Davies, Jones; Buchanan, K Phillips, Young, Richards, *R Moriarty, Collins (Sutton 40), P Davies, P Moriarty.
SCORERS: *Try:* Devereux. *Con:* Thorburn.
Sent off: Richards.
Referee: Kerry Fitzgerald (Australia)

An inside view of the 'best match ever'

1987 WORLD CUP SEMI-FINAL • FRANCE v AUSTRALIA

Serge Blanco was one of the great stars of the first World Cup. Here he recalls with typical French passion the events of June 13, 1987, when some people say the greatest rugby match of all time took place

BY SERGE BLANCO

France went to the first World Cup full of confidence. In the Five Nations, we had just taken the Grand Slam, and we had beaten New Zealand in Nantes. Had we set off for the World Cup with the sole aim of winning it, we could have done. But, paradoxically, our main aim was to disprove all the predictions that the Final would be between Australia and the All Blacks. More than anything else, we wanted to reach the semi-final against Australia and beat them. So, although we achieved a place in the Final, we lacked any real desire to be the world champions.

But this was a team that was capable of great things, of producing the extraordinary. On our day, we were unbeatable. Daniel Dubroca was the latest in a line of good captains of France. I myself started playing with Jean-Pierre Rives, then Philippe Dintrans, and then Dubroca. We had a generation of players who felt they could rely on one another – a generation of friends who were straight with one another – and Daniel was the link between us all. He brought the team to life. He knew how to make us understand what he was aiming for. He was a great captain.

"This was a team that was capable of great things, of producing the extraordinary. On our day, we were unbeatable."

Our opening match was against Scotland at Christchurch. We knew that if we lost we would have to face New Zealand in the quarter-final – and that would have been catastrophic. So when Patrice Lagisquet scored what seemed like a perfectly good try and it was disallowed, we were upset. Even worse, Scotland scored an equaliser right at the end which should have been disallowed because Matt Duncan had actually gone out of play, apparently unseen by the referee.

The entire crowd was supporting the Scots, who played fiercely, with a great desire for revenge because of the '87 Grand Slam, when they gave us a scare in Paris. They were very, very hard to beat that day. One could say that they were filled with aggression, in a sporting sense, but aggression all the same. They wanted to get their own back.

In the end, the scores finished level at 20-20, but because we had scored three tries to two, we would head the group. So our third try was an important one. France had been awarded a penalty, and I recall that Pierre Berbizier had been injured, so the referee had stopped play to call the medical people on to the pitch. Berbizier went off, and with the referee standing beside them they had a discussion about whether he should continue to play. Then the referee said to me: "OK, you can carry on playing now."

When I turned round, I saw that the Scottish forwards were all huddled together in a circle listening to their scrum half or their captain, Colin Deans. They carried on talking and talking. So I asked the referee: "Can I start play now?" He said to me: "Carry on."

It was in quite an awkward position, so I had to decide whether to kick the penalty, run the ball or go for touch. I opted for a tap penalty, went past the first line of the defence and found myself in front of Gavin Hastings. I went on his inside quite easily and took the ball and scored between the posts. Someone else might have played the penalty differently, but I saw an opportunity and just went for it. Perhaps that was the French way of doing things.

But then the Scots made a last-minute effort and went through our defence, into our territory and flung themselves over for Duncan to equalise. We were in almost total disarray, knowing we might lose, even though we had scored more tries. As we waited for Gavin Hastings to convert, you can imagine how we were feeling. We were unhappy about the try and if Gavin converted, the match was theirs. But the kick was right on the touchline, in the dying moments of a very hard match, and for once he missed.

We were relieved, because we had gone to this World Cup without a kicker – in fact, in that match, I was the kicker. But that problem was solved in our third pool game against Zimbabwe. I didn't play, because I had picked up an injury in the second game, a 55-12 victory against Romania. The match against Zimbabwe allowed all those players who hadn't yet played to have a game ... and something fantastic happened. A lad called Didier Cambérabéro, who had joined the group only at the last minute because Jean-Baptiste Lafond was injured, was man of the match with 30 points – a world record which is still the French record today.

It was a turning point for him and a bonus for the French, who won the game 70-12.

After the pool games we changed hotels. I have read that it was because of all the girls at the Mon Désir, but that just makes me laugh. The hotel was so full of people that it was more like Club Med – great for having a good time but not so good for concentration and serious preparation.

The quarter-final against Fiji was a strange match because I was not sure I was fully fit. I played with my thigh strapped up. The French team were expecting an easy win, but they were rather taken by surprise by the Fijians, who played with great skill and confidence and knew how to pass the ball out to the wings. There was one particularly telling moment. It came right at the end of the game, when we knew we were going to win, but we let in a silly try. The Fijian wing Damu dropped the ball but still managed to score. We were really flagging and it made us realise that we could be out of the tournament if we didn't make more effort. It gave us the impetus to refocus and really prepare for the semi-final against Australia. It has been described as the best rugby match ever. Well, I don't know about that, but it was certainly outstanding. All the ingredients were there: the weather was fine, there was a good crowd, two strong teams, the 'great and the good' of the press and TV. The scene was set for a great game – even Hitchcock couldn't have planned it better!

We felt rather isolated because the entire world expected Australia to reach the Final, and our performance against Fiji had only served to reinforce their expectations. But it turned out to be a real cliffhanger. No one in France, or in Australia for that matter, will ever forget it. That kind of match – where anything and everything might happen – is

Pierre Berbizier picks up the pieces and launches his unpredictable backs on another attack

the sort of game that I hope tomorrow's rugby will give us.

I had the pleasure of playing against David Campese. Firstly, he is my friend, but more than anything, he is a great player. We French felt that he was the one player who would be quite at home in our team. His game, like that of the French perhaps, could be described as poetry. Initially, watching as David Campese began to develop his game, one might have felt a little threatened by it, but in fact we were both moving forward in the same way.

On that particular day, we came under a lot of pressure but we never doubted ourselves for one second, even when we were trailing 9-0. Late on, Australia scored a try from a lineout which was, shall we say, somewhat contentious, but we never let it get to us. We knew we were going to succeed. David Campese scored their first try, to put them 15-12 ahead, so we had to come back quickly. I sidestepped past Campese, passed inside, wrong-footing the opposition, and suddenly Patrice Lagisquet found himself on the open road, as it were – *un grand boulevard*. All he had to do was run to score a try. That put us back into the game and showed us that we could play well and score tries.

Blanco describes David Campese's game as "poetry" – but Blanco himself was the poet laureate

The worst moment was David Codey's try, which made it 21-21, after a throw-in at the lineout which was not straight. I complained to the referee but in rugby the referee never changes his mind! It was especially important because, earlier, we had had a try disallowed. But that's how it goes sometimes. So instead of complaining any more, as we stood under the posts we said to ourselves: "Let's go!" We got on with the game.

We were already in injury time when Michael Lynagh kicked a penalty to make it 24-21, but we couldn't let anything get to us; we mustn't let self-doubt begin. We got into the Australian half and – boof! – a penalty in our favour. We said a quick "thank you, God" because this was a chance for Didier Cambérabéro to equalise and keep our dreams alive. Everything rested on Didier, who had been such a revelation in the match against Zimbabwe. He came up and calmly kicked it over and we had equalised. 24-24. Magic!

That was the best moment of the match. By now it was deep in injury time and we were waiting and waiting for the referee to blow for full-time, but play went on … and on! And then came a sequence of play which was something else. There were so many of us involved, one after another – to me, to Lagisquet – a pass to the right, to the left – we lost the ball, we got it back – me, Patrice Lagisquet, Rodriguez – and so the ball went on and on, and from Rodriguez back to me. What a moment for me! I was absolutely inspired by this great rolling wave of play to make a supreme effort. I threw myself over the line … and that was it! Victory!

Didier converted. It was quite a moment for French rugby; for everyone who had had faith in us.

After the final whistle, back in the changing room, we were the happiest men in the whole world. We had accomplished a great feat because the Australians had been out-and-out favourites but we, the French, had done it. Everyone would have liked to have been in our shoes, but not everyone could have played like we did. It was a moment of extreme happiness – an extraordinary moment of rapport and communication.

After showering and changing, we gave a press conference, by the end of which time the stadium was in complete darkness.

We all went out on to the pitch, we did a lap of honour, and we sang! We sang Basque songs for half an hour. It was a way to re-experience the emotions through our voices, because the voice is the instrument of the feelings. There was absolutely no one else there. Just us. It was our little secret. Our special time, a really quite extraordinary moment that was ours alone. It was a moment of sheer magic which is difficult to describe. The feelings, the emotions. So happy, so proud of what we had done. Yes, the happiest men in the whole world.

And so to the Final. There was a pivotal moment in that match. We were stronger in the scrum than New Zealand and just before half-time we had three consecutive scrums on their line. We drove the scrum backwards, the Blacks turned the scrum, the Blacks collapsed the scrum but the referee didn't even give a penalty. We thought it should have been a penalty try. We just could not believe it. That unsettled us.

"Long after the match, when the stadium was in darkness, we all went out on to the pitch. We did a lap of honour, and we sang! We sang Basque songs for half an hour. It was a way to re-experience the emotions through our voices, because the voice is the instrument of the feelings. There was absolutely no one else there. Just us. It was our little secret. Our special time. The feelings are difficult to describe. So happy, so proud of what we had done."

It was then that we realised that we could not win this match. For New Zealand it was a home game, they were a great team, they had the big names – John Gallagher, John Kirwan, Grant Fox, whose kicking game was so strong. There were other things as well, to tell the truth. Perhaps we did not prepare as well as we should have done. We were in a rather relaxed state of mind, almost happy just to be in the Final. We didn't have a strong enough desire to win the match. New Zealand deserved to win.

They say that the All Blacks were a machine, but that's not true – not if by 'machine' one means 'mechanical'. They had a generation of great players who complemented each other. I didn't often win when I played against them. In that World Cup, the Blacks were unstoppable.

We talk nowadays of Jonah Lomu, but Kirwan was a phenomenal player. He was the equivalent of Lomu except that Kirwan could do quite exceptional things with his hands. You couldn't afford to give away a penalty because Grant Fox would place the ball and – ping! – an almost guaranteed three points. Not only that, but he had a coolness, a sense of calm, which was outstanding. David Kirk was the link between the forwards and the three-quarters – a great leader and a player of exceptional talent.

After the match, I can remember as if it was yesterday Albert Ferrasse presenting the Cup to David Kirk. And I can truly say that, even as he lifted the World Cup, there was not one Frenchman who was really sad. We were disappointed to have lost – one couldn't be happy to have lost the Final of the World Cup – but we were happy for the Blacks, because one can retrace the last 50 years of rugby history through the standard of All Black play. There would have been a great injustice if they hadn't won.

1987 THE PLAY-OFF FOR · THIRD PLACE ·

This is the fixture no one wants to play. The losing semi-finalists are the forgotten teams. Who remembers them? For Andrew Slack, Australia's captain, it was a waste of time.

"It's a Test match, we are fair dinkum about it. We don't ever devalue the status of the jersey."
AUSTRALIA COACH ALAN JONES on the eve of the third-place playoff match

Wales, after all their injuries, were having to patch together a pack of forwards. Richard Webster was on holiday in Australia and playing for Teacher's North Club in Canberra, as had David Young. With crippling injuries to the Welsh team, both players, under 20 years of age, had been recruited into the squad and found themselves winning their first caps for their country. Young had already played twice in the tournament and Webster was chosen to play in the World Cup's penultimate match in Rotorua.

No one gave Wales a chance. Bets were taken only on the number of points Australia were likely to amass. But the sceptics were to be confounded. If doubts had been expressed beforehand as to the worthiness or otherwise of this play-off fixture, the success of the game in Rotorua ensured that it remained part of the tournament. A big crowd turned up and quite a spectacle followed.

Above: Wales captain Richard Moriarty with the trophy that would go to David Kirk. Right: Nick Farr-Jones clears from a maul

Australia were reduced to 14 men after only four minutes. David Codey, the flanker, ignoring a previous warning, decided to continue taking the law into his own hands by using the bodies of opponents as a resting place for his studs. He was sent off.

If this diminished his team's resources, the depletion, as so often happens, can stiffen a team's resolve. A resolve which was reinforced when Nick Farr-Jones replaced the wing, Peter Grigg, in the 47th minute The three-quarter line was rejigged with Farr-Jones going to his customary position, while Brian Smith, who started at scrum half, went to the wing.

It proved a tight contest. Cutler and Coker in the second row were crucial in denying Wales the ball so that the brilliantly astute Lynagh at outside half pinned back Wales for long periods.

Thorburn and Lynagh began by exchanging successful penalties and then each failing with an attempt before Wales broke the deadlock. If some of their adventurous play did not always show good judgement, they were eventually rewarded. A firm Welsh drive was carried on by the ubiquitous Jones at scrum half for Gareth Roberts to be pushed over by the rest of his pack. But every time Wales seemed to be making headway they overplayed their hand and committed errors.

Burke and Grigg were the beneficiaries with a try each. Paul Moriarty responded with the best try of the match after a long movement that involved Webster, Alan Phillips and Buchanan. With the three tries converted, Australia took the interval lead at 15-13. The respective kickers exchanged two more penalties before Lynagh seemed to settle the result with a drop goal to give a 21-16 lead.

As the match reached a climax, in the fourth minute of injury time Jonathan Davies hoisted a treacherously high ball to his opponents' 22-metre line. Devereux jumped high to recover it. He succeeded. Ieuan Evans took it, ran in-field to join Mark Ring and Thorburn. The full back sent in Adrian Hadley for the score near the corner flag.

It still needed the conversion to win the game. This was left to Paul Thorburn. In a long and prolific kicking career, he had accomplished many a fine strike, but none was to prove better than this. With a superb kick from the touchline and under intense pressure, the full back did what was needed. The large section of the Rotorua crowd who had given their support to Wales throughout gave an ecstatic cheer as the ball sailed through the posts: 22-21.

• 3RD PLACE PLAY-OFF •

WALES 22 AUSTRALIA 21
18 June 1987 • Rotorua International Stadium
WALES: Thorburn; I Evans, Devereux, Ring, Hadley; J Davies, Jones; Buchanan, A Phillips, Blackmore, *R Moriarty, Sutton, Roberts, Webster, P Moriarty.
SCORERS: *Tries:* Roberts, P Moriarty, Hadley. *Cons:* Thorburn (2). *Pens:* Thorburn (2).
AUSTRALIA: Leeds; Grigg (Farr-Jones 46), Burke, *Slack, Campese; Lynagh, Smith; Lillicrap (Rodriguez 76), Lawton, McIntyre, Cutler, Coker, Poidevin, Codey, Tuynman.
SCORERS: Burke, Grigg. *Cons:* Lynagh (2). *Pens:* Lynagh (2). *DG:* Lynagh.
Sending off: Codey.
Referee: Fred Howard (England).

Richard Moriarty of Wales fingertips the ball away from rival lock Troy Coker of Australia in the tightly-contested third-place playoff match. Left: Wales fly half Jonathan Davies makes a break in the bold style that made him a great player in both union and league

The thriller in Rotorua

THIRD PLACE PLAY-OFF • AUSTRALIA v WALES

Many observers said that Jonathan Davies of Wales was the best player in the first World Cup. Here he recalls the pulsating match against Australia that sent Wales home as heroes

BY JONATHAN DAVIES

I enjoyed the 1987 World Cup both on and off the field. We had a lot of characters in that Wales side and were really good mates. Playing in the World Cup fulfilled a dream: it was one thing I wanted to do before I went to rugby league. The irony is that when we got there they sat us down and made us sign a form saying we wouldn't write any articles or books or make any commercial gain from the tournament. So we signed, then settled back to watch the opening game between New Zealand and Italy on TV – and the first advert had All Blacks captain Andy Dalton promoting four-wheel quad bikes. The second showed John Kirwan advertising cream. It made it seem like a bit of an uneven playing field.

Our first game was against Ireland in Wellington, which was like Wales but windier. Ireland's Donal Lenihan won the toss and elected to go with the wind, which was incredibly strong. In fact it was the deciding factor, because we used it better. Ireland started as favourites, having beaten us in Cardiff during the Five Nations. But we played well, kicking low and hard against the wind in the first half to keep the score down to 6-0, then attacking in the second.

Mark Ring scored a try after a move in which he was involved twice, and then I dropped two goals. A tight game, but we controlled it well. I sat out most of a rugged encounter with Tonga, coming on with 20 minutes to go when Malcolm Dacey was injured.

In the next match, against Canada at Invercargill, I achieved a personal ambition. Richard Moriarty was rested and I captained my country for the first time. Canada were a very strong side, but I had one of my better games. I was fortunate enough to make a few breaks which set up tries and in the end it was one-way traffic.

"It was an exciting finish. Too exciting. Winning third place wasn't everything but at least we ended among the medals"

I also enjoyed that game immensely because I was playing against Gareth Rees who had been quite cocky in the run-up. We struggled in the first half, with their forwards on top and the wind against us, but in the second half we ran in seven tries to win 40-9 and finish top of the group.

The quarter-final against England was in Brisbane. I was carrying a dead leg that I had picked up against Canada and shouldn't really have played. But I went through the motions because they said that if I didn't participate, it would give a psychological advantage to England. To be fair, Robert Jones dictated that match because he knew I was injured. He looked after me.

Conditions were poor, which was surprising for Brisbane, and it was a dour game. Because I was injured, I couldn't do the crazy things I liked to do with the ball. The two teams knew each other so well, and there was so much riding on it, that it was a rather dull affair and people were very critical of it. We scored three tries, the first when Gareth Roberts dived on the ball after a scrum which England actually won.

Then there was a break where I did a scissors with Bleddyn Bowen, he carried it on, the ball went to ground, Robert Jones kicked through and won a foot race with England scrum half Richard Harding. Finally,

John Devereux took a good interception pass off England fly half Peter Williams and drove it in easy.

The semi-final against the All Blacks was a different kettle of fish. Their scrums, their rolling mauls and their rucks annihilated us, and then their back line just ran us ragged. They were the best side in the World Cup, though not the best side I have ever played against. That honour goes to the same New Zealand side a year later, when they had matured as players and as a team, and flogged us in both Tests.

The third place play-off took place at Rotorua, where they have big geysers and the place smells of sulphur. It's a Maori area steeped in rugby, with a great stadium in a natural bowl.

All week, the locals were supporting us because they hate the Aussies – it's like England coming to play Scotland in Cardiff; all the Welsh fans would be supporting Scotland. We also knew that the Aussies didn't want to be there, because they were so disappointed after losing the semi-final to France on home ground. So we thought we could be in with a shout.

Robert Jones prepares to hoist an up-and-under as the Australian defence bears down on him

I can't remember what the attendance was, but it seemed to be thousands and thousands. And it was a nice day. It was a strange game – both teams had chances, and there were lots of breaks going on. We played extremely well. It doesn't matter what they say about not wanting to be there, the Australians still did not want to lose.

They were far stronger than us up front, but when David Codey was sent off after just four minutes, we gained some parity.

Our strength was in the back line, but in the earlier matches we never had enough ball. This time, having parity in the forwards allowed us to play the expansive game we wanted to play – even though one of their tries came from Mark Ring and myself trying to be over-elaborate.

I remember that Michael Lynagh and I had a couple of right old ding-dongs. He clipped me off the ball when I was supporting Robert Jones's break, and then I left an inside gap for him and took his head off. The last try came when we were 21-15 down. I hoisted a high kick into their 22 and I'm not sure what happened after that because it was so frantic. We managed to get the ball back and they were in disarray.

John Devereux touched it and suddenly he was away. Paul Thorburn handed somebody off and flipped the ball to Adrian Hadley, who just snuck in at the corner. Then Paul Thorburn had the easy task of converting from the touchline to win the match. As we told him, there was never any pressure on the kick because nobody thought he was going to get it...

Even then Australia could have won it because I remember Campo charging towards the line and being brought down by an ankle tap – I'm not sure if it was by me or somebody else.

So it was an exciting finish. Too exciting. Winning third place wasn't the be-all-and-end-all, because the biggest prize was on the following Saturday, but it's always nice to finish in the medals. We knew we weren't good enough to win the World Cup, but we came back with our heads held high and with a lot of confidence. And we went on to win the 1988 Triple Crown.

1987

EDEN PARK

·THE FINAL·

> "If you knock a few guys around, that's part of the game. It's a physical game and the harder it is, the more I thrive on it."
>
> NEW ZEALAND No 8 WAYNE SHELFORD looking forward to the Final against France

Although they had amassed 269 points in their five tournament matches, allowing only 43 to pass their iron grip, the All Blacks had not seemed to play with any of the freedom of movement these figures suggest. They had scored 40 tries by this stage, playing traditional All Black rugby. They had a formidable pack to which everyone else should play servant. Everything should be efficiently geared to a tight control; simple and direct.

The principles of their game were incarnated in the dynamic form of Wayne Shelford, their No 8. On the field, he seemed to marshal the team.

David Kirk, by and large, was a quiet presence – but, in view of the turmoil which had engulfed New Zealand rugby, all the more potent for that. There was a latent authority which was impressive. He appeared an elfin in the midst of the tyrannous power around him; the still, small voice of reason against the roar and bluster. Nonetheless, he was unquestionably the "guvnor", endowed with an intelligence that effortlessly set aside the merely peripheral to emphasise and analyse the main elements of the day's play. Grant Fox outside him was the outside half, or first five-eighths as they prefer to be called in New Zealand, for whose place-kicking exploits the word 'metronome' was first coined. His accurate kicking was to

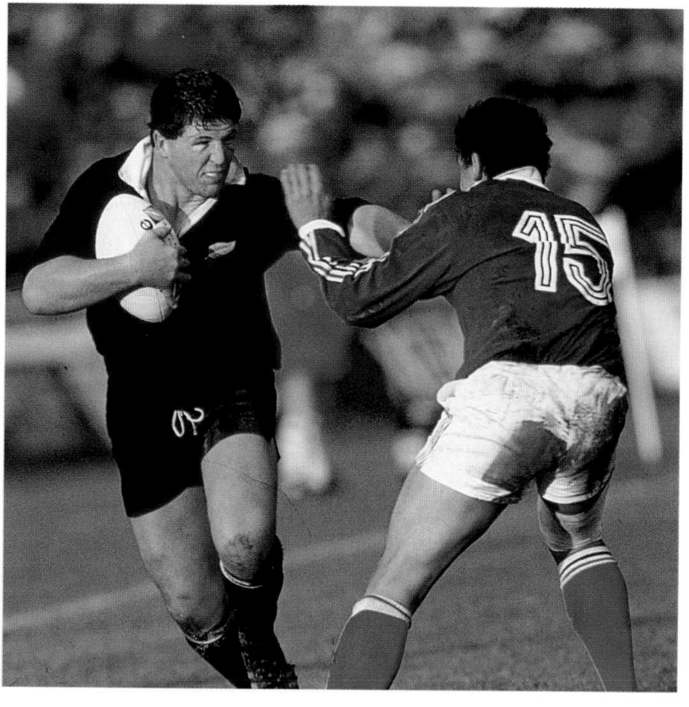

All Blacks hooker Sean Fitzpatrick hands off Serge Blanco

COULD FRANCE CLIMB THE MOUNTAIN AGAIN?

• Captain Daniel Dubroca on the eve of the Final •

'We have only a 25 per cent chance of winning. We attach a lot of importance to playing on the home ground. The All Blacks have the normal 50 per cent chance, plus 25 per cent because they play on their own field. To win we need a new type of commitment, a superior form of mental concentration. We are immensely fit and eager, the only problem is our spirit. Can we do two in a row? I know that all the hard work we've put into it, the way we've sacrificed our families and personal lives, has been worthwhile. We are in the Final and I hope we'll do well. I'm not a star myself. I'm just a rugby player who has been given the honour to captain his country. Rugby is a team game and the star is the team. If we win on Saturday, it is France, not Dubroca."

John Kirwan stands tall in the tackle as Patrice Lagisquet tries to bring him down. Fittingly, Kirwan scored the final try of the 1987 tournament

collect him 109 points in the five matches. Both half backs were efficient and well-disciplined. Outside this pair and behind Shelford's pack, the three quarters were a supporting act. They played classic All Black rugby.

Above all, the team had resilience. They did not suffer many injuries and so had no need to change their personnel, as Australia had to. What did prove irksome was the failure of Andy Dalton, the original captain, to recover. When he did, Sean Fitzpatrick was performing so well that in the end, Dalton did not play at all.

France had worries aplenty. Neither Blanco or Lorieux, both of whom had played magnificently in the semi-final, were fully fit for the Final, although they did make the line-up. It had been touch and go.

But more than that, it was evident by June 20 at Eden Park in Auckland that the spark which sustains French rugby had left them. After so much rugby in the previous months and the strain of the semi-final, France looked to be a tired team and proved to be so. For them it was a game too far. Apart from the occasional swift French riposte, it was a match dominated by the All Blacks.

There was no colour, only a grim determination by New Zealand to get their hands on the Webb Ellis Cup. For the most part France were engulfed by black jerseys, the most prominent being those in the back row, among whom Jones was the most conspicuous. After Fox's attempt at a drop goal was charged down and Lagisquet failed to gather, Jones latched on to the wayward ball to score the first try. Then, Fox, after converting this score, succeeded with his second attempt at a drop goal. So the

"Shelford is an extraordinary player. It is him who drives the All Black train. He is the locomotive. And you can't stop the train unless you stop the locomotive."

FRANCE No 8
LAURENT RODRIGUEZ
on his New Zealand opposite number, Wayne Shelford

The only Englishman to win the World Cup

THE 1987 WORLD CUP FINAL

John Gallagher took the rugby world by storm with his pioneering style of his play – a full back coming into the three-quarter line like an express train. You couldn't miss his red hair. You also couldn't miss his London accent…

BY JOHN GALLAGHER

We had no preconceptions about what the World Cup would be like. All we knew was that it was being played on New Zealand soil, so we had to win it. I say "we", although I hadn't actually played for the All Blacks at the time, and the very fact that I was there at all still struck me as something of a miracle, as I was born and brought up in London and didn't go to New Zealand until I was 20. I went for six months to play rugby for a small club side, and got picked for Wellington while six of their All Blacks were touring Australia. But then I came back to England, where I ended up joining the police.

While at Hendon police college I started playing for the Met with Paul Ackford, but I really didn't enjoy the rugby. I had eight games at centre and only saw the ball three times. So I went back to New Zealand to play for Wellington.

"I didn't enjoy the rugby in England. I had eight games at centre and only saw the ball three times. So I went back to New Zealand…"

I was brought into the World Cup squad because I could cover a number of positions – wing, full back and centre – and I was lucky enough to get the nod at full back for the first Test against Italy. Winning my first cap in the first game of the first World Cup was fantastic.

I had played four midweek games for the All Blacks on the 1986 French tour and never scored a try. Then we beat Italy by 70 points in the World Cup opener and I still didn't score. I was beginning to wonder if I was ever going to. But I scored four times in the second World Cup match against Fiji. I remember my first international touchdown as if it was yesterday. Grant Fox went for a penalty shot and actually hit the post. The ball bounced out and we hit a couple of rucks and then the winger Craig Green – who also scored four tries – put me over in the corner. It was exhilarating.

Kieran Crowley was at full back for the third match against Argentina, but I got the call for the quarter-final against Scotland and held the place for the rest of the tournament. By then we were on a roll. Andy Dalton, the captain, missed the early games with a hamstring injury. After we reached the semi-finals the selectors didn't want to change a winning team. It was tough for Andy but he was brilliantly supportive. David Kirk continued as on-field captain.

It was an incredible team, particularly for a back. From the start of the World Cup we went 50 games undefeated, including 23 Tests, with one draw against Australia in 1988. I think it's difficult for anyone on the outside to understand what made it such a good team. The All Blacks may have appeared arrogant, but they were actually very modest, down-to-earth – and totally loyal. People referred to us as the "All Black machine", but it certainly wasn't mechanical. The key to our success was our ability to change the gameplan; there was such close utility within the team that we could play any way we wanted.

Auckland had been playing 'total rugby' since 1984, and with 11 of their players in the Test side it was easy for the four others to fit in. People tell me I was a new style of full back, but it came naturally. I had played a lot of rugby at centre and I was very aware that if you have a full back coming into the line it makes the centre's job that much easier because the defence is caught in two minds. There's an automatic overlap, and if the defence's full back comes up, then you just kick it and gain ground with the boot. Whether the centre actually gave me the ball was irrelevant. I knew I had to be there every time. I couldn't understand why it hadn't been done before.

Our toughest match was the quarter-final against Scotland, which we won 30-3. We scored two tries, one of which came my way after Michael Jones latched on to the ball at the back of a lineout and took off. He fed it inside to Gary Whetton, who gave it to Wayne Shelford, who nearly scored. Then everybody piled over the top, the ball came wide and I picked the line off Joe Stanley and went in under the posts. It was a good team try.

The All Blacks' English full back John Gallagher is tackled by Pierre Berbizier in the Final

The day before the semi-final against Wales in Brisbane, we saw France beat Australia in Sydney on television. We had a real love-hate relationship with the Aussies, so we were delighted that France had got through. Now only Wales stood between us and the World Cup Final – and we were surprised to find they were one of the weaker teams we had met in the tournament. By the time we were about 27 points up after 30 minutes, we knew the game was over. Jonathan Davies has since told me he was annoyed that when they got home they were treated as heroes because they had beaten Australia for third place, whereas he was disappointed to have lost 49-6 to the All Blacks.

I picked up an injury in that game when I took a high ball and John Devereux came through with his knee up. I lasted the game but couldn't walk for three days, and it was touch-and-go whether I would make the Final. To say I was desperate would be an understatement. We were pleased to be facing France in the Final because we had lost in Nantes the year before, and that rankled with the guys who had played in that game. I was really looking forward to facing Serge Blanco in the World Cup Final, because he was my hero – the player I aspired to be.

Unfortunately, the weather on the big day was miserable, and the game carried on in the same vein. It was drizzling throughout, which made it very difficult to play a decent standard of rugby. The match was won by the forwards and Grant Fox. Wayne Shelford had a fantastic game, as did Michael Jones and Alan Whetton. The midfield tackled superbly.

There was a great try at the end which started with David Kirk, who had just scored a try himself. From the kick-off Kirky made a break up the short side which was carried on by Buck Shelford, who gave it to John Kirwan. He had a foot-race with Philippe Sella and beat him to the corner. That made it 29-3 with 15 minutes to go and we knew the game was won.

Andy Dalton had been on the bench, and when David Kirk went up for the trophy he called Andy over to lift it with him. We couldn't do a lap of honour because the field had been invaded, so we just sat in the changing room, congratulated ourselves and let it sink in. Many of the players felt sheer relief, because there is a hell of a burden of expectancy from the New Zealand public, who think the All Blacks will always win.

The Monday after the Saturday Final I was back at work as a policeman. It was difficult to do my job because I was recognised all the time. Being a World Cup winner had some good spin-offs, but I never did any undercover work again...

THE BUSINESS

A total of 355,500 people watched 21 games in New Zealand – an average of 17,000 a match. In Australia, 126,000 people watched 11 games – an average of 11,500.

score at the interval was 9-0. In the second half, Cambérabéro reduced the deficit with his only opportunity of a penalty all afternoon. But more often than not, the game was played in his team's half. Fox kicked four penalties.

In among these kicks the ever-present Jones made the influential break which led to Kirk's try. And from the restart the scrum half, leaving the French defence as mere spectators, slipped away for 60 metres to give Kirwan his eighth try of the tournament.

There was no way back for the French. They did get a consolation try courtesy of Pierre Berbizier, who was

four times in the movement which led to only the fourth try that the All Blacks had conceded during the month-long campaign.

The New Zealanders were dour but brilliant executioners in their 29-9 victory. And if they could be ungracious and there was little humour in them, what of that? No doubt they would feel it is the combat that is important; the desire for the spoils that is the motive force. Keep your smiles and gentlemanly conduct.

But the lasting image of the first World Cup was of New Zealand's captain, David Kirk, a Peter Pan figure, holding aloft the Webb Ellis

French flanker Eric Champ tries to break the All Black chains. Above: New Zealand kicker Grant Fox, the top scorer in the 1987 World Cup with 126 points

· 1987 STATISTICS ·

INDIVIDUAL SCORING RECORDS

Most points in tournament:
126 **G J Fox** (New Zealand)
82 **M J Lynagh** (Australia)
62 **A G Hastings** (Scotland)

Most tries in tournament:
6 **C I Green** (New Zealand)
6 **J J Kirwan** (New Zealand)

Most dropped goals:
3 **J Davies** (Wales)

Most points in a match:
30 **D Cambérabéro** (France v Zimbabwe)
27 **A G Hastings** (Scotland v Romania)
26 **G J Fox** (New Zealand v Fiji)

Most tries in a match:
4 **I C Evans** (Wales v Canada)
4 **C I Green** (New Zealand v Fiji)
4 **J A Gallagher** (New Zealand v Fiji)

New Zealand's acting captain David Kirk accepts the Cup

"We played our Final in Sydney."

FRANCE COACH JACQUES FOUROUX after losing the Final in Auckland to New Zealand

Cup. With a whole face that smiled and an extra twinkle in his eye, you could imagine Kirk captivating the hearts of those who held rugby in less than an endearing embrace. Physically slight and unintimidating, he was as untypical an All Black as could be imagined.

But the graze and the trickle of blood on his left eyebrow as he received the Cup from Albert Ferrasse of France, chairman of the IRFB, were evidence that he had survived a bruising afternoon. He was no softy. He could be as tough, physically and mentally, as men with a more menacing demeanour.

After the South African visit to New Zealand in 1981 and the controversial Cavaliers tour to the republic in 1986, Kirk was the very acceptable face of All Black rugby. He was a walking public relations campaign. This was no small consideration, especially as New Zealand's brand of rugby was unlikely to win many friends. We admired them but we were not charmed by them. But all in all, the All Blacks were, by far, the best team in the tournament. They had not been seriously challenged for their crown, as the scores testify. The 1987 Cup really did belong to them.

· THE FINAL ·

NEW ZEALAND 29 FRANCE 9
20 June • Eden Park, Auckland
NEW ZEALAND: Gallagher; Kirwan, Stanley, Taylor, Green; Fox, *Kirk; McDowell, Fitzpatrick, Drake, Pierce, G Whetton, A Whetton, Jones, Shelford.
SCORERS: *Tries:* Jones, Kirk, Kirwan. *Con:* Fox. Pens: Fox (4). *DG:* Fox.
FRANCE: Blanco; Cambérabéro, Sella, Charvet, Lagisquet; Mesnel, Berbizier; Ondarts, *Dubroca, Garuet, Lorieux, Condom, Champ, Erbani, Rodriguez.
SCORERS: *Try:* Berbizier. *Con:* Cambérabéro. *Pen:* Cambérabéro.
Referee: Kerry Fitzgerald (Australia).
Attendance: 48,500.

1991

THE WEBB ELLIS CUP

In Great Britain, Ireland and France

AFTER THE SUCCESS OF THE FIRST WORLD CUP, THE NORTHERN HEMISPHERE COUNTRIES GINGERLY DIPPED A TOE IN THE WATER – AND FOUND IT WAS LOVELY

"Watch out, Dean, they're doing the haka again!"
Dooley and Richards get a shock during the 1991 World Cup Final

4
9

IT'S COMING HOME, IT'S COMING HOME...

The 1991 World Cup was centred on Twickenham, but it ventured far afield, from Béziers to Pontypridd. As southern hemisphere stars such as Lynagh, Campese and Kirwan got ready to dazzle, the unknown Western Samoans checked in to Cardiff

"The World Cup has brought a more professional approach from all teams. The only team that has not improved is New Zealand, because they got it right last time. By 1988 it was clear that the second World Cup was going to be nothing like the first, that it would be the biggest global sporting event of the year."

AUSTRALIA COACH BOB DWYER

Although the Rugby World Cup was still rather an unknown quantity, it was widely believed that. since the idea had sprung from the International Board countries of the southern hemisphere, they were the ones likely to dominate the tournament. The evidence from 1987 was that Europe had been left behind by the New World.

The technical and tactical style of play of the All Blacks and the Wallabies, and indeed the quality of their intelligence, was far ahead of anything happening in the northern hemisphere.

By October 1991, Europe's hopes rested squarely with England. Wales were in disarray. In the preceding two years they had had three national coaches. In July they had returned from a disastrous tour of Australia, triggering another sequence in the coaches' musical chairs which saw Ron Waldron replaced by Alan Davies only weeks before the World Cup was due to begin. No one quite knew what to make of Wales any more. Sympathy was the kindest response, ridicule the harshest. There were those who longed for them to regain their eminence, others who would be glad to see them finally buried as their payback for their arrogance of the past. For sure, they had fallen from a great height.

The ceremonial rugby ball from Rugby School arrives at Twickenham, where Prince Edward launched the 1991 Rugby World Cup, left

Ireland, for all their excitable potency and devil-may-care, could not be relied upon to sustain their efforts. They could turn the tables once on their opponents, but evidence suggested they could not repeat the feat. They played on a whim and a prayer. Of all the national teams, Ireland is the one that most people would like to see do well. Former players tend to hold it in particular affection, as Ireland is the most popular rugby country to visit – but none of those

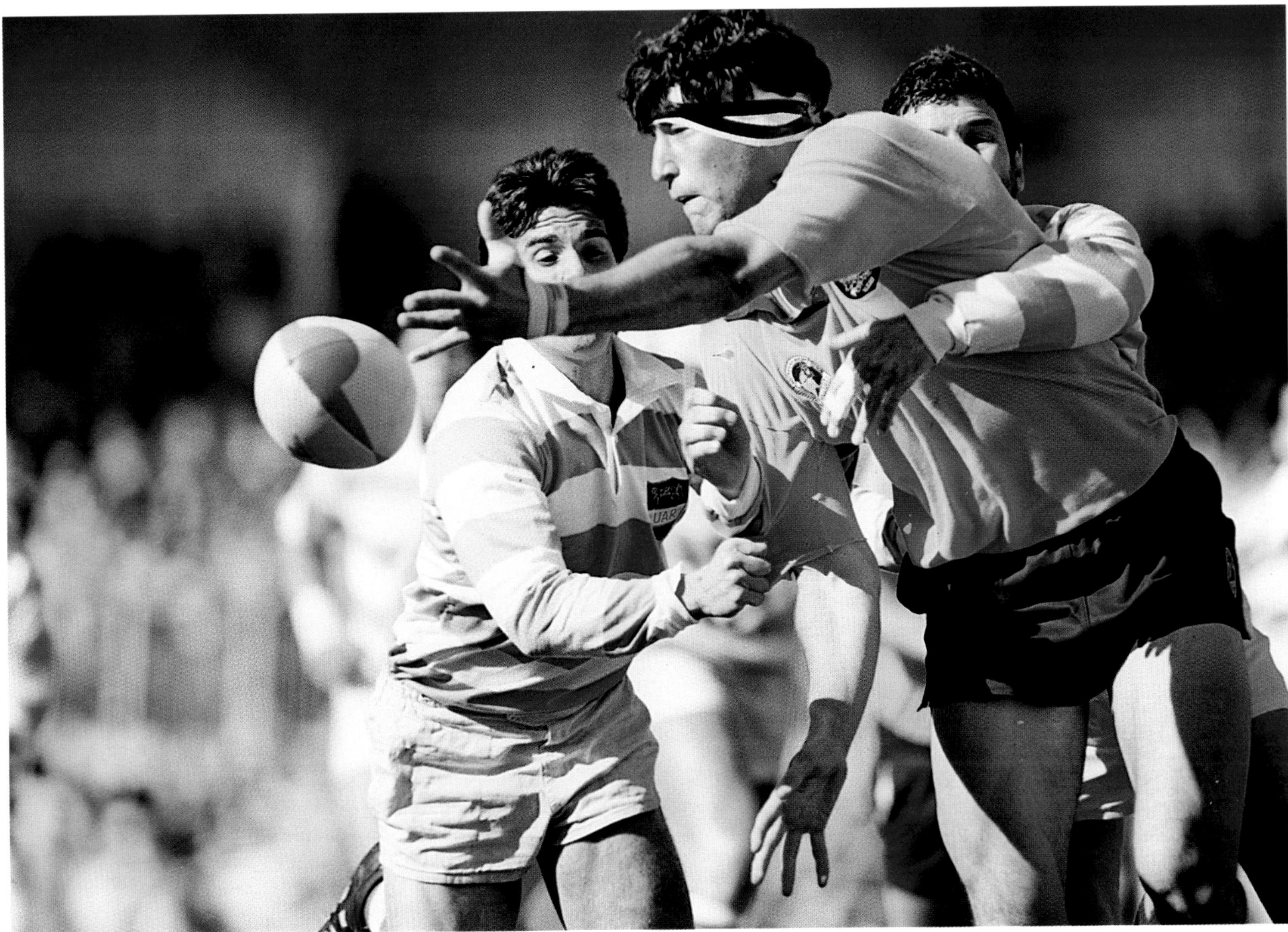

John Eales, the highly effective lock for Australia, in action against Argentina

ex-players plying their trade in the prints were expecting to be toasting the World Cup winners in Guinness.

Scotland, despite winning the Grand Slam in 1990, enjoyed brilliant but fragile success. If only, one felt, they could muster enough players to share the burden; if only they had the strength in even moderate depth; if only, if only... More often than not they had a crowd of workaday players mingled with some of genuine greatness.

Of all the teams, though, they managed – when the Thistle was on their breast and *Flower of Scotland* in their ears – to get the maximum out of each player when called upon. They could play a beautifully fluid game.

For all of France's silvery brilliance, no one felt confident they could maintain their panache from one match to the next, let alone for a whole month's competition. When they did so it came as a surprise to everyone. They could just as easily disappoint us. In an aesthetic sense they could be the best rugby players of all. They could turn a brutish sport into a beautiful one. A new resilience appeared to have entered their rugby soul, but history being what it is, and national characteristics being what they are, hardly anyone felt they could truly trust it.

England, on the other hand, were a team with a military discipline, imbued with the Bulldog spirit. They had overcome the rush of blood which had once inspired a trio of players to play football with the Calcutta Cup along Princes Street in Edinburgh. Such aberrations were no longer part of the regime. In March, Will Carling's men had won the Grand Slam for the first time since Bill Beaumont's team in 1980.

That this period was to become a golden age of English rugby was confirmed a year later when they won a second consecutive Grand Slam which equalled the achievement of Wavell Wakefield's team of 1924. Undoubtedly, there was a supreme confidence in the air. Perhaps there was too much of it. Self-belief is one thing, hubris quite another. Failure to distinguish between the two had cost them dearly at Murrayfield in 1990 when both the home team and England contested the Grand Slam. England were the strong favourites but it was Scotland who won.

"We didn't really aim to do that well in the Five Nations. Our main worry is peaking twice within a year, as our main target is the World Cup."
FRANCE MANAGER HENRI FOURES

American tourists in Yorkshire – the USA team run out at Otley for their match against Italy, which the Italians won 30-9

The English had acquired a resolve to go with their ambition. Furthermore, the incentive of being the host nation, with a final at Twickenham, was high. So was the expectation. There was a sense of gathering momentum and strengthening reputation. Geoff Cooke, the coach, was an astute strategist. He was a shrewd and sympathetic manager of men; a Cumbrian who knew what he wanted and understood, more often than not, how to get it.

Cooke was the architect of England's glory days. If these were in their dawning period as yet, this year might go some way to indicate the firm grip they could have on European rugby over the next few years. Cooke was practical and unsentimental, although touched, on occasion, by too much presumption. Within his winning ways there could be a failure to respect the opposition enough. He and his captain had miscalculated at Murrayfield in 1990. And, in the 1991 Five Nations Championship, after England's first victory in Cardiff since 1963, he made himself appear ungracious, even disdainful, when he and Carling failed to turn up at a scheduled after-match press conference.

Cooke, after a major reshuffle at Twickenham, had been installed in his position following the first World Cup and in time would transform the whole perception of the game in England. His appointment represented a firm statement of intent and would recreate for English rugby the much longed-for palmy days of its past.

There had been such a contrast between the English and Welsh response to the events of 1987. In reaching the semi-finals in that year and beating England on the way, Wales crowed about achieving third place. This might have been fine had they also agreed that being third was not good enough. The Welsh Rugby Union, instead of recognising their failures and redoubling their efforts, carried on as if they had little to learn.

England, on the other hand, after losing in the quarter-finals to Wales, went home, did their homework and, having lost the battle, they set out determinedly to win the war. They put into place a system from which they were to reap rich rewards over the next decade or so.

The management team in 1991 along with Cooke, now manager, included the formidable presence as coach of

Roger Uttley, a fine and greatly admired man. The team was recognisably a team, with the same familiar faces forming a considerable and unchanging core of strength. There was a real sense of optimism that England had it within their capacity to break the stranglehold of New Zealand and Australia.

There was, however, a nagging question at the back of England's mind. They had conquered Europe by beating the other four countries in the winter, but their celebrations had been short-lived. Having left these shores as northern hemisphere champions, their sense of well-being was deflated when they visited Australia and Fiji in the summer. They lost three of their matches in Australia, including the one Test. This last in Sydney was by a record margin of 40-15. Their only consolation was that Wales, the previous week in Brisbane, had succumbed to a humiliating 63-6 defeat.

Scrum half Gary Armstrong was central to Scotland's successful run. At the end of the decade, he would lead them to Five Nations glory

Australia had also played two matches against New Zealand, sharing a victory each. But the Aussies were the more impressive of the two teams and were rightly ranked as favourites to win the 1991 World Cup.

This year's competition had a considerably higher profile than the first. If the 1987 World Cup was a modest affair, it was nevertheless a hugely successful one. The Rugby World Cup could not be thought of in the same way as the Olympics, nor the World Cup in soccer. But in rugby's own unpretentious terms it was a success. The show had been put on the road and though it may have been provincial and low-key in scope, higher things beckoned.

Encouraged by the success of the 1987 tournament, which had been initiated by the bolder Antipodeans, the Europeans welcomed the competition four years later. One conclusion drawn after the first World Cup was that it was an unhappy decision to split the competition between two countries. Logistics, ease of administration, concentration and focus all argued in favour of a single base.

Nevertheless, it was agreed that in 1991, though England would be the official host, the other four International Rugby Board members in Europe were also to be involved. The 24 pool matches would be spread across all the countries: Pool 1 in England, Pool 2 in both Scotland and Ireland, Pool 3 in Wales and Pool 4 in France. The quarter-finals would be held in France, Scotland and Ireland. The semi-finals would be at Lansdowne Road and Murrayfield, the third place play-off at Cardiff Arms Park, and the Final at Twickenham. In all, there would be 19 venues, as opposed to 11 in 1987.

It was thought that extending the scope of the tournament to include places such as Otley, Gloucester and Pontypridd, which are not normally associated with international rugby, would help promote the game in those areas. Rugby needed to spread itself about.

Domestically, this was a laudable aim. But to do it with an international tournament was a policy not universally embraced with great enthusiasm. Television, whose tentacles reach every corner, did not much like it either.

Unquestionably, there were those who were sceptical of extending rugby's embrace; to allow other nations to join. Privately, it was believed that it would be far better to keep rugby to the narrow but comfortable field that they knew. In their enclosed world, the traditionalists felt no great need to go beyond the eight member nations of the

"We will have to play a lot better and a lot faster than we did to win the Grand Slam. We also have to make a lot fewer mistakes. This event will be played at more pace by fitter and more practised sides."

ENGLAND CAPTAIN WILL CARLING

MARKETING RUGBY IS AS EASY AS ABC1

• Marcel Martin, commercial director, on selling the Cup •

'We are trying to bring rugby to non-rugby people. So we must ask ourselves if we are doing better than 1987 in terms of media exposure. And already the answer is yes. Thousands of words have been written and many more will be written over the next month about rugby. Secondly, are we going to generate a surplus sufficient to permit the development of rugby in the coming years? So long as we make enough to be able to satisfy our ambitions for the game, then the tournament will be a success. The third criteria for success is, will we have full houses for every game? We have deliberately chosen not to play all the games in the national stadia of the five host countries and that will help ensure success on that front.

We are just rookies in this international business, but once we have established RWC and have the financial muscle, we could decide to hold the tournament one year in a country where it is assured of making money then, four years later, take it to a country which loves rugby but where money-making would not be the prime objective. But whatever we do, we must not lose control of the game.'

"We are not building New Zealand up into a monstrous side. Many of the players have not played against us, either, and they will not be sure what to expect. Several of our players have had the opportunity, as individuals, to compare themselves with the All Blacks and they know they are only human. It's essential for them to get off to a good start, because if they lose, there will be more criticism from their own country."

ENGLAND MANAGER GEOFF COOKE
before the opening game against New Zealand

International Board. Who knew what that new world might bring? The world as they knew it was secure and so was their administrative power. Amateurism needed constant vigilance. Expansion might threaten that code. By 1991, this grip was loosening. Other forces were entering the game.

Of no small significance as an indication of an expanding interest, and of changed perspectives, in rugby football was the awarding of the host broadcasting rights to ITV. Previously, the BBC had been the sole broadcaster of rugby for three decades, and its 1987 contract was worth £1million. Now, in 1991, the ITV contract with ancillary facilities had leapt to £7 million, and for the first time the commercial television companies would show rugby live throughout the network.

Twenty-four of the 32 matches would be screened, filling 100 hours of TV time. In 1987, the BBC had broadcast only 28 hours. Times were changing.

The marketing people had arrived, as had advertising agencies, and with them a new seductive voice began insinuating itself into the ear of the chairman of the Rugby World Cup organising committee, Mr John Kendall-Carpenter, a distinguished headmaster of Wellington School.

There was talk of merchandising and licensing, of marketing and exploiting commercially "an honourable sporting event". Rugby had "an upmarket image" and, along with golf and skiing, was purported to be the sport most likely to attract an ABC1 audience.

At that time it was felt necessary to explain, since so much of this advertising science was new, what all this was supposed to mean. Fortuitously, the ABC1 group was composed of people just like those on the rugby committee – white-collar professionals. For the advertisers, and their niche marketing, this was a very desirable target group.

Some committee members, hearing this kind of talk for the first time, must have become convinced that the £3 million raised in 1987 was a paltry sum, simply chicken feed. But for the majority, talk of blatant professional commercialism could only induce apoplexy or paranoia, as they contemplated the Saatchi and Saatchi world that their cherished amateur sport was about to welcome into its reluctant bosom.

In 1987, it had been very late in the day before the tournament organisers found a sponsor, the Japanese telecommunications company KDD. This time, sponsors were queuing in the wings so that with other commercial deals, the 1991 Rugby World Cup was expected to make ten times as much profit as its predecessor.

This was wealth beyond rugby's dreams. The experts were anticipating an audience of two billion in 65 countries. All that was required was for the players on the field to deliver rugby of quality to match the expectations.

Before the competition was due to start, and true to rugby's social and comradely traditions, all the countries were invited to an inaugural dinner, as they had been in Sydney and Auckland in 1987.

It was held at the Royal Lancaster Hotel in London, and the gathering was not universally welcomed. Those who counted themselves as among the favourites to win felt that such a bash was very nice and all that, but it did rather intrude into their serious preparations.

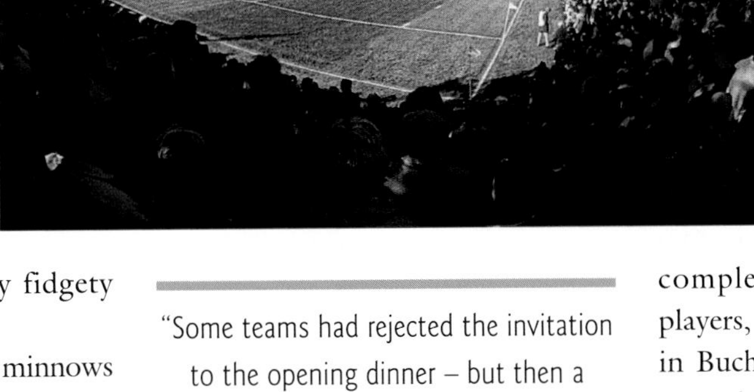

Indeed, some of them had rejected the invitation in the first place. Then a three-line whip was imposed. Once there, they were manifestly fidgety and solemn.

"Some teams had rejected the invitation to the opening dinner – but then a three-line whip was imposed. Once there, they were fidgety and solemn."

On the other hand, the minnows of the tournament could barely contain their sense of excitement at being among the big fish. They were simply glad that they had made it to the party. Everything for them was a bonus.

For the French, there was no joy at all. They had been summoned all the way from their training camp in Béziers. They arrived shortly before the dinner began at 7.30pm, and departed at 10pm to arrive back whence they came at 3am. They were not, shall we say, best pleased.

The French, along with Australia, England and New Zealand, made up the quartet among whom the spoils were expected to be challenged.

Scotland were thought to have a good outside chance by virtue of a favourable draw, which meant that within their pool they would play Ireland, their stiffest opposition in the early stages, at Murrayfield. If they won their pool, their quarter-final fixture would also find them at home – as, indeed, they would then be if they reached the semi-finals.

In addition, Scotland had in Ian McGeechan, Jim Telfer and Derrick Grant a trio of experts whose experience and coaching talent were second to none. Indeed, the more the Scottish scenario was scrutinised, the more favourable the narrative looked. The plot lines were persuasive, the characters strong and appealing.

In the interests of broadening both the appeal of rugby and the travel experiences of its performers, the World Cup took the players of Italy and the United States to Otley in Yorkshire

In the trail leading into the World Cup, Scotland had experienced a couple of unsettling results. Their largely experimental team lost 24-18 to Canada in their early summer tour, although they beat the USA 41-12.

Not long after their return, and with a fuller complement of their first-choice players, they lost 18-12 to Romania in Bucharest. However, they would not wish to dwell on these results, preferring instead to point to their display of the previous year on their tour of New Zealand, where they had given a fine account of themselves in that most testing of arenas. They lost both international matches, but the second in Auckland was a close call at 21-18.

Scotland had a clutch of talented players whose experience of the hot-house atmosphere of international rugby was invaluable and irreplaceable. There was a possibility, depending on the wins and losses in Pools 1 and 2 and the resultant quarter-finals – where Scotland anticipated facing Wales, a strategic point they were soon forced to reassess – that Scotland might have the chance to settle the score with England in the semi-final.

Indeed, we would have a good idea of the likelihood of this at the end of the opening match. This was between the host nation and the winners of the Webb Ellis trophy in

A clash of the titans in the very first game of the 1991 tournament as England's steamroller runs into New Zealand's runaway train – from left: England scrum half Richard Hill, All Black prop Richard Loe, and wing John Kirwan

"Defensive styles will reduce the spectacle of this World Cup and England should definitely set standards of attractive rugby."

ITALY COACH BERTRAND FOUCARDE
after England's failure to play a more attacking game against the All Blacks

1987: England versus New Zealand. The opening match of the 1987 inaugural World Cup, with its attendant ceremony, had been held on a Friday. With hindsight, the organisers realised they would have preferred it to take place on a Saturday. Perversely, this recommendation was ignored in 1991 and the first game was arranged for October 3, a Thursday.

This was extraordinary. Who would turn up? Would the ABC1s reschedule their commitments and take time off from the office? Or would their presence at the proliferating corporate hospitality suites count as Thursday's work? For sure, they had a better chance of being at Twickenham than the Ds and Es, the allegedly non-decision makers, of this world...

As the many golden oldies paraded behind their national flags at the opening ceremony, the stadium was some 300 short of capacity. This was due to a last-minute mishandling of 2,000 unsold tickets which Dudley Wood, the RFU secretary, managed to distribute in the days leading up to the first fixture.

Messages on the rugby ball which had started its journey from Rugby School in June with an inscription from the headmaster, Michael Mavor, were read by Prince Edward at Twickenham. The game of rugby, he hoped, would be the winner.

But it was too much to ask that the first match, all nerves and trepidation, would be full of thrills. However, there were spills – mostly from England. In a cautious game, the All Blacks were awarded 19 scrums to the home side's five. There were also 27 penalties.

These statistics indicated that the referees – in this case Jim Fleming of Scotland – were going to heed the directive from the International Rugby Football Board, which had issued strict guidelines to avoid the possibility of diverging interpretations. The upshot was that this first game was inhibited by too frequent use of the referee's whistle.

For sure, the referee is a man who can never win. The "man in the middle" not only adjudicates between two teams, he is also caught in the crossfire between those who insist that he operates strictly according to the game's laws and those who believe he is a killjoy for not allowing the game to flow. This is an unenviable and perennial tension in rugby.

At any rate, the scrummage count gave the All Blacks a huge advantage. That they scored only one try, the only one in the game, scored by Michael Jones, their tirelessly dynamic flanker, suggested a nervousness one rarely sees in them. They can be as tense as the next team, but they dare not let it show as others conspicuously do – and as they did at Twickenham on that opening day.

In retrospect, these were the early signs that all was not entirely as it should be in the All Blacks camp. They played well, but not with their usual masterly knowledge and control, which they were to display only sporadically during the whole tournament.

Neither team felt content with their performance. There were four penalties and a conversion for Grant Fox, and three to Jonathan Webb and, as we were to come to expect, a drop-goal from Rob Andrew which gave his team the half-time lead.

It was a game, as Alex Wyllie, New Zealand's coach said, of the kind that opens a tour. Above all else you need to have a win under your belt. It is not a matter of whether you play well. It is a matter, quite starkly, of whether you win. In which case, England's dressing room was the gloomier place to be after their 18-12 defeat. But first outings are notoriously unpredictable affairs, often clumsy.

The following day at Llanelli, Australia found the full

"People were not composed and didn't look to have too definite a game plan. We know we have to show more composure."

AUSTRALIA CAPTAIN NICK FARR-JONES after watching the opening game between New Zealand and England at Twickenham

Philippe Marocco throws into the floodlights at Béziers during France's opening fixture against Romania

Toshiyuki Hayashi of Japan tries to re-enact the famous 'lineout punch' picture during their 47-9 defeat by Scotland, while Ray Nelson of the USA feels the collar of Stefano Barba of Italy

80 minutes not quite to their liking. They had, after all, lost on tour to Argentina in 1987. If it was a mundane first half, Australia seemed to be doing enough to put Argentina quietly aside. They led 16-7 and in Tim Horan and David Campese, who had scored tries in the first half, they had players of a class unmatched in their opponents.

No one ever quite gets the better of the Argentinians and while their scrum holds true they believe they are in with a chance. So it was against the Wallabies. That they did well in the lineout was a bonus. Obstinately, and not without a few surprises, Argentina nibbled away at the lead to such effect that entering the last quarter of the game they found themselves only four points adrift, leaving their opponents hot, bothered and bewildered. The Australians were later to find themselves in similar straits in even more dramatic circumstances in the quarter-final.

But they were not so bewildered as not to get themselves out of a sticky spot. In their midst they had a player who, however desperate the circumstances, could be relied upon to leave the opposition rooted to the spot, like so many rabbits in the glare of the headlights.

David Campese stamped his mark on the game. He scored a marvellous try for himself and then created one for Horan, to put the result at 32-19 beyond all doubt.

"Realistically speaking, we are not in the class of Ireland and Scotland, though we will start both games trying to win. But I believe that we can beat Zimbabwe. We are faster, more skilful and better organised."

JAPAN COACH HIROAKI SHUKUZAWA

This was the first of his statements. There would be others. By the end of Rugby World Cup 1991, David Campese would have created the most enduring image of all.

The one other player likely to challenge the Australian for flamboyance was Serge Blanco, France's charismatic full back and captain. He could make little impression in their muted first match in Béziers. France dispatched Romania but while the 30-3 score was convincing, their style in an error-strewn game was not. They were on track, however, to the quarter-final confrontation that everybody expected with England.

There was not, as yet, reason to raise any eyebrows. Events and results were going much according to plan.

The Fijians, a nation expected to make strides forward in world ranking, were to prove disappointing. They lost to Canada 13-3, which included three penalty goals by Gareth Rees. Fiji's reputation was due almost exclusively to their mastery of the sevens version.

Thus, with a yawn and sceptical nod, the conclusion was that, yes, it is all very well to encourage the emerging rugby nations but really we will have to wait until the quarter-finals before the World Cup really begins. People were hard-pressed not to be patronising.

In an attempt to drum up a good story we were reminded that Japan had in fact beaten Scotland 28-24 in Tokyo two years earlier. But on the Saturday, David Sole's team put them to the sword, this time by a margin of 47-9.

On the same day, Italy in their first match against the USA won a splendid game at Otley (30-9) which included a brilliant individualist try including a devastating sidestep from Ivan Francescato and a fine kicking demonstration from Diego Dominguez. The following day, at Lansdowne Road, Ireland would score more than a half century of points (55-11) against Zimbabwe. But sandwiched in between these results, with a one o'clock kick-off on Sunday, was the bombshell score from Cardiff Arms Park – Wales 13, Western Samoa 16.

This reversed all expectations, capsizing an already uncertain vessel to cast all Welsh souls adrift. This was a staggering turn-up for the book. Quite a few Welsh players were left staggering too. There were times during the match when the high, fierce tackling, testing the borders of legitimacy, left Welsh players strewn all over the pitch and in need of attention. Phil May, Tony Clement and Richie

"Money, money and money."

ZIMBABWE CAPTAIN BRIAN CURRIN when asked what is needed to bridge the gap between the so-called second division majority in international rugby union and the small, eight-strong first division elite

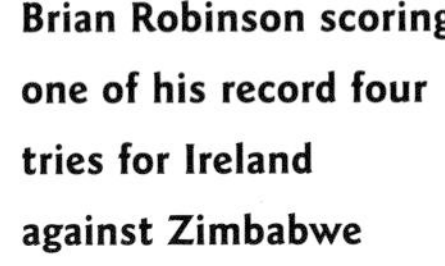

Brian Robinson scoring one of his record four tries for Ireland against Zimbabwe

Before the match, Welsh fans had a good laugh dressing up as Western Samoans – but Stephen Bachop and his team-mates ran away with the game, leaving Wales lock Phil May sitting on the sidelines with a dislocated shoulder

Collins suffered the most and had to be replaced.

Wales claimed that the referee – here we go again! – had awarded a try to Too Vaega when it seemed, as the television pictures confirmed, that Robert Jones, Wales' scrum half, had touched down the ball first. But, overall, the Pacific islanders deserved their victory.

"It's been pretty difficult to raise morale. Some of the players were so nervous before they went on the pitch against Western Samoa, it was obvious the pressure had got to them. We've spent two days discussing what went wrong."

WALES COACH ALAN DAVIES

Under the coaching eye of Bryan Williams, the great All Black winger and the first Western Samoan to wear the jersey, they had exploited Wales' weaknesses and uncertainty. In declaring beforehand that this match was the most important in Wales' 110-year history, an extra burden was placed on the Welsh players which they seemed incapable of shouldering. This upset caused a stir. The error had been in underestimating the Western Samoans. If previous experience was anything to go by, no one should expect any shocks at this stage of the World Cup. But closer scrutiny of the Western Samoan squad and of the provenance of their players might have suggested something in the offing. Although Western Samoa has a population of only 250,000, a further 150,000 live overseas, mainly in New Zealand. Thus they are weaned on rugby football, a game which comes naturally to their physique and footballing talent.

Indeed, a player who was to make an impression in this tournament, Frank Bunce, was soon thereafter to wear the All Black jersey and to do so with distinction during the Nineties. He was a key figure for New Zealand in the 1995

World Cup. When the Western Samoan manager, Tate Simi, was asked before the 1991 competition to define his country's rugby strengths, he answered with a broad smile that, surely, the other rugby nations did not believe they had any. After their performance at the Arms Park, the Welsh were left in no doubt what they were. Power, enterprise, flair, but above all, their fearsome tackling which derived from Australian rugby league.

The other countries who were to play the Western Samoans went back to their rooms to rethink their misconceptions and to revise their prejudices. Back in Samoa, more than 15,000 people had flocked into the rugby stadium in the capital, Apia, to watch the game transmitted live on television at 1am.

As Bryan Williams, their technical adviser, said afterwards: "We have found our place in the sun." Suddenly, Western Samoa were the centre of attraction. Since they had encouraged scarcely a thought hitherto, people – at least those who were willing to admit their ignorance – turned to their pristine atlases to find out where exactly on the planet was Western Samoa. The joke going the rounds was: "If Western Samoa could give Wales such a hiding, imagine what the whole of Samoa would have done!"

Anyway, it was Australia's turn in the next pool game, and then Argentina. Beyond that, there were tremors north of the border. These were caused by Scotland's team management scurrying back into the classroom where the flip charts outlined details of how they were to bring the downfall of Wales in the quarter-final. They were having second thoughts about that.

After Wales's humiliation in Brisbane in the summer, they could not entertain any sensible hope of a victory

"The success of the Western Samoa team has been based on a style of play superior to anything I have seen from Wales or Ireland in four years. It is by no means rash to suggest we may see Samoa in the Final."

DAVID KIRK
the man who lifted the World Cup in 1987, getting a little carried away

Zimbabwe scrum half Ewan MacMillan gets his pass away during their 51-12 defeat by Scotland

Philippe Sella launches himself over the line for one of his two tries in France's 33-9 victory against Fiji, while hat-trick hero Iwan Tukalo leads the charge as Scotland beat Zimbabwe 51-12

against Australia. This being the case, with the possibility of two defeats staring at them, the Welsh had to rely on others, Western Samoa most probably, to stumble and fail if Wales were to progress further than the pool stage.

The pool games carried on their merry way but there had been a noticeable shift in perception. It was not as it was expected to be. The mould had cracked. A team outside the pack of favourites was likely to reach the quarter-final stage. An underdog was having his day. So were the feature writers on the newspapers. They were looking for a colourful piece. Western Samoa provided it.

Scotland, with a much changed team from that which beat Japan, defeated Zimbabwe 51-12, with Iwan Tukalo scoring a hat-trick of tries. It was only 21-12 at half-time. Ireland, with a second-string pack, beat an all-running, all-passing Japan by 32-16, but not before Japan had crossed their line three times to Ireland's four.

England scored four tries against Italy in a 36-6 victory. France were hardly convincing in their 33-9 win over Fiji which ended the Fijians' interest in the competition. A lack of cohesion in New Zealand's 46-6 win at Gloucester against a very plucky USA raised further doubts about the form of the All Blacks.

But all eyes and ears were fixed on Pontypool Park where the heroes from the south Pacific – the location by now was more widely known – were to play the Wallabies, who had their off-shore neighbours to thank for providing Willie Ofahengaue, their marvellous flanker. Yet though they were close neighbours, this was the first encounter between the two countries.

Pontypool's park is a stunning venue for a rugby match when the autumn colours are aflame but, on this day, mist and rain thwarted any hope of an aesthetic display. The same could be said of the game. It was a grinding, mauling contest. There were no tries, only four penalties (3-1 to Australia). But not at any stage could it be thought of as dull. It was a titanic tussle of bone and muscle with the match result remaining in doubt until the end.

Australia paid a heavy price. Nick Farr-Jones, their scrum half, injured his medial ligament in the ninth minute of the first half. He would be cutting it fine to make the quarter-finals. Australia would miss him. They would miss

his leadership. Away from his rugby kit he looked like a misfit, as if he should be somewhere quieter, poring over an obscure text in a library, perhaps; or studiously cataloguing rare species in his laboratory. Swottish in his gold-rimmed spectacles, you imagined him a charmer in a college tutorial, making the odd don lament why the counterculture refuseniks he so often had to contend with in their perpetual state of dishabille, could not be more like Farr-Jones. Like David Kirk for New Zealand in 1987, Farr-Jones possessed intelligence and an engaging personality. He articulated the game's finer points with precision. Sadly, his injury meant he would have plenty of time for his books.

Michael Lynagh took the captaincy, as he often had to do, with admirable composure against Western Samoa. He kicked all of his side's points and breathed a sigh of relief at surviving the attritional test. Lynagh, like Bjorn Borg, the great tennis player, had competitiveness sealed in his narrow eyes. As Shakespeare noted in *Macbeth*: *"There's no art/ To find the mind's construction in the face"*. Lynagh's was a very combative stare. His short-stepped walk from scrum to lineout had a business-as-usual briskness. He

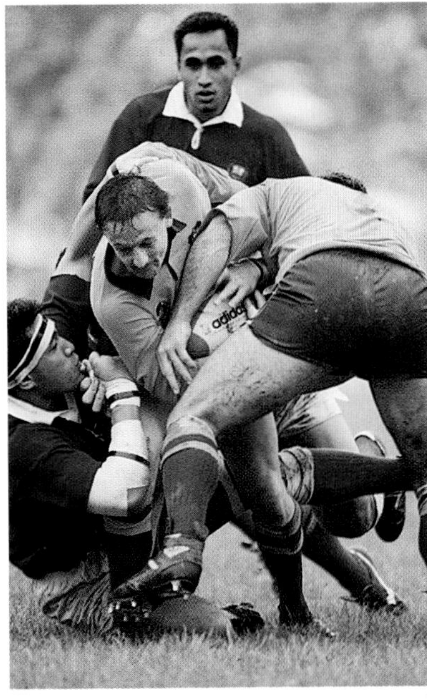

Australia full back Marty Roebuck finds the going tough in the 9-3 victory over Western Samoa, while Paul Ackford rises above Italy's forwards as England win 36-6

"I have never awarded so many penalties against one team in the whole of my refereeing career, at any level. I repeatedly spoke to the Italian captain but it was water off a duck's back."

BRIAN ANDERSON
Scottish referee, after England were left frustrated by the stream of penalties awarded against the Italians

showed his steadiness of nerve in difficult conditions in Pontypool, as he was to do throughout the tournament. He was to have a great World Cup.

Nerves were exposed elsewhere. They were tight as banjo strings in the Welsh camp. Fearful of an early exit, Wales, on the same day, had accounted for Argentina 16-7.

Execution had been delayed. It was a waiting game.

Interest now centred on Pool 3, where there were any number of different permutations hanging on the winners and losers of the final two matches. Wales beating Australia would produce one set of conclusions, Argentina winning their last game would produce another.

Since Wales were not seen as likely conquerors of Australia, who would then be unbeaten at the head of the pool, the outcome of the Argentina and Western Samoa fixture would determine second position. Thus, Wales' fate lay in the hands of another team. In the event, Australia – after embarrassing Wales in the summer – were so finely tuned, particularly in the second half, that they won by the biggest margin – 38-3 – for an international at the home of Welsh rugby. This beat the record of 34 points shared by Scotland (1982) and New Zealand (1989). In the Samoa-Argentina match at Pontypridd, tempers were so frayed that it brought the first sendings-off of the tournament. Mata'afa Keenan (Western Samoa) and Pedro Sporleder (Argentina) were dismissed by referee Jim Fleming for fighting on the field. Fleming had replaced his Scottish compatriot Brian Anderson, who had retired hurt.

Argentina strongly condemned what they saw as the dangerous tackling of the Western Samoans. After trailing 12-9 in the early stages, the Western Samoans ran out comfortable winners in the end, 35-12. Wales were out.

Thierry Lacroix hands off Pat Palmer during France's hard-fought 19-13 victory over Canada. Opposite: England's flying ace Rory Underwood and the USA's flying scrum half Mark Pidcock, in a game England won 37-9

Thus for the first time, one of the original members of the International Rugby Board failed to make the cut. There were signs that the World Cup was coming of age and that it might be achieving one of its stated aims. Two emerging countries had reached the final eight. Fiji had done so four years earlier but, sadly, this time they failed to win a game.

Romania, who were expected to make significant advances, had become a declining force. Their only success was against Fiji, whom they defeated 17-15.

Instead, it was Canada's turn. Over the same weekend they put up an impressive display against France in Agen where they lost narrowly 19-13. They had won their previous two matches against Romania (19-11) and Fiji (13-3).

Mark Wyatt and Gareth Rees had contributed 33 of the 45 points scored by the Canadians, thus ensuring that Canada qualified to play New Zealand in the quarter-final. France would face England, who had beaten the USA 36-6. This would be a repeat of the Grand Slam finale of the previous season. France, drawn at home, relished the prospect.

Meanwhile, Scotland beat Ireland in a wonderful game so typical of their fixtures over the years and one in which Gary Armstrong proved to be the key player for the home team. This meant that the Scots came top of their group and had the dubious reward of meeting Western Samoa in the quarter-final tie which, according to pre-tournament theory, would be the supposedly easier fixture.

Peter Fatialofa, Western Samoa's captain, and his hard-hitting colleagues had changed everybody's

Rees's pieces

BY
GARETH REES
The only man to play in all four Rugby World Cups

The 1991 opening dinner was at London's Royal Lancaster Hotel. It was a massive affair with the teams all sat at long tables. The England team sat opposite us, the Canadians. One of our guys made a joke to Will Carling about his private life and the other English players looked amazed that we would have the nerve to do that. I think that summed us up, but it also said a bit about them. They were very tense and I think they were feeling the pressure of hosting the World Cup

All the current players' tables were at the front, and to go to the toilet you had to weave your way to the back through what would normally be the cheaper tables. But sitting at those tables you had your Gareth Edwards, your Barry Johns – all these great players of the past. As the evening wore on, the front tables emptied because the current players wanted to go and talk to the greats from the past.

Our pool, with France, Fiji and Romania, took place in France, which we were quite frustrated about, because we didn't feel we got the exposure we would have liked. We beat Fiji 13-3 in the first match and I didn't have a beer after the game, which was probably the first time I'd ever done that after a rugby match. I went down to the lobby to have an orange juice and found six or seven others who had obviously also seen the writing on the wall, saying, "Hang on, this is only half a job done." We went up against Romania and won 19-11, and qualified for the quarter-finals.

Before the game against France, we all arrived in our number ones – our infamous bright red blazers. The French were typically chic with their double-breasted blazers. And then one member walks in with his tracksuit and trainers on, and smoking. That was Serge Blanco, the great one. Everyone loved watching him and you kind of got a glimpse of it there, breaking the rules off the park as well as on. He did things that you weren't supposed to do.

'We were in our bright red blazers, the French looked typically chic. Then in walks one in a tracksuit, smoking. Blanco, the great one…'

We had a very experienced pack, very physical, and the style of the game in '91 suited that. I scored a drop goal with a very good kick, but my opposite number Didier Cambérabéro was also on form… until Dan Jackart, our prop, hit him with a massive tackle and he had to be carried off. The scoreline finished up quite close – we only lost 19-13.

We had been on the road for a long time with no financial reward and very little recognition, slogging away and we were getting quite grumpy. Guys were really bitching about the food and the big men didn't have any large beds to sleep in. All the standard tour complaints. But then we went to Vimy Ridge, the site of probably the greatest victory in Canadian military history from World War I. We saw the battlefield, the memorials to the Canadians, and the tunnels where these men fought and the conditions they lived in. It put everything in perspective.

Maybe the bed where the second-row forward's feet were sticking out at the end wasn't the worst thing in the world, and the diced carrot salad that you seemed to get before every meal wasn't really that bad.

We played New Zealand at the Lille football stadium in a torrential downpour. I remember going out before the game to practise drop-outs and Grant Fox was doing the same thing beside me. There was a layer of water on the pitch and the ball simply wouldn't come up for the kick. We just looked at each other as if to say, "How the hell are we supposed to play on this?" There's no question that New Zealand were the biggest team we had faced in a World Cup. I don't know if they were the happiest team, but a great deal was expected of them.

They did their haka and I remember Inga Tuigamala smiling as it was going on, although you knew that inside the fires were burning. We had a wonderful start. We put a lot of pressure on and Chris Tynan, our scrum half, dummied and went on his own when there was probably an overlap on and in the end we didn't come away with any points. To have scored the first try against the All Blacks would have been amazing, but they were far more clinical and won 29-13.

It was a very physical game, and we would like to think that one of the reasons that the All Blacks did not go through against Australia was because we had taken quite a lot out of them.

"The days when we could be treated condescendingly are gone. We have proved ourselves. There was a healthy lack of respect for the established nations in our approach. And who are those nations anyway? Wales? Ireland? I was born in Cornwall while Ian Birtwell (the coach) was born in the north of England. In both these regions there is a healthy disrespect for London rugby, the old boy network and what it represents. This is the feeling in the Canadian team about the condescending way we have been treated by the European nations. We are fed up with the old pat on the shoulder ... well done, boys ... we are fed up with the raised eyebrows of the so-called establishment, when we do well. New Zealand and Australia have been very supportive. There has been a marked difference between their attitude and that of the European nations."

CANADA MANAGER MIKE LUKE
after his team's narrow 19-13 defeat by France

preconceptions. Their rugby was New Zealand-inspired. Along with their captain and Keenan, Pat Lam, Frank Bunce, Timo Tagaloa and Stephen Bachop had all played their rugby in New Zealand. They were not exactly naive players from some far-flung and isolated island.

Ireland were doomed, so all the stars foretold, to be mesmerised by the slick and sleight-of-hand brand of rugby of Australia. Seeing that New Zealand were far from being their true selves, Australia had by this time become favourites to win the Cup.

The All Blacks were indeed out of sorts. After setting a standard of discipline and efficiency against an England side admittedly racked with nerves, they progressed in pedestrian and clumsy fashion through their next two matches. In front of a capacity 12,000 crowd at Gloucester, New Zealand stumbled their way past a spirited USA side who simply harried and tackled all afternoon.

"You just have to reach down and grab your guts" was the way Gary Hein, their winger, explained a performance in which New Zealand were held for 22 minutes before taking the lead. With six minutes to go the score stood at 28-6. That New Zealand added a further 18 points before the end could not deflect anyone from thinking that this was a well below par All Blacks performance. The New

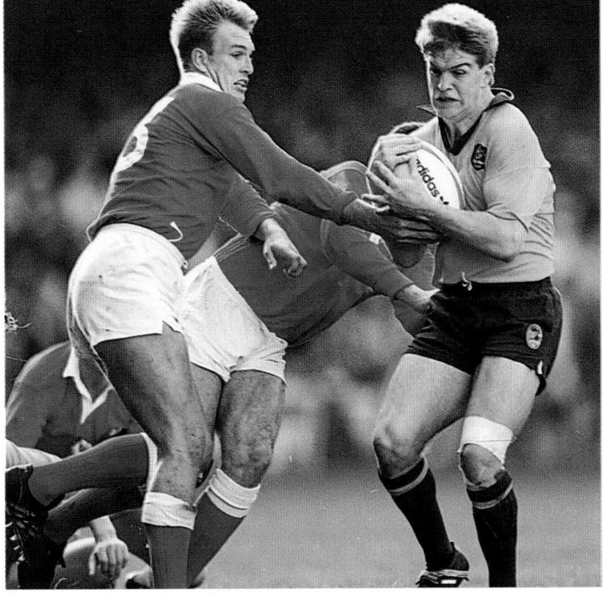

Wales centre Mike Hall battles with Australia centre Tim Horan, while, far left, Filimone Seru of Fiji gets away in the 17-15 win over Romania. Above: A Canadian fan wears a maple syrup

"We're not running the ball well in the first phase. But we will, even though I'm not sure when."
AUSTRALIAN COACH BOB DWYER
dissatisfied with his team's record win over Wales

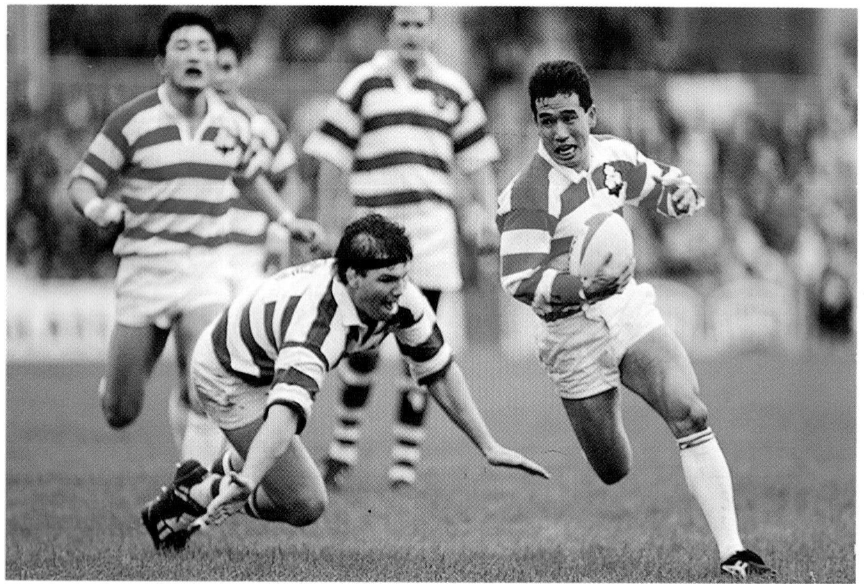

Ireland's Rob Saunders is hauled down as Scotland win 24-15 to avoid a quarter-final with Australia. Left: Katsuhiro Matsuo of Japan scores a try in their 52-8 demolition of Zimbabwe

Zealanders could not puff out their chest after the next encounter, either.

Italy had been accused of playing a destructive style in their earlier games. It was a style reflected in the number of penalties awarded against them (an extraordinary, perhaps unparalleled, figure of 37 in the England game which allowed Jonathan Webb to create a new England record of 24 points in an international). But Italy were to present a far more polished display at Leicester.

The final score showed that they held New Zealand to a 10-point margin (31-21), but in fact they outscored their illustrious opponents by 18-15 in the second half. Italy's two tries by that wonderful wing Marcello Cuttitta – who

Paolo Vaccari of Italy is about to get Tuigamala'd as Va'aiga homes in during the All Blacks' 31-21 win. Right: Argentine fans can't watch as Mark Ring kicks a penalty in Wales' 16-7 victory

had created such an impression in the first World Cup – and Massimo Bonomi were the first in the tournament to breach the All Blacks defence.

The last time the teams had met was in the opening match of the 1987 tournament when New Zealand established a world record of 70 points. This was a satisfying return match for the Italians.

The disconcerted winners, unusually sensitive, were left to complain about how Italy played on the fringe of the laws. Fortunately for all Europeans, the referee, Kerry Fitzgerald, was Australian. Normally, they see eye to eye in the southern hemisphere. Clearly, all was not well. The All Blacks would face Canada next.

POOL 1 FINAL TABLE

	P	W	D	L	F	A	Pts
New Zealand	3	3	0	0	95	39	9
England	3	2	0	1	85	33	7
Italy	3	1	0	2	57	76	5
USA	3	0	0	3	24	113	3

POOL 2 FINAL TABLE

	P	W	D	L	F	A	Pts
Scotland	3	3	0	0	122	36	9
Ireland	3	2	0	1	102	51	7
Japan	3	1	0	2	77	87	5
Zimbabwe	3	0	0	3	31	158	3

POOL 3 FINAL TABLE

	P	W	D	L	F	A	Pts
Australia	3	3	0	0	79	25	9
W Samoa	3	2	0	1	54	34	7
Wales	3	1	0	2	32	61	5
Argentina	3	0	0	3	38	83	3

POOL 4 FINAL TABLE

	P	W	D	L	F	A	Pts
France	3	3	0	0	82	25	9
Canada	3	2	0	1	45	33	7
Romania	3	1	0	2	31	64	5
Fiji	3	0	0	0	27	63	3

"Everything the supporters feel, we feel ten-fold. I haven't got the personality or strength of character to bear the weight of all Welsh ills."

WALES COACH ALAN DAVIES
after his team's 38-3 drubbing by Australia at Cardiff Arms Park

Grant Fox was already the world's top points-scorer before the 1991 World Cup began, but that didn't stop the All Blacks' relentless fly half getting his kicks. Below: Centre Jeremy Guscott scored two tries as England beat Italy 36-6

· POOL 1 RESULTS ·

NEW ZEALAND 18 ENGLAND 12
3 Oct • Twickenham
NEW ZEALAND: Wright; Kirwan, Innes, McCahill, Timu; Fox, Bachop; McDowell, Fitzpatrick, Loe, I Jones, *G Whetton, A Whetton, M Jones, Brooke (Earl 69)
SCORERS: *Try:* M Jones. *Con:* Fox. *Pens:* Fox (4)
ENGLAND: Webb; Underwood, *Carling, Guscott, Oti; Andrew, Hill; Leonard, Moore, Probyn, Ackford, Dooley, Teague, Winterbottom, Richards.
SCORERS: *Pens:* Webb (3). *DG:* Andrew.
Referee: J M Fleming (Scotland)

ITALY 30 USA 9
5 Oct • Cross Green, Otley
ITALY: Troiani; Vaccari, Gaetaniello, Barba, Marcello Cuttitta; Dominguez, Francescato; Massimo Cuttitta, Pivetta, Properzi Curti, Favaro, Croci, Saetti, Checchinato, *Zanon
SCORERS: *Tries:* Barba, Francescato, Vaccari, Gaetaniello. *Cons:* Dominguez (4). *Pen:* Dominguez (2).
USA: Nelson; Hein, Williams, Higgins, Whitaker; DeJong, Daily; Lippert, Flay, Paoli, Swords, Leversee, *Vizard (Lipman 58), Farley, Ridnell.
SCORERS: *Try:* Swords. *Con:* Williams. Pen: Williams.
Referee: O E Doyle (Ireland)

NEW ZEALAND 46 USA 6
8 Oct • Kingsholm, Gloucester
NEW ZEALAND: Wright; Timu, Innes, McCahill, Tuigamala; Preston, Bachop; McDowell, Fitzpatrick, Purvis, I Jones, *G Whetton, A Whetton, M Jones, Earl
SCORERS: *Tries:* Earl, Wright (3), Purvis, Timu, Tuigamala, Innes. Cons: Preston (4). *Pens:* Preston (2).
USA: Sheehy; Hein, Williams, Burke, Whitaker; O'Brien, Pidcock; Lippert (Manga 50), Johnson, Mottram, *Swords, Tunnacliffe, Sawicki, Lipman, Ridnell.
SCORER: *Pens:* Williams (2).
Referee: E Sklar (Argentina)

ENGLAND 36 ITALY 6
8 Oct • Twickenham
ENGLAND: Webb; Oti, *Carling, Guscott, Underwood; Andrew, Hill; Leonard, Moore, Probyn (Rendall), Ackford, Redman, Teague, Winterbottom, Richards.
SCORERS: *Tries:* Underwood, Guscott (2), Webb. *Cons:* Webb (4). *Pens:* Webb (4).
ITALY: Troiani (Bonomi 46); Vaccari, Gaetaniello, Barba, Marcello Cuttitta; Dominguez, Francescato; Massimo Cuttitta, Pivetta, Properzi Curti, Favaro, Croci, Saetti, Giovanelli, *Zanon.
SCORERS: *Try:* Marcello Cuttitta. *Con:* Dominguez.
Referee: J B Anderson (Scotland)

ENGLAND 37 USA 9
11 Oct • Twickenham
ENGLAND: Hodgkinson; Heslop, *Carling, Halliday, Underwood; Andrew, Hill; Leonard, Olver, Pearce, Redman, Dooley, Skinner, Rees, Richards.
SCORERS: *Tries:* Underwood (2), Carling, Skinner, Heslop. *Cons:* Hodgkinson (4). *Pens:* Hodgkinson (3).
USA: Nelson; Hein, Williams, Higgins (DeJong 40), Sheehy; O'Brien, Pidcock; Manga, Flay, Mottram, *Swords, Tunnacliffe, Lipman, Farley (Wilkinson 75), Ridnell.
SCORERS: *Try:* Nelson. *Con:* Williams. *Pen:* Williams.
Referee: LJ Peard (Wales)

NEW ZEALAND 31 ITALY 21
13 Oct • Welford Road, Leicester
NEW ZEALAND: Wright (Philpott 73); Kirwan, Innes, Little, Tuigamala; Fox, Hewett; McDowell, Fitzpatrick, Loe, I Jones, *G Whetton, A Whetton, Carter, Brooke
SCORERS: *Tries:* Brooke, Innes, Tuigamala, Hewett. *Cons:* Fox (3). *Pens:* Fox (3).
ITALY: Vaccari; Venturi, Gaetaniello, Dominguez, Marcello Cuttitta; Bonomi, Francescato; Massimo Cuttitta, *Pivetta, Properzi Curti (Grespan, 44), Favaro, Croci, Bottacchiari, Giovanelli, Checchinato.
SCORERS: *Tries:* Marcello Cuttitta, Bonomi. *Cons:* Dominguez (2). *Pens:* Dominguez (3).
Referee: Kerry Fitzgerald (Australia)§

· POOL 2 RESULTS ·

SCOTLAND 47 JAPAN 9
5 Oct • Murrayfield
SCOTLAND: G Hastings; Stanger, S Hastings, Lineen, Tukalo; Chalmers (Wyllie 68), Armstrong; *Sole (D Milne 75), Allan, Burnell, Gray, Weir, Jeffrey, Calder, White.
SCORERS: *Tries:* S Hastings, Stanger, Chalmers, PT, White, Tukalo, G Hastings. *Cons:* G Hastings (5). *Pens:* Chalmers, G Hastings (2).
JAPAN: Hosokawa; Masuho, Kutsuki, *Hirao, Yoshida; Matsuo, Murata; Ohta, Kunda, Takura, Hayashi, Tifaga, Kajihara, Nakashima, Latu.
SCORER: *Try:* Hosokawa. *Con:* Hosokawa. *Pen:* Hosokawa.
Referee: E Morrison (England)

IRELAND 55 ZIMBABWE 11
6 Oct • Lansdowne Road, Dublin
IRELAND: Staples; Geoghegan, Cunningham, Curtis, Crossan; Keyes, Saunders; Popplewell, Smith, D Fitzgerald, Lenihan, Francis, *Matthews, Hamilton, Robinson.
SCORERS: *Tries:* Robinson (4), Geoghegan, Popplewell (2), Curtis. *Cons:* Keyes (4). *Pens:* Keyes (5).
ZIMBABWE: *Currin; Brown, Tsimba, Letcher, Walters; Kuhn (Schultz 30), Ferreira; Hunter, Beattie, Garvey; Demblon, Martin, Botha, Dawson, Catterall.
SCORERS: *Tries:* Dawson, Schultz. *Pen:* Ferreira.
Referee: K H Lawrence (New Zealand)

IRELAND 32 JAPAN 16
9 Oct • Lansdowne Road, Dublin
IRELAND: Staples; Clarke, Mullin, Curtis, Crossan (Cunningham 63); Keyes, Saunders; J Fitzgerald, *Kingston, Halpin; Galwey, Francis, O'Hara, Hamilton, Mannion.
SCORERS: *Tries:* O'Hara, Mannion (2), Staples. *Cons:* Keyes (2). *Pens:* Keyes (4).
JAPAN: Hosokawa; Masuho, Kutsuki, *Hirao, Yoshida; Matsuo, Horikoshi; Ohta, Fujita (Kunda 52), Takura, Hayashi, Oyagi, Tifaga (Miyamoto 75), Kajihara, Latu.
SCORERS: *Tries:* Hayashi, Kajihara, Yoshida. *Cons:* Hosokawa (2).
Referee: L Colati (Fiji)

SCOTLAND 51 ZIMBABWE 12
9 Oct • Murrayfield
SCOTLAND: *Dods; Stanger (Chalmers 78), S Hastings, Lineen, Tukalo; Wyllie, Oliver; Watt, K Milne, Burnell, Cronin, Weir, Turnbull, Marshall, White.
SCORERS: *Tries:* Tukalo (3), Turnbull, Stanger, Weir, White, S Hastings. *Cons:* Dods (5). *Pens:* Dods (2). *DG:* Wyllie.
ZIMBABWE: *Currin; Schultz, Tsimba, Letcher, Walters (Chimbima 56); Brown, MacMillan, Nicholls, Beattie, Garvey (Hunter 45, Roberts for Hunter 78); Martin, Nguruve, Muirhead, Dawson, Catterall.
SCORERS: *Tries:* Garvey (2). *Cons:* Currin (2)
Referee: D Reordan (USA)

SCOTLAND 24 IRELAND 15
12 Oct • Murrayfield
SCOTLAND: G Hastings; Stanger, S Hastings, Lineen, Tukalo; Chalmers (Shiel 47), Armstrong; *Sole, Allan, Burnell, Gray, Weir, Jeffrey, Calder, White.
SCORERS: *Tries:* Shiel, Armstrong. *Cons:* G Hastings (2). *Pens:* G Hastings (3). *DG:* Chalmers.
IRELAND: Staples; Geoghegan, Mullin, Curtis, Crossan; Keyes, Saunders; Popplewell, Smith, D Fitzgerald, Lenihan, Francis, *Matthews, Hamilton, Robinson.
SCORERS: *Pens:* Keyes (4). *DG:* Keyes.
Referee: Fred Howard (England)

JAPAN 52 ZIMBABWE 8
14 Oct • Ravenhill, Belfast
JAPAN: Hosokawa; Masuho, Kutsuki, *Hirao, Yoshida; Matsuo, Horikoshi; Ohta, Kunda, Takura, Hayashi, Oyagi, Tifaga, Kajihara, Latu.
SCORERS: *Tries:* Horikoshi, Yoshida (2), Masuho (2), Kutsuki (2), Tifaga, Matsuo. *Cons:* Hosokawa (5). *Pens:* Hosokawa (2).
ZIMBABWE: *Currin; Schultz, Tsimba, Letcher, Walters; Brown, MacMillan, Nicholls, Beattie, Garvey (Snyder 68); Martin, Botha, Nguruve, Dawson, Catterall.
SCORERS: *Tries:* Tsimba, Nguruve.
Referee: R Hourquet (France)

Scrum half Gary Armstrong cuts a dash in Scotland's 47-9 jamboree against Japan while, below, Ireland's outside half Ralph Keyes kicks for touch in the 55-11 win over Zimbabwe, in which he landed five penalties and four conversions

· POOL 3 RESULTS ·

AUSTRALIA 32 ARGENTINA 19
4 Oct • Stradley Park, Llanelli
AUSTRALIA: Roebuck; Campese, Little, Horan, Egerton; Lynagh, *Farr-Jones; Daly, Kearns (Nucifora 49), McKenzie, McCall, Coker, Poidevin, Ofahengaue, Eales.
SCORERS: *Tries:* Campese (2), Horan (2), Kearns. *Cons:* Lynagh: (3). *Pens*: Lynagh (2).
ARGENTINA: del Castillo; Teran, Laborde, Garcia Simon, Cuesta Silva; Arbizu, Camardon; Mendez, Le Fort (Bosch 41), Cash, Sporleder, Llanes, *Garreton, Santamarina, Carreras.
SCORERS: *Tries:* Teran (2). *Con:* del Castillo. Pen: del Castillo. *DG:* Arbizu (2).
Referee: DJ Bishop (New Zealand)

WESTERN SAMOA 16 WALES 13
6 Oct • Cardiff Arms Park
WESTERN SAMOA: Aiolupo; Lima, Vaega, Bunce, Tagaloa; Bachop, Vaea; *Fatialofa, Toomalatai, Alaalatoa, Birtwistle, Keenan, Vaifale, Perelini, Lam.
SCORERS: *Tries:* Vaega, Vaifale. *Con:* Vaea. *Pens:* Vaea (2)
WALES: Clement (Rayer 47); *I Evans, Gibbs, Hall, E Lewis; Ring, R Jones; Griffiths, Waters, Delaney, May (Morris 30), Moseley, A Lewis, Collins (Jenkins 51), P Davies.
SCORERS: *Tries:* Emyr, I Evans. *Con:* Ring. *Pen:* Ring.
Referee: P Robin

AUSTRALIA 9 WESTERN SAMOA 3
9 Oct • Pontypool Park, Pontypool
AUSTRALIA: Roebuck; Campese, Herbert, Horan, Flett; Lynagh, *Farr-Jones (Slattery 11); Lillicrap, Kearns, Crowley, Coker, Cutler, Miller, Nasser, Eales.
SCORERS: *Pens:* Lynagh (3)
WESTERN SAMOA: Aiolupo; Lima (Tagaloa 50), Vaega, Bunce, Fa'amasino; Bachop, Vaea; *Fatialofa, Toomalatai, Alaalatoa, Birtwistle, Keenan, Paramore, Kaleopa, Perelini.
SCORERS: *Pen:* Vaea.
Referee: E Morrison (England)

WALES 16 ARGENTINA 7
9 Oct • Cardiff Arms Park
WALES: Rayer; *I Evans, Gibbs, Hall, E Lewis; Ring, R Jones; Griffiths, Jenkins, Delaney, Arnold, Moseley, A Lewis, Webster, P Davies.
SCORERS: *Try:* Arnold. *Pens:* Ring (3), Rayer.
ARGENTINA: del Castillo; Teran, Laborde, Garcia Simon, Cuesta Silva; Arbizu, Camardon; Mendez, Le Fort, Molina, Sporleder, Llanes, *Garreton, Santamarina, Carreras.
SCORERS: *Try:* Garcia Simon. *Pen:* del Castillo.
Referee: R Hourquet (France)

AUSTRALIA 38 WALES 3
12 Oct • Cardiff Arms Park
AUSTRALIA: Roebuck; Campese, Little, Horan, Egerton; *Lynagh, Slattery; Daly, Kearns, McKenzie, McCall, Eales, Poidevin, Miller, Ofahengaue.
SCORERS: *Tries:* Roebuck (2), Slattery, Campese, Horan, Lynagh. *Cons:* Lynagh (4). *Pens:* Lynagh (2).
WALES: Clement; *I Evans, Gibbs (Rayer 79), Hall, E Lewis (D Evans 77); Ring, R Jones; Griffiths, Jenkins, Delaney, Arnold, Moseley, A Lewis, Webster, P Davies.
SCORER: *Pen:* Ring.
Referee: KH Lawrence (New Zealand)

WESTERN SAMOA 35 ARGENTINA 12
13 Oct • Sardis Road, Pontypridd
WESTERN SAMOA: Aiolupo; Lima, Vaega, Bunce, Tagaloa; Bachop, Vaea; *Fatialofa, Toomalatai, Alaalatoa, Birtwistle, Keenan, Vaifale, Perelini, Lam.
SCORERS: *Tries:* Tagaloa (2), Lima (2), Bunce, Bachop. *Cons:* Vaea (4). *Pen:* Vaea.
ARGENTINA: Angaut (Meson 52); Teran, Laborde, Garcia Simon, Cuesta Silva; Arbizu, Camardon; Aguirre, Bosch, Cash, Sporleder, Buabse, Irarrazaval (Carreras 58), *Garreton, Santamarina.
SCORERS: *Try:* Teran. *Con:* Arbizu. *Pens:* Laborde, Arbizu.
Referee: JB Anderson and JM Fleming (Anderson off with injury at half-time)

Australia captain Nick Farr-Jones rouses his troops for a tough battle against Ireland, which the Wallabies won 19-18. Below: Emyr Lewis of Wales on the charge against Western Samoa, during their sensational match in Cardiff

Jean-Baptiste Lafond scored France's first try in their 19-13 victory over Canada at Agen. Below: The Fijian haka at the start of their game against France in Grenoble – it appears it didn't bring them much luck, as they lost 33-9

· POOL 4 RESULTS ·

FRANCE 30 ROMANIA 3
4 Oct • Stade de la Méditerranée, Béziers
FRANCE: *Blanco; Saint-André, Lacroix, Mesnel, Lagisquet (Lafond 48); Cambérabéro, Galthié; Lascube, Marocco, Ondarts, Cadieu, Roumat, Champ, Cabannes, Benazzi.
SCORERS: *Tries:* PT, Saint-André, Roumat, Lafond. *Con:* Cambérabéro. *Pens:* Cambérabéro (4)
ROMANIA: Dumitru; Sasu, Lungu, Sava, Racean; Nichitean, Neaga; Leonte, Ion, Stan, Ciorascu, Cojocariu, Dinu, Guranescu, *Dumitras.
SCORER: *Pen:* Nichitean.
Referee: LJ Peard (Wales)

CANADA 13 FIJI 3
5 Oct • Parc Municipal Saint-Leon, Bayonne
CANADA: S Stewart; Palmer, C Stewart, Lecky, Gray; Rees, Tynan; Evans, Speirs, Jackart, Robertsen, Hadley, Charron, MacKinnon, Ennis.
SCORERS: *Try:* S Stewart. *Pens:* Rees (3).
FIJI: Koroduadua; Seru, Aria, Nadruku, Lovo; Serevi, Tubulutu; *Taga, Naivilawasa (Baleiwai 75), Naituivau, Savai, Domoni, Kato, Dere, Tawake.
SCORER: *DG:* Serevi.
Referee: Kerry Fitzgerald (Australia)

FRANCE 33 FIJI 9
8 Oct • Stade Lesdiguières, Grenoble
FRANCE: *Blanco; Lafond, Sella, Mesnel, Saint-André; Cambérabéro, Galthié; Lascube, Marocco, Ondarts, Cadieu, Roumat, Champ, Cabannes, Benazzi.
SCORERS: *Tries:* Sella (2); Lafond (3), Cambérabéro. *Cons:* Cambérabéro (3). *Pen:* Cambérabéro.
FIJI: Koraduadua; Seru, Aria, Naisoro, Lovo; Serevi, Vosanibole (Tabulatu 40); *Taga (Volavola 10), Baleiwai, Vuli, Savai, Domoni, Naruma, Dere, Tawake.
SCORERS: *Try:* Naruma. *Con:* Koroduadua. *Pen:* Koroduadua.
Referee: WD Bevan (Wales)

CANADA 19 ROMANIA 11
9 Oct • Stade Municipal, Toulouse
CANADA: *Wyatt; Palmer, S Stewart, Lecky, C Stewart; Rees, Graf; Evans, Svoboda, Jackart, Van den Brink, Hadley, Breen, MacKinnon, Ennis.
SCORERS: *Tries:* MacKinnon, Ennis. *Con:* Wyatt. *Pens:* Wyatt (2). *DG:* Rees.
ROMANIA: Dumitru (Sava 37); Sasu, Lungu, Fulina, Racean; Nichitean, Neaga; Leonte (Vlad 70), Ion, Stan, Ciorascu, Cojocariu, Dinu, Doja (Brinza 20), *Dumitras.
SCORERS: *Tries:* Lungu, Sasu. *Pen:* Nichitean.
Referee: AR McNeill (Australia)

ROMANIA 17 FIJI 15
12 Oct • Stade Municipal, Brive
ROMANIA: Racean; Sasu, Lungu, Fulina, Colceriu; Nichitean (Ivanciuc 51), Neaga; Stan, Ion, Vlad, Cojocariu, Ciorascu, Dinu, Marin, *Dumitras.
SCORERS: *Tries:* Ion, Dumitras, Sasu. *Con:* Racean. *Pen:* Racean.
FIJI: Turuva; Seru, Nadruku, Naisoro, Vonolagi; Rabaka, Tubulutu; Vuli, Baleiwai, Volavola (Naituivau 31), Savai, Nadolo, Tawake, *Dere, Olsson (Narumu 41).
SCORERS: *Pens:* Turuva (2). *DG:* Rabaka (2), Turuva.
Referee: O E Doyle (Ireland)

FRANCE 19 CANADA 13
13 Oct • Stade Armandie, Agen
FRANCE: *Blanco; Lafond, Sella (Sadourny 47), Mesnel, Saint-André; Cambérabéro (Lacroix 40), Galthié; Lascube, Marocco, Ondarts, Cadieu, Roumat, Champ, Cabannes, Benazzi.
SCORERS: *Tries:* Lafond, Saint-André. *Con:* Cambérabéro. *Pens:* Cambérabéro, Lacroix (2).
CANADA: *Wyatt (S Stewart 46); Palmer, C Stewart, Woods, Gray; Rees, Tynan; Evans, Svoboda, Jackart, Robertsen (Van den Brink 23), Hadley, Charron, MacKinnon, Ennis.
SCORERS: *Try:* Wyatt. *Pens:* Wyatt, Rees. *DG:* Rees.
Referee: SR Hilditch (Ireland)

The match that put Samoa on the map

THE 1991 WORLD CUP

Western Samoa's very first World Cup game remains the greatest upset in the tournament to date. Pat Lam of Northampton remembers every minute of one of most exciting events in his nation's history

BY
PAT LAM

I was born in New Zealand, where every kid wants to be an All Black, and I was no different. By 1990, I was was already captain of the New Zealand Under-21 team. At that time Samoa weren't on the world stage, so there was nothing for a young player like me to aspire to. But whenever I visited my family in Samoa I would play for my local club, and so when they asked me if I would be available for the 1991 World Cup, I jumped at the chance to represent my heritage.

Our first World Cup match was the most famous we ever played – the 16-13 victory against Wales at Cardiff Arms Park. It was the last opening game of the World Cup, nearly two weeks after we arrived in Britain. We just seemed to be training and training without having a game, so by the time the match came we were bursting to get out on the field.

Whenever people ask me what my most memorable game was, I always name that game against Wales. I remember walking on to the Arms Park and thinking, "Wow, I can't believe we're here." By the kick-off, the boys were on fire. The game seemed so easy. It all went our way. We were running on pure adrenalin, enjoying the occasion and putting in the big hits.

Back in Samoa, if you go down to the local rugby ground, you'll see plenty of big hits. Samoan players would rather put in a big tackle than score a try. We just love the physical confrontation, being able to put someone on their backside and really drive them to the ground. I don't think Wales were prepared for that. In that match, and in many games since, you can see the way it affects players' concentration. All of a sudden they are looking for the hit coming in and not concentrating on the pass.

'To see one player go off with a dislocated shoulder, then the next go down groggy – it put a bit of fear into the Welsh players'

We rattled them. To see one player go off with a dislocated shoulder and then the next go down groggy – it put a bit of fear into the players. They began making mistakes, which we were able to pounce on.

The turning point was the tackle on Phil May by Apollo Perelini. The game was stopped for a good three or four minutes ... and then he walked off holding his arm. I think it shook the Welsh team. You could see that they were not as confident when they were running with the ball.

When we scored our second try to go 16-9 ahead, if you look at the video, you can see the emotion of all the players, because we knew we were in the driving seat. We let in a soft try at the end, which was disappointing, but obviously you forget about it when you win a game like that. And when the final whistle went the party really began.

I remember going into the changing room, all the hugs and tears; we had our team prayer and then started singing our Samoan traditional songs and hymns. We partied until all hours of the morning.

Suddenly we were headline news and everything seemed to improve day by day. We had the same sponsors as the All Blacks, but had been given only half the clothing they received. After that win, boxes of gear arrived. You had to laugh – but it also made you realise that if you do the business on the field, things happen for you off. Food was another example. In Wales, there were 26 full-grown men about to play the biggest tournament of their lives, and in the hotel restaurant we were on the set menu. It was very hard for a lot of us. But that changed when we made the quarter-finals. Suddenly you get a flash hotel with buffet meals and the boys can eat what they like.

On the morning of our second match, against Australia, I got a blood infection in my big toe and had to pull out. That was tough. I was lying in bed, sick and feverish, watching it on TV. It was very frustrating because the boys went down 9-3 in a game they could have won. And of course Australia eventually took the title, so we would have loved to have beaten them.

After the game I said to the coach, you've got to get me to the best hospital or you might as well send me home. They took me to the top surgeon in Wales at a private hospital, dug into my foot and found that I had collected a stone deep in a blister. Once that was cleared out, with a few pain-killers, I was able to play against Argentina.

We knew that if we beat Argentina we were in the quarter-finals. That day, we trained well. We were very confident, but we struggled early on against the Argentina forwards. At half-time our veteran full back Anatolia Aiolupo said: "Why are we kicking everything? Let's play." We really opened up in the second half and scored some very good tries to win it 35-12. After the game, that was the biggest celebration because we knew we had made history.

In Wales, we were based in a hotel called The Angel, right next to Cardiff Arms Park. When we arrived we were able to walk around in our tracksuits that said "Western Samoa" and people wouldn't give us a second look. Or they might come up and say, "Western Samoa, where's that?" There were hardly any reporters at our training sessions, and we could happily get on with our own thing.

The change when we got to Scotland, having reached the quarter-finals, was unbelievable. We certainly couldn't go out in our tracksuits any more. There were TV crews in the hotel, at the training ground, and in a way all the distractions led to our downfall.

Of course, we couldn't take Scotland by surprise. Their coach Ian McGeechan, who is now my coach at Northampton, says they really did their homework on us. We lost the toss, which was crucial because there was a strong wind. But the biggest thing they did was to pressurise us right from the start and fight fire with fire. Gavin Hastings came running straight at us early on. They laid down their platform and they played really well.

We were used to playing in front of 20-30,000 at the most. All of a sudden we were playing in front of 56,000 at Murrayfield, a full house with lots of noise, and for the first time ever we were in an atmosphere where we couldn't hear our lineout calls. It was overwhelming, and our inexperience at that level cost us the game. Scotland deservedly won 28-6.

'In Samoa, 20,000 people packed into our national stadium to watch the game at 3am. Many had been there since the afternoon'

But it was superb for our country. Back in Samoa, 20,000 people packed into our national stadium to watch the match live at three o'clock in the morning. They were coming into the ground at four in the afternoon just to get a seat – all that time sitting in the Samoan heat. I remember the tears the boys shed when we saw that footage back at our hotel. The room was wallpapered with faxes. We were so proud of what we had achieved for our nation as Samoans and Polynesians.

The thing I was pleased about as a school teacher was that before that, the Samoan kids in New Zealand used to say, "I want to be an All Black", but after that they said, "I want to play for Samoa".

When the final whistle went at Murrayfield, and we did our lap to thank people for their support, some of the Scottish crowd were crying. They gave us a great send-off. For a lot of us it is still the highlight of our careers. After that came the harsh reality: we were on the first plane home the next day.

We arrived in Samoa at about six o'clock in the morning, when it was still dark, but we were welcomed by the Prime Minister. And then we saw all these floats outside. We thought, "What are they doing here at six o'clock in the morning?" It turned out they wanted one player per float.

From the airport to the hotel in the town is 33 kilometres, which is quite a long drive, and as soon as we left the airport there was this massive cheer and all 33 kilometres were lined with people welcoming us back, throwing money, throwing food, throwing leis round our necks. The whole country had come out to welcome us home.

Then we had a big march from the hotel to the government buildings. We had a massive party, national holidays, the works. It was an amazing time.

THE 1991 ·QUARTER-FINALS·

Prop Steven McDowell leads the haka in New Zealand's quarter-final confrontation with Canada while, right, Iwan Tukalo evades To'o Vaega as Scotland meet Western Samoa. Opposite: John Kirwan leaps to conquer, and the Canadians bid farewell to Lille after their 29-13 defeat

Two schools of thought existed about the quarter-finals. In one there was speculation about whether an underdog, a developing nation, might have his day. In the other, old fully fledged members of the International Board maintained confidence.

In the first grouping there was fear and trepidation at Murrayfield where Scotland were to be confronted not by Wales, as had been expected, but by Western Samoa. On their way to the later stages the Pacific islanders had not so much cut a fluid swathe as run madly amok. Like a wayward juggernaut out of control on the highway, knocking cones to right and left, they left a trail of destruction in their wake. It was an image which Scotland might have had in mind as they contemplated this new and unpredictable phenomenon.

The other match in this group was played in Lille. New Zealand, for their part, were no longer so much concentrating on the forces ranged against them, as attempting to assuage the aggravating demons which were afflicting their own game. They were not playing well; not creating the clear daylight between them and their opponent, as they were so confidently fond of doing. This was, unusually, navel-gazing time for the All Blacks; a habit which is as much a stranger to their fearless, unconquerable spirit as contemplating a dancing, will-o'-the-wisp, finger-tipping passer at second five-eighths. It was out of character.

So that, suddenly, their opponents seemed to be a problem when, normally, Canada would be – to take liberties with Shakespeare's *King Lear*: *"As flies to wanton boys would Canada be to the Blacks/ They kill them for their sport."*

But not now. Not in Lille in 1991.

These two matches represented the day of the underdog. In the other group stood the member nations of the

International Rugby Board. The big contest was in Parc des Princes in Paris: France v England. This fixture had begun to acquire the aura that had once belonged to Wales v France matches. France had held supremacy during most of the Eighties, but England had beaten France on every occasion in the past three years. In their last encounter at Twickenham in the final match of the Five Nations Championship in March, England had won to secure their first Grand Slam since 1980. France were looking to take revenge on their own patch. This had the makings of a colossal struggle.

Finally, Australia would encounter Ireland in Dublin. The Antipodeans had dispatched Ireland unceremoniously in 1987. In 1991 it hardly mattered that the Irish were already at home. They were set to receive the same treatment. But Lansdowne Road was due for a match that was the stuff that myths are made of.

In the end, the underdog was to have his day neither in Lille nor in Edinburgh. Even if Canada did make New Zealand work for their 29-13 victory, the tables were not turned on the favourites, and at Murrayfield Western Samoa's colourful adventure reached its journey's end in a 28-6 defeat. For the All Blacks the match again indicated, somewhat ominously, that the machine was far from being finely tuned. The contest was too much like hard work. The New Zealanders do not mind that at all, indeed they thrive on it, provided the rich rewards are reaped. In 1991 it was not like that. There were rumours of a malaise, of a management not able to agree on which style of play to adopt. And in the absence of Wayne Shelford, the man who had led them to unprecedented success in the previous three years, no strong character was available to instil a new sense of direction. It was a team under stress.

A spate of scores in the first half secured the victory but Canada, like Italy, could boast of having won the second half 10-8. This was not something the All Blacks cared to contemplate.

Meanwhile, Scotland won comfortably in a match in which Gavin Hastings was in magnificent form, giving a fine display of the full back's art, kicking one prodigious penalty from 10 metres within his own half. He spearheaded the momentum from the start, casting aside the burgeoning reputation of his opponents.

There were many passages of ebullient movement from

the Pacific islanders which left an indelible memory. To show their joy in what they had achieved they ran a lap of honour and gave one final rendering of MANU SAMOA. Then, they went home to a raptuorus welcome in Apia where 20,000 people had watched the match live on several television screens in the rugby stadium. The Rugby World Cup was reaching parts which rugby hitherto had not reached.

In Paris and Dublin the tournament was back on more usual territory. Two magnificent contests unfolded, each with its own distinctive flavour.

At Parc des Princes, France and England played a contest of unremitting physical challenge. This was an eyeball-to-eyeball sort of game; the crunch of bone and muscle against unyielding muscle. A match for tough bodies and even tougher minds (one in which, as a result, Daniel Dubroca, the French coach, was to lose his).

The match would be Serge Blanco's last game, his 93rd appearance for his country. One of rugby's greatest full backs, he had embellished the sport with his instinctive flair and risk-taking flamboyance and encouraged others to follow. This match turned on the fact that France ignored these special qualities, for the most part, and attempted to play England at their own game. It became a macho trial of strength.

The close-quarters game had come to belong to England. France, misguidedly, set out to prove that they were better. With Eric Champ, their flanker, the epitome of in-your-face, won't-step-back aggression, supported by Marc Cecillon and Laurent Cabannes and the rest, they might have had every right to think so. But when it became 'red meat' time, when bodies had to be sacrificed for the greater good of Albion, the clever money had to be on the camp where dwelt the three doughty undissembling men of the soil, honest and true, as they seemed: Mick Skinner, Peter Winterbottom and Mike Teague. They were men to go into the jungle with; not only knowing you would survive the ordeal but in doing so would have a lot fun on the way.

Not that there was much fun to be had in Paris that

"This World Cup was meant to be a festival of rugby, but it is turning into a festival of referees. On my first touch of the ball, I was used as a foot mat. The second time, when I made a mark, Heslop crashed into me, hoping to hurt me. I reacted, unfortunately, outside the rules of rugby. The referee warned me that I would go for another punch, but he said that he was a good friend of mine and it was his duty to see that I did not leave the field that way. There was another bizarre situation when I took a stiff-arm tackle and the decision was only a scrum."

SERGE BLANCO
after France's quarter-final defeat by England

Rory Underwood celebrates at the end of a match which also spelt the end of the road for French legend Serge Blanco, left. Opposite: Mickey Skinner thunders into Thierry Lacroix, and Underwood dives in to score England's first try

Incredible game, wrong result

THE 1991 WORLD CUP QUARTER-FINAL • AUSTRALIA v IRELAND

On October 20, 1991, Ireland were less than four minutes away from a place in the World Cup semi-finals. Simon Geoghegan was only 21, and took it all for granted – but now he can't believe they let it slip away

BY SIMON GEOGHEGAN

We had a really successful season in the 1991 Five Nations, even though we didn't win a game! We drew against Wales, lost the other matches by agonisingly narrow margins, and scored about ten tries. That year, everything happened very quickly for me. I won my first cap in France: there I was, only 21, playing against Blanco and Lagisquet and people like that. As the season went on, I found myself facing Ieuan Evans, Rory Underwood and the Hastings brothers – guys who had been playing rugby when I was at school. I scored tries in three of the Five Nations matches and it all seemed like a dream.

Perhaps because my first season had gone so well, I didn't really appreciate what a good a side we had. Certainly it was the best back line I ever played in for Ireland. When the World Cup started in the autumn, we were in good heart – particularly as our first two games were at home. Lansdowne Road may not be as nice to look at as somewhere like Twickenham, but it's a great atmosphere with the crowd so close to you, and they really get behind the team.

'At the time I didn't really appreciate how close we had come to beating Australia. We could have won, and probably should have done.'

We got off to a good start by beating Zimbabwe 55-11 – the second-highest Irish total ever. Brian Robinson scored a record four tries and Ralph Keyes kicked 23 points, also an Irish record at that time. We then beat Japan 32-16, and felt we were unlucky to lose 24-15 to Scotland at Murrayfield, particularly as it meant that we would have to face Australia in the quarter-final. Keith Crossan was injured against Scotland, and there was a lot of talk about me switching wings to play against David Campese, but it never happened.

The quarter-final was on a Sunday. I was sharing a room with Jim Staples, the full back, and it was his birthday that day. I remember that we were woken up by the telephone at 8 am. He picked up the phone and it was a 12-year-old girl supporter wishing him happy birthday!

For some reason we only arrived at Lansdowne Road half an hour before the kick-off. But maybe that was one of the reasons why we did so well – we didn't have time to think about it.

It was an incredible game. Campese scored a great early try when he came between the centres to touch down under the posts, but after that we played very well. Phil Matthews was an exceptional captain and he got the boys wound up before the game. The great Irish support increases the adrenalin, too.

Everything boded well, but the Aussies moved the ball brilliantly. Martin Roebuck at full back was very good at coming into the line, while the centres, Tim Horan and Jason Little, always looked likely to score when they moved the ball wide. Campese scored their first two tries. For one of them, he went past a lot of Irish players with no one even managing to get a tackle in. The second was a loop-round with Horan, which was almost as good as the try Campese created for Horan in the semi-final against the All Blacks in Dublin: he was so good at making space for the players around him. The other winger, Robert Egerton,

Ireland's jinking genius Simon Geoghegan brushes off a challenge from Australia's Rob Egerton, who is left to contemplate the grass

was an exceptional footballer, too, even though he's not so well remembered. We competed very well up front, but in terms of moving the ball, they were streets ahead of us.

I didn't see much of the ball. It was frustrating because in the Five Nations we had moved it so well. But then fly half Brian Smith moved on and they brought in Ralph Keyes, and although he did a very good job, it's always difficult when you have a new cog in the wheel.

At the time I didn't really appreciate how close we had actually come to beating Australia. We could have won the game, and probably should have done. To be fair to the Australians, when flanker Gordon Hamilton scored a try in the left-hand corner to put us 18-15 ahead with only six minutes to go, I think we would have beaten any other side in the world.

But then Rob Saunders dropped a clanger which we still give him stick about. Rob had the chance to kick the ball out but he missed touch. It was run back and ended up with a lineout and scrum – and then Michael Lynagh scored in the corner.

The Australians deserved to win because of their willingness to throw the ball around when they were under the cosh. But for us it was very disappointing. So near and yet so far.

"It is hard to imagine England winning the tournament. In the crunch, I don't believe they can dominate sufficiently to win the World Cup playing that way. The French forwards were very short on the basics against England, but the Scottish pack will be much stronger in basic skills. I am a little disappointed with England's philosophy. They just restrict their game, but it is up to them. They have more capability than they show and it seems a shame not to utilise that potential."

AUSTRALIA COACH
BOB DWYER
before the semi-finals

afternoon. With Paul Ackford and Wade Dooley in commanding form in the lineout, England were dominant. Rory Underwood and Will Carling, the wing and centre respectively, scored the tries with Jonathan Webb kicking three penalties and a conversion. Against these, Jean-Baptiste Lafond scored a try and Thierry Lacroix kicked two penalties. But the contest belonged to the two mighty packs of forwards. It may have been "the death of romanticism" according to Jean Trillo, the backs coach of France, but the suffocating pressure imposed by England was a joy to Roger Uttley, their coach, as they won 19-10.

Frustration boiled over into acrimony in the tunnel leading from the field. Daniel Dubroca called the referee David Bishop, from New Zealand, 'a cheat' and the French coach was accused of assaulting him. There were witnesses to the manhandling but they were no more, according to French sources, than fraternal gestures. Albert Ferrasse, the president of the French Rugby Federation, maintained that Dubroca's English was not good enough "to abuse the referee seriously". No action was taken by the World Cup committee. Soon afterwards, however, Dubroca resigned.

With this defeat, Serge Blanco, who himself had been involved in the first of the afternoon's fracas, retired from the game he had graced so luminously to become a living expression of rugby's capacity for rhapsody and adventure. It is always a sadness to witness the departure of such a romantic figure from the game. Who would replace him in the crowd's affections? Who is there to inspire the young?

A different mood was set in Dublin. The match developed into a pulsatingly feverish affair. The contest very nearly reversed all the wiseacres' prophecies into airy nothing. If 1987 had the Australia-France semi-final to lift the competition to simmering levels of excitement and febrile tension, then the 1991 tournament could boast of this momentous game at Lansdowne Road. The thrilling

"We put up a tremendous display. I have always felt that this is a good Irish side, capable of winning the Triple Crown, and there is cause for a great deal of optimism for the Five Nations Championship."

IRELAND CAPTAIN PHIL MATTHEWS after the Australia game

drama which was to unfold with cliff-hanging, nail-biting heroics had begun with a no-nonsense, bare-knuckle saloon-bar brawl. It was down-to-earth, spit-and-sawdust stuff. The only way was up. Then, with hot-tempered turbulence out of the way, the stage was set for passion and glory.

David Campese was the most prominent personality of the 1991 World Cup. He set Dublin alight with the first of his two tries when, taking an angled 30-metre run, he crossed over in the 17th minute. Lynagh converted. Ralph Keyes kept Ireland in close contact with penalty goals so that the teams were level 6-6 at half-time.

Lynagh kicked a penalty. A drop goal from Keyes. Then with Campese's second try and Lynagh's conversion, Australia opened a six-point lead: 15-9. This looked, despite Ireland's magnificent performance, to be enough. But Keyes was persistent with his kicks and reduced the deficit back to three points. Pulses were racing. So indeed was Gordon Hamilton, the Ballymena flanker, as he chased after the ball to score what looked like a winning try. Keyes converted with barely five minutes remaining. 18-15.

Yet Australia were resourceful enough when Ireland disastrously failed to kick themselves out of their own territory and safely – surely – into folklore. The Aussies ignored a penalty attempt at goal and Lynagh, acting captain after Farr-Jones had left the field injured, opted for a 15-metre scrum instead. This took great nerve and composure. It is what made Australia into a fine team. Campese, from one of their pre-planned moves, ran, was held, and passed to ... who else but Lynagh for the winning try.

You felt that that this near-miss would return to haunt the Irish players. They would reflect on the glory that was so nearly theirs and will never come again. Etched forever on their memories will be 19-18 on Sunday October 20, 1991.

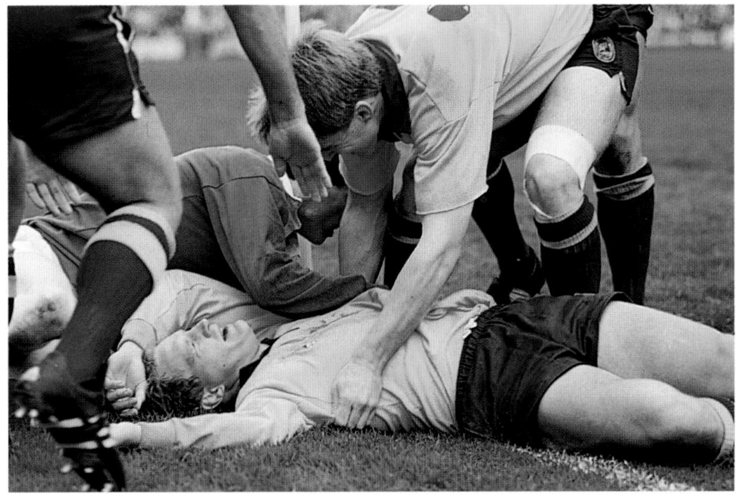

Michael Lynagh of Australia collapses after clinching the match against Ireland. Opposite: A juggling act by Marty Roebuck and Tim Horan

· QUARTER FINALS ·

SCOTLAND 28 WESTERN SAMOA 6
19 Oct • Murrayfield
SCOTLAND: G Hastings; Stanger, S Hastings, Shiel, Tukalo; Chalmers, Armstrong; *Sole, Allan, Burnell, Gray, Weir, Jeffrey, Calder, White.
SCORERS: *Tries:* Stanger, Jeffrey (2). *Cons:* G Hastings (2). *Pens:* G Hastings (4)
WESTERN SAMOA: Aiolupo; Lima, Vaega, Bunce, Tagaloa; Bachop, Vaea; *Fatialofa, Toomalatai, Alaalatoa, Birtwistle, Ioane, Vaifale, Perelini, Lam.
SCORERS: *Pen:* Vaea. *DG:* Bachop.
Referee: WD Bevan

ENGLAND 19 FRANCE 10
19 Oct • Parc des Princes, Paris
ENGLAND: Webb; Heslop, *Carling, Guscott, Underwood; Andrew, Hill; Leonard, Moore, Probyn, Ackford, Dooley, Skinner, Winterbottom, Teague.
SCORERS: *Tries:* Underwood, Carling. *Con:* Webb. *Pens:* Webb (3).
FRANCE: *Blanco; Lafond, Sella, Mesnel, Saint-André; Lacroix, Galthie; Ondarts, Marocco, Lascube, Roumat, Cadieu, Champ, Cabannes, Cecillon.
SCORERS: *Try:* Lafond. *Pens:* Lacroix.
Referee: DJ Bishop (New Zealand)

AUSTRALIA 19 IRELAND 18
20 Oct • Lansdowne Road, Dublin
AUSTRALIA: Roebuck; Campese, Little, Horan, Egerton; Lynagh, *Farr-Jones, (Slattery 18); Daly, Kearns, McKenzie, McCall, Eales, Poidevin, Miller, Ofahengaue.
SCORERS: *Tries:* Campese (2), Lynagh. *Cons:* Lynagh (2). *Pen:* Lynagh.
IRELAND: Staples; Geoghegan, Mullin, Curtis, Clarke; Keyes, Saunders; Popplewell, Smith, D Fitzgerald, Lenihan, Francis, *Matthews, Hamilton, Robinson.
SCORERS: *Try:* Hamilton. *Con:* Keyes. *Pens:* Keyes (3). *DG:* Keyes.
Referee: JM Fleming (Scotland)

NEW ZEALAND 29 CANADA 13
20 Oct • Stade du Nord, Lille
NEW ZEALAND: Timu; Kirwan, Innes, McCahill, Tuigamala; Fox, Bachop; McDowell, Fitzpatrick, Loe, I Jones, *G Whetton, A Whetton, Henderson, Brooke.
SCORERS: *Tries:* Timu (2), McCahill, Brooke, Kirwan. *Cons:* Fox (3). *Pen:* Fox.
CANADA: *Wyatt; S Stewart, C Stewart, Woods, Gray; Rees, Tynan; Evans, Speirs, Szabo, Van den Brink, Hadley, Charron, MacKinnon, Ennis.
SCORERS: *Tries:* Tynan, Charron. *Con:* Rees. *Pen:* Wyatt.
Referee: Fred Howard (England)

1991 THE · SEMI-FINALS ·

Strong tradition applied to both the semi-final matches, so did an intense and localised rivalry. The fixtures went back a long way; the nations lived on each others' doorsteps. After 92 encounters, Australia and New Zealand, who compete for the Bledisloe Cup, were playing each other on a neutral ground for the first time. Since 1903, New Zealand had won 64 times, Australia 24. England, who play Scotland for the Calcutta Cup, have faced each other 108 times since 1871 with the English succeeding 52 times to Scotland's 39.

In their most recent encounter, Australia had lost in Auckland. On their last visit to Murrayfield, England had also lost in a Grand Slam decider.

As with the previous weekend, they were contrasting matches. On the Saturday in Edinburgh, England, in the same grim mood that they had shown in Paris, ground out a victory against Scotland. The past weighed heavily on this encounter. A run of 13 matches since 1988 meant that England were fearful of what might be thought of as "Fortress Murrayfield".

England's experience was not a happy one. They were not about to take any chances there. Knowing their superior power at forward and exercising it to the full, they tormented and frustrated Scotland into submission. It took the Scots 20 minutes just to win their first lineout. Despite playing to their known strengths, however, England, still only managed to survive by the skin of their teeth. Even with a free flow of possession, a huge territorial advantage which left Scotland reeling on their heels, and expert control by outside half Rob Andrew, England could have lost the match. Full back Jonathan Webb was off-key with his early kicks, and England failed to build up the kind of lead which might have given a cushion of comfort and which the likes of Ackford and his solid front row had prepared for them.

With Finlay Calder, Derek White and John Jeffrey such persuasive influences in Scotland's back row, anything was possible. In support was Gavin Hastings, who was in mischievously adventurous mood when the moment allowed. Indeed, Scotland could have stolen the prize from under their old enemy's noses. Had Hastings in more

Scenes from the Murrayfield semi-final, from opposite left: The Gavin Hastings fan club; England's twin towers Wade Dooley and Paul Ackford; Mike Teague celebrates the final whistle; and Rob Andrew scores the winning drop goal

conventional mode kicked what was for him a penalty of mere formality, his team and not his opponents who would have gone into a 9-6 lead in the last quarter. But he missed the crucial kick which would surely have given his team a Final place.

Thus England's was a fragile eminence. Often, they could not put the game out of a struggling opponent's reach. They would leave open, however slightly, a window of opportunity; the whiff of a chance. This is always dangerous and the phenomenon, like the ghost at the feast, would return at intervals to scupper their ambitions.

> "England wanted to strangle the game; we wanted to keep it alive."
>
> SCOTLAND COACH IAN McGEECHAN
>
> "We would love to have cut the Scots to pieces with scintillating back-play, but it's not quite as easy as that."
>
> ENGLAND TEAM MANAGER GEOFF COOKE
>
> "The ruination of rugby."
>
> NEW ZEALAND COACH JOHN HART

In their midst, England had a player who knew how to win a game, and often did so. Rob Andrew was disciplined, efficient, highly motivated and had an icy rugby temperament. He was unflinching in his understanding of the parameters within which Geoff Cooke's England should play. In the purely determining physical sense of match play, he captained the team; he ran the show.

There were times when you wished he would chance his arm a little more and extend the limits he had imposed on his talent. Such men of chance are few. But Andrew, if unable to fulfil other people's expectations of him, invariably could point to the scoreboard and feel vindicated.

He was to do so against Scotland. As an act of vengeance against the country which had denied him and

Scenes from the Lansdowne Road clash of the titans, from left: John Eales outjumps All Black Ian Jones; David Campese drags down John Timu; and Eales grapples with centre Bernie McCahill

his team the Grand Slam a year previously, Andrew, after Rory Underwood's run along the touchline, dropped the goal in the dying minutes to put England through to, and Scotland out of, the Final of the 1991 World Cup.

The following day in Dublin, the tournament witnessed a vibrant game of pulsating movement. The difference lay in the fact that the teams at Lansdowne Road won the ball to attack while at Murrayfield the team that won most of the possession was motivated mainly in denying it to the other side.

Australia, in a fashion that hardly seemed possible, bearing in mind their opponents' stature in rugby, gave New Zealand the run-around. The All Blacks had not played with their distinctive and overwhelming power in the World Cup in 1991. Even so, it was never imagined that they could be so outplayed. Bob Dwyer's team were in outrageously commanding mood. They left New Zealand

"I hope the rugby public saw at Lansdowne Road what rugby can do and the way it can be played. It was awfully important for the tournament this game was played the way it was. We participated in a great game of rugby where both sides showed they can use the ball. I believe the game is played to run the ball, to move it, not just kick and chase it. If any side can win the ball as England did and not move it past first five-eighth [stand-off half], I wonder why we're playing rugby. I don't believe rugby has been promoted all the time in this World Cup but I would like to think it was promoted today."

JOHN HART

New Zealand co-coach on Australia's winning performance against New Zealand in the semi-final

"I'm astonished looking at our players in the swimming pool. They look like athletes. That was not always the case!"
AUSTRALIA COACH BOB DWYER

with nowhere to turn. No one, it was thought, could put the All Blacks so out of sorts as to leave them bereft and ragged. Michael Lynagh, Tim Horan and Jason Little tied down the midfield.

Despite Ian Jones' magnificent efforts in the lineout, the All Blacks pack were outplayed in the loose and close quarters. Rarely, if at any time in their whole history, can an All Blacks team have been so reduced to impotence. If they had the territorial advantage, they hardly found themselves in a position to threaten the Wallaby line in the second half. It was not until after the interval that Grant Fox had his first chance to aim at goal to indicate the distance that Australia maintained between their line and their Tasman Sea neighbours.

Indeed, almost from the start New Zealand were left to chase an Australian lead. After seven minutes David Campese had scored a superlative try by entering the three-quarter line in the outside half position and running in a long, diagonal sweep towards the try-line. The All Blacks stood off him. No one committed himself to the tackle. Onwards the charismatic wing went. Lulled by the thought that he might do something – change direction, halt, start, vary his speed, throw a 'goose-step' or two as was his wont

Below: A pointed message which, for the time being, the rest of the world cannot easily deny

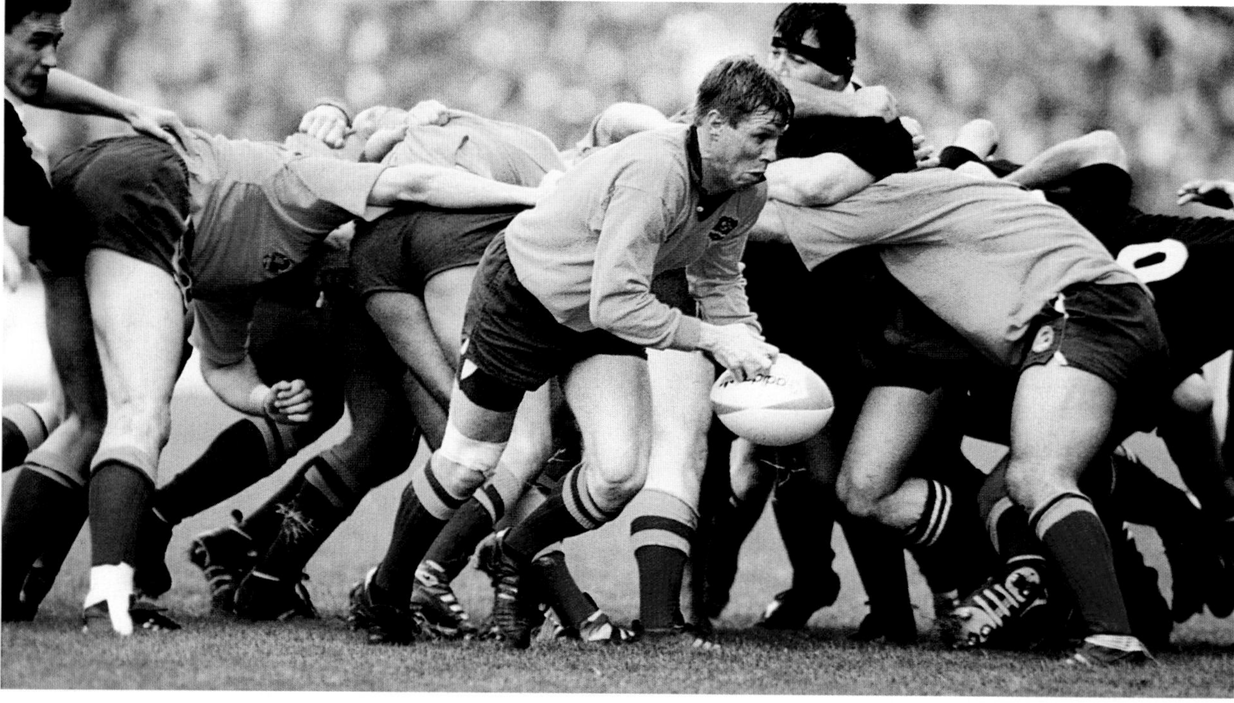

Nick Farr-Jones, the Australia captain and scrum half, takes the attack to the All Blacks in a surprisingly comfortable victory

"Having made the Final, we now have every prospect of winning it. Whatever people may say, for the England side to beat France and Scotland away on successive Saturdays is a magnificent achievement. The Final is at Twickenham and it's who gets it right on the day."

ENGLAND MANAGER GEOFF COOKE

· SEMI-FINALS ·

ENGLAND 9 SCOTLAND 6
26 Oct • Murrayfield
ENGLAND: Webb; Halliday, *Carling, Guscott, Underwood; Andrew, Hill; Leonard, Moore, Probyn, Ackford, Dooley, Skinner, Winterbottom, Teague.
SCORERS: *Pens:* Webb (2). *DG:* Andrew.
SCOTLAND: G Hastings; Stanger, S Hastings, Lineen, Tukalo; Chalmers, Armstrong; *Sole, Allan, Burnell, Gray, Weir, Jeffrey, Calder, White.
SCORER: *Pens:* G Hastings (2).
Referee: Kerry Fitzgerald (Australia)

AUSTRALIA 16 NEW ZEALAND 6
27 Oct • Lansdowne Road, Dublin
AUSTRALIA: Roebuck; Campese, Little, Horan, Egerton; Lynagh, *Farr-Jones; Daly, Kearns, McKenzie, McCall, Eales, Poidevin, Ofahengaue, Coker.
SCORERS: *Tries:* Campese, Horan. *Con:* Lynagh. *Pens:* Lynagh (2).
NEW ZEALAND: Crowley; Kirwan, Innes, McCahill, Timu; Fox, Bachop; McDowell, Fitzpatrick, Loe, I Jones, *G Whetton, A Whetton, Carter, Brooke.
SCORER: *Pens:* Fox (2).
Referee: JM Fleming (Scotland)

– they watched as Campese glided past, virtually at the same uniform speed. By the time New Zealand realised that they had been hoodwinked, the Australians were four points up.

Lynagh kicked a penalty before the Lynagh/Campese combination manufactured a second try. Lynagh chipped, Campese gathered. While he veered slightly in-field, the wing in the same movement flipped an outrageous pass over his shoulder and blind to where intuition hinted to him that Horan might be. The centre gratefully accepted the pass and scored. Thirteen-nil and the All Blacks had hardly been in the match.

The New Zealanders were forced to play catch-up rugby. John Kirwan had his moments but whenever he managed to avoid one player he was soon swamped by the Australian defence. To what extent they missed Michael Jones, the flanker, who refused to play on Sundays, was a matter of debate. In truth, though, New Zealand had lacked their usual conviction in their other performances.

Thus, the two teams who had deserved to reach the Final had, in fact, done so – even if by contrasting means.

THE PLAY-OFF FOR

· THIRD PLACE ·

This is the fixture of which no one dares speak its name. Not, anyway, with any enthusiasm. This contest, if the word is appropriate, emphasised the resigned air with which New Zealand and Scotland played at the Cardiff Arms Park. Forty thousand people turned up but it might just as well have been one man and his dog. The All Blacks' performance of the haka was intimidating enough, with the advancing Va'aiga Tuigamala looking threatening. But John Jeffrey only smiled. The battle was over. It really was time to go home. Coming third was of no great moment to either country. By winning 13-6, the All Blacks were not going to go back to their homeland feeling satisfied that they were third in the world.

Walter Little scored the game's only try. It had remained something of a mystery why the New Zealand management had failed to give proper recognition to the centre from North Harbour. He had shown speed off the mark, a delicate handling touch and an eye for the gap which had made the others seem journeymen. He showed these qualities in abundance in this game and his play was probably the only quality ingredient to emerge from a match which otherwise was full of mistakes and shoddy play. Jon Preston and Gavin Hastings kicked five penalties between them. Sadly, it was the time to say a regretful farewell to Finlay Calder and John Jeffrey of Scotland's tormenting back row, the scourge of so many well-laid plans. They were about to retire. Their names had grown familiar to everyone and in Jeffrey's case his blond hair could so easily be picked from the anonymity of a steaming mêlée. The White Shark, as he was called, suggested his deadly predatory instincts. We would not hear again their names roll off Bill McLaren's Borders brogue commentating on the Five Nations Championship.

So close were they to everything that mattered that their names were forever bracketed together like those two inveterate cricket enthusiasts, Charters and Caldicott, in Alfred Hitchcock's *The Lady Vanishes*.

Jeffrey and Calder had played their last.

· 3RD PLACE PLAY-OFF ·

NEW ZEALAND 13 SCOTLAND 6
30th October • Cardiff Arms Park
NEW ZEALAND: Wright; Kirwan, Innes, Little, Tuigamala; Preston, Bachop; McDowell, Fitzpatrick, Loe, I Jones, *G Whetton, Earl, M Jones, Brooke.
SCORERS: *Try:* Little. *Pens:* Preston (3).
SCOTLAND: G Hastings; Stanger, S Hastings, Lineen, Tukalo; Chalmers, Armstrong; *Sole, Allan, Burnell, Gray, Weir, Jeffrey, Calder, White.
SCORER: *Pens:* G Hastings (2).
Referee: S R Hilditch (Ireland)

Left: New Zealand say hi to their third place playoff opponents while, below, Scotland hooker David Sole gets the bum's rush

The plan that saved Australia's World Cup

THE 1991 WORLD CUP QUARTER-FINAL • AUSTRALIA v IRELAND

It looked like the Wallabies were down and out. Against all the odds, Ireland had them on the rack. Michael Lynagh describes how he and his team pulled off one of the greatest escape acts in rugby history

BY MICHAEL LYNAGH

What was it like to win the World Cup? I have been asked this question so many times since the victory over England at Twickenham on November 2, eight years ago. To this day I still haven't been able to come up with an adequate response. "Great, good and fantastic" don't seem to be the appropriate answer when you are trying to describe the feeling of being part of the best team in the world at that moment in time in your chosen sport.

For me the best moment throughout the 1991 World Cup happened two weeks before at Lansdowne Road against Ireland in the quarter-final. To be even more specific, the last four minutes of that game were for me one of the highlights of my rugby career.

A bit of background first on Australia's progress to reach this point in the World Cup in 1991.

We had come through the initial games without too much trouble or fanfare. We accounted for Argentina in the first match, had a 35-point victory at Cardiff Arms Park against Wales and won a close, rain-sodden contest with a very physical Western Samoan outfit in Pontypool. This set up a quarter-final against Ireland at their home ground in Dublin. The winner of this match was scheduled to meet the favourites, the New Zealand All Blacks, at the same venue.

We were undoubtedly the favourites for this match against Ireland. It started like that and felt like that all the way through the game. We seemed to be scoring pretty easily and in control throughout the contest. Yet the Irish kept pegging us back with penalty goals to stay in touch. We never really pulled away from them, yet, as I said, we seemed to be in control. Then Gordon Hamilton, the Irish flanker, received the ball with clear passage to the try line.

'With four minutes to go, I had to avoid any negative talk, like "Don't panic". I kept saying to myself: "Do not use the word don't".'

Mayhem! Suddenly we were one point behind. There were Irish supporters all over the pitch celebrating the seemingly impossible, but now very realistic, chance of an Irish victory.

I was acting captain, as Nick Farr-Jones was off the field injured. I had to come up with a plan. There were four minutes to play and we had to win the game or we would be on the plane back home to Australia the next morning wrapped in failure. This is what happened.

I had to have all the information I could gather before I could start to construct a plan. I went to the referee and asked him how long there was to go before full-time. Jim Fleming's response was "four minutes". As I trotted back to the team, I formulated the bare bones of a plan. I got all the guys together behind the goal line and started by telling them that there were four minutes to go, which was plenty of time. I then said very specifically what we were going to do. We will kick off long, the Irish will then kick into touch giving us a lineout throw around the halfway mark. We would then win that lineout and I would call the appropriate backline moves, which I already had in my own mind.

The last thing I said to the guys before we went back to restart the game was: "If you have the ball in your possession and are in any

The crucial try – Michael Lynagh drives for the line with despairing Irish captain Phil Matthews in tow

doubt about what to do, hold on to it and run towards the opposition goal-line. But above all, hold on to the ball." All pretty simple stuff, but I intentionally wanted to avoid at all costs any negative talk, like "Don't panic". I kept saying to myself: "Do not use the word don't." I wanted to keep the instructions as simple as possible. Not because rugby players are simple, but in times of stress the simpler and shorter the directive, the easier it is for people to absorb it.

As it turned out, the Irish bungled their kick into touch and we had the throw-in on their 25-metre line. I called a move, which brought David Campese back inside the centres. I called this move for two reasons. One, we had scored from it in the first half and secondly, if Campo didn't get through it would bring him closer to the supporting forwards, which is what actually happened.

Normally Campo was like most backs – as soon as he got tackled he would throw the ball away and get the hell out of the way. On this occasion, however, he held on to it and pushed with the rest of the forward pack towards the opposition try line. In so doing, we were assured of possession at the next set-piece. Exactly as I had instructed the players to do in my goal-line chat.

I remember thinking at the time that if Campo had been paying attention, then there was a fair chance that everyone must have been. We got the scrum put-in. I called another move, which we had practised throughout the week at training. We had identified a weakness in the Irish defence by studying them on video and come up with a ploy to exploit it. I called it. We broke through and I was in support to cross the line after Campese had been brought down just short. We had won the match.

We beat the All Blacks a week later in our best performance of the tournament and then went on to take the title against England at Twickenham. I was relieved at the end of the game at Lansdowne Road – and very relieved after the game at the Twickenham.

My command of the English language still does not allow me to express my feelings much more than this obviously feeble attempt; even after all these years.

1991

THE · FINAL ·

In the days leading up to the Final at Twickenham the focus of attention sharpened on England. Australia seemed to be fulfilling their promise and accomplishing a rounded game and, as witnessed in their previous two matches, doing so under pressure.

England apparently were not. They were on the threshold of one of English rugby's greatest moments, perhaps *the* greatest moment, and yet there was a nagging criticism. 'Wonderful accomplishment and all that but, tut, tut, what about the style?' It is not a conundrum that would take too much of a New Zealander's time. Indeed after winning the Cup in 1987, a similar proposition was put to David Kirk, the All Blacks captain, after his team's success. "You Brits," he responded. "You make me laugh..." and the answer trailed away as if he did not feel the need to amplify further. In other words, why worry with such finery as style; a matter which so preoccupies the 'Brits' and hardly anyone else. The object of the exercise is to win and to do so in the manner best suited to the team and the circumstances in which they find themselves.

In fact, it was all a question of style. But not in any cosmetic sense; not in the sense of making something look good. Rather, England's plan was transparently monotone. The tactics were there for all to see; unchanged from first to last. England's forwards, according to Geoff Cooke, were looked upon with fear "or at least with respect". In this he was quite right. Indeed, this 'respect' was to remain in 1995, too, but it is not enough, based as it is on past performance.

But did the rest of the rugby world hold England's threequarters in the same respect ? That was the dilemma. What of Jeremy Guscott and Will Carling in the centre?

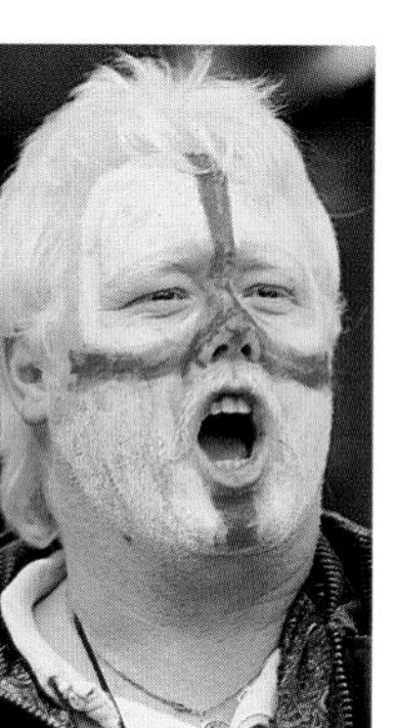

"Aw no...!" England fans groan as the Australian forwards deliver possession to Nick Farr-Jones

"I feel a bit sorry for England. I didn't think any team apart from New Zealand was capable of winning in Paris and Edinburgh. They would be stupid to depart from the game which has won matches for them. If I find it boring, then I find it boring, but that's not a criticism. If England won the World Cup it would have a terrifically positive effect on the game here."

AUSTRALIA COACH
BOB DWYER
before the World Cup Final

What of Rory Underwood and Simon Halliday on the wings? We were not to know. They had big reputations but very little had been seen of them during the tournament. They had not been allowed to ask any questions of the opposition. So far, it was potential unfulfilled, which Geoff Cooke in his pre-match interviews seemed to acknowledge. The team, during Cooke's four-year tenure, had won 23 of their last 33 fixtures.

On the other hand, we had all witnessed Little and Horan for Australia. They had strutted their stuff. We had marvelled at Campese's devastating high-jinks. Martin Roebuck, too, had had his scintillating moments from full back. Michael Lynagh,

Troy Coker jumps against Mick 'The Munch' Skinner and, left, Tim Horan clears as Will Carling closes in

The Aussies were there for the taking...

THE 1991 WORLD CUP FINAL • AUSTRALIA v ENGLAND

England were in the World Cup Final, thanks largely to Messrs Leonard, Moore, Probyn, Ackford, Dooley, Skinner, Teague and Winterbottom. So why weren't they asked to finish the job? Theirs is a rage that still burns...

BY PAUL ACKFORD

They were there for the taking. As each minute of the second half ticked by, the Australian forwards grew ever more tired. By the end of the match they were surviving on will power alone. And what did we do? Instead of driving though the heart of them, battering them senseless, we continued to move the ball wide. Not much was at stake. Only immortality as the first northern hemisphere side to win the World Cup.

The die was cast months before when England toured Fiji and Australia in preparation for the 1991 World Cup. We squeezed past Fiji, only to be smashed 40-15 by Australia in Sydney. If the margin of defeat was bad enough, the manner was worse. We could not cope with the pace and continuity of the Australians and we could not dominate the ball for long enough to get our own style of game going.

The next day, back at our hotel, we gathered in the team room for a debrief. There we resolved that, if ever we met up with Australia again, we would match them for speed and ingenuity. None of this up-the-jumper, grind-forward rugby which had clinched England's first Grand Slam in a decade. That was not going to be good enough. And, in any case, we reasoned, wasn't it about time to unleash the sublime talents of Rory Underwood, Will Carling and Jeremy Guscott? They were just as good as Michael Lynagh, Nick Farr-Jones and that Campese bloke.

The mistake was not to play that way from the start of the competition. In the group games of the World Cup, and for the quarter-final against France and the semi-final against Scotland, we reverted to type. Catch and drive, bang up the middle, regroup, inch forward, secure the scrum and begin the whole process once again. It had worked six months previously during the Grand Slam campaign and it worked once more.

'Not much was at stake. Only immortality as the first northern hemisphere side to win the World Cup.'

Suddenly we were in the Final at Twickenham. The Queen was guest of honour and all over the country millions of folk who had never watched rugby and hadn't heard of Wade Dooley, Jason Leonard and Mike Teague were switching on their television sets.

The final sessions in the week leading up to the match were slick as we remained true to our pledge. This running rugby lark wasn't that difficult. Quite good fun, in fact. Rory and Jerry and Will looked in fine fettle and the handling particularly sharp. Australia, who were expecting the usual strong, stolid England, were going to get the shock of their sporting lives.

So much for the theory. When it came to the big day we found we could not transfer the excellence of the unopposed training sessions to the intensity of the live match. Passes were dropped, opportunities went begging. But that wasn't the whole story. Around half-time, when we started to get on top of the big Aussie forwards, we should have thrown the running rugby option out of the window. We didn't, and the rest is history.

appearing for the 53rd time with his partner Nick Farr-Jones at half back, could run and score tries, too. In John Eales, the lock, Australia had the kind of forward who ideally conformed, physically and mentally, to the kind of adaptable player who should adorn teams as the Millennium turns. He was comfortable in any situation; never gauche or awkward. Perceptive, he was endowed with most of the skills. These players, singly or in combination, could change the complexion of a match. Australia had choices.

The Australian forwards had more than matched New Zealand but could they account for England in the same manner? And if they could, what would the English response be?

England entered the Final with what appeared to be the one plan, established and proven. There had been little evidence of another. And if they did have a Plan B, would they dare declare it in the final, with such glory to be won in the last game, when, hitherto, they had so ignored it? Would they, could they, take such a radical shift? England were in a dilemma. They were not short of advice from the pundits in the media and the rosy-hued experts in the fug of four-ale bars.

On the day, England failed to resolve this dilemma. Or if they did, they did so by choosing at the critically decisive moment, not to be true to their known selves. They ran the ball in the way so many of their own followers had wished, but it did not win the game.

Australia, gaining so little possession against the magnificent Ackford and Dooley, were often forced for long periods to defend. For a team who had a reputation for appreciating the movement of rugby and for 15 players to feel the ball in hand, their performance relied a great deal on controlled defence.

The Australian try-line was crossed only three times throughout the whole tournament (twice by Argentina in their first game). And it was their defensive network that won the day at

"I think England will win because the Australian pack will not be mature enough to handle them."

FORMER BRITISH LIONS CAPTAIN FINLAY CALDER, BEFORE THE FINAL

"I'll approach the final like any other Test. I play the same, whatever the game."

DAVID CAMPESE OF AUSTRALIA, BEFORE THE FINAL

"This World Cup Final is the greatest event in English rugby union history. The players, to a man, feel pride and privilege at being in the squad which will contest it. We are desperate to win and determined that we will enjoy ourselves."

ROB ANDREW OF ENGLAND, BEFORE THE FINAL

John Eales of Australia does battle with the England forwards

John Eales and Tony Daly celebrate victory, Nick Farr-Jones collects the Cup from the Queen, and Will Carling salutes the crowd

Twickenham. Yet, for all England's running and handling, it was Australia with a bit of push-and-shove from a line-out who crossed for the only try of the game, accorded to Tony Daly.

But while Jonathan Webb, with the wind at his back, failed with two penalties, Lynagh kicked the conversion and a penalty to give his side a 9-0 half-time lead. This was vastly against the run of play. Lynagh and Webb kicked three penalties between them in the second half to give a final score of 12-6 and the Cup to Nick Farr-Jones.

> "Around the England dressing room at Twickenham, players were slumped on the benches in a mixture of sheer fatigue and dismay. In the immediate aftermath of the game, exhaustion crept on us: heads were held in hands, most of us stared inconsolably into space, reflecting on what we had come through these last five weeks. Was it really only a game?"
>
> ROB ANDREW

Were Australia worthy world champions? In a marvellous Final they stuck it out through gritted teeth but they had displayed in the month a flexible capacity to adjust their game. They had shown admirable composure against Argentina, whose surprising fightback might have unsettled

· 1991 STATISTICS ·

INDIVIDUAL SCORING RECORDS

Most points in tournament
68 **RP Keyes** (Ireland)
66 **MP Lynagh** (Australia)
61 **AG Hastings** (Scotland)

Most tries in tournament
6 **DI Campese** (Australia)
6 **J-B Lafond** (France)

Most points in a match
24 **JM Webb** (England v Italy)
23 **RP Keyes** (Ireland v Zimbabwe)

Most tries in a match
4 **BF Robinson** (Ireland v Zimbabwe)
3 **TJ Wright** (New Zealand v USA)
3 **I Tukalo** (Scotland v Zimbabwe)
3 **J-B Lafond** (France v Fiji)

FAIR PLAY AWARD:
Zimbabwe: No penalties conceded for foul or dangerous play.

"At the end, the team was exhausted. Against the All Blacks we felt we could have gone on another 40 minutes. England ran at us so many times, we had to make so many tackles that it was a far more tiring game. I just lay in the bath for 30 minutes afterwards. I was so absolutely exhausted."

NICK FARR-JONES
after Australia's 12-6 victory in the Final against England

many another team. In unfamiliar wet conditions they overcame an aggressive Western Samoan team when they had lost their captain through injury. Given only moderate opposition, they ran away with the game against Wales. Then there were the famous contests against Ireland and New Zealand. The Australian players were magisterial in both of them.

But in all of this hustle and bustle, tensions and pressure, they had the seemingly infinite capacity to summon a spirit from deeper recesses which are unknown to lesser teams. They did so to conjure an extraordinary victory in Dublin when it all seemed to have been lost. Their strength of will and the undying belief, until the final whistle blows, that the match is still there to be won, was testimony to their status as world champions.

A remarkable confidence exuded from the young side. They risked everything to fashion a try for Michael Lynagh in Dublin's fervid atmosphere. This alone marked them as worthy winners of the 1991 World Cup.

· THE FINAL ·

AUSTRALIA 12 ENGLAND 6
2 Nov • Twickenham
AUSTRALIA: Roebuck; Campese, Little, Horan, Egerton; Lynagh, *Farr-Jones; Daly, Kearns, McKenzie, McCall, Eales, Poidevin, Ofahengaue, Coker.
SCORERS: *Try:* Daly. *Con:* Lynagh. *Pens:* Lynagh (2).
ENGLAND: Webb; Halliday, *Carling, Guscott, Underwood; Andrew, Hill; Leonard, Moore, Probyn, Ackford, Dooley, Skinner, Winterbottom, Teague.
SCORER: *Pens:* Webb (2).
Referee: WD Bevan (Wales)
Attendance: 56,208

"As a special treat for the winners, you can have a sachet of shampoo each..." Simon Poidevin, Phil Kearns and Michael Lynagh bask in victory

1995

THE WEBB ELLIS CUP

In South Africa

THE FIRST MAJOR SPORTING EVENT IN POST-APARTHEID SOUTH AFRICA WAS ALWAYS GOING TO CARRY ADDED SIGNIFICANCE. BUT COULD THE RUGBY WORLD CUP LIVE UP TO THE WEIGHT OF EXPECTATION?

The Terminator: Jonah Lomu charges, Rob Andrew dives in vain

A TOURNAMENT TO TRANSCEND RUGBY

President Nelson Mandela threw his weight behind South Africa's return to the world sporting stage, taking the 1995 World Cup to a new level. The event was spectacular – even before the phenomenon known as Jonah Lomu blasted his way into rugby history

"Sporting a baseball cap and wearing the green and gold jersey of South Africa – identical to the captain's – with the leaping Springbok on his breast, Nelson Mandela epitomised reconciliation."

The evening of June 24, 1995, should have been a time of unalloyed celebration. But Louis Luyt, President of the South African Rugby Football Union, very nearly spoilt the atmosphere of good fortune and euphoria which had engulfed his country. With an almost comic sense of mistiming, Luyt – inured from what the rest of the world might think by the skin of a pachyderm – blundered. Standing to speak at the post-match dinner to close the 1995 tournament, he announced brazenly that the Rugby World Cup was now in the hands of those to whom it rightly belonged. And, he went on in a cataract of shameless effrontery: "We boasted in 1987 that the real World Cup could not be won in New Zealand because we were not there. It was the same in England in 1991. In 1995 we have proved that if we were there, we would win."

Furthermore, ignoring Ed Morrison, the English referee who had officiated in the Final, Luyt presented the Welsh referee Derek Bevan with a special tournament award for best official. This was not only bad manners to the other officials and particularly insulting to Morrison, but it might have been perceived as something more unsavoury. It was Bevan who had been in charge of the semi-final which saw South Africa, in less than straightforward circumstances, overcome France in Durban. This was a delicate moment and placed Bevan in an embarrassing position that very nearly compromised his integrity.

Aghast at Luyt's rudeness, the All Blacks walked out; others felt equally aggrieved but stayed. The dinner which was meant to be a joyous occasion was spoiled. The rest of the evening deteriorated into puzzlement and acrimony. Thus one man's arrogance nearly betrayed a nation.

Hours earlier, in inspiring contrast, a frail black man who had been incarcerated in Robben Island by white supremacists for over a quarter of a century had now, in the declining years of the Millennium, so flourished as to become an icon of 20th-century statesmanship. Nelson Mandela had dignified Rugby World Cup 1995 with his noble presence. Without pomp or vainglory, he had presented the World Cup to François Pienaar, the highly esteemed Springbok captain and flanker, in front of a jubilant Ellis Park crowd. Sporting a baseball cap and wearing the green and gold jersey of South Africa – identical to the captain's – with the leaping Springbok on his breast, Mandela epitomised reconciliation. Not even these motley garments could deny the President his

grandeur. Rather they enhanced his lustre. Nothing, after all, was as representative of the past injustices of apartheid as rugby union. This was the white man's sport; the Springbok jersey was a metaphor for the old regime.

Such benign harmony and grace were not in Louis Luyt's mealy-mouthed lexicon of Afrikaner understanding – but his kind, it was fervently hoped, were being left behind. The rainbow nation was emerging gradually after 40 years of bigotry. In this way, a rugby event was transformed.

Rugby World Cup 1995 assumed a dimension above and beyond the trivialities which we normally attribute to sport. These frivolous pastimes are made more potent by the exaggerated emotions we attach to them. The emotions revealed in Johannesburg on June 24 may have been

The showdown the world was waiting for: South Africa face the All Blacks' haka before the World Cup Final

"There were not just 63,000 cheering us on; there were 43 million."

SOUTH AFRICA CAPTAIN FRANÇOIS PIENAAR after the opening game against Australia

Right: The finalists in the national anthem karaoke competition – from top: Western Samoa, Japan, England, Ireland, New Zealand. Above: Young fans peer through the fence at East London, where Western Samoa beat Italy 42-18. Opposite: South African supporters show the flag, and the Ivory Coast's mascot packs his trunk for the World Cup

extravagant, but they were not out of proportion with an afternoon which had begun, immoderately, with the vast bulk of a Boeing 747 – with the legend "Good luck Bokke" on the wing – flying so low that it was seriously in danger of giving a fleeting kiss to the roofs of the Ellis Park stands.

After that, how could anything that followed be considered over-the-top? It was all of a piece. So that when Pienaar, moments after the final whistle, said "There were not just 63,000 cheering us on out there; there were 43 million", no one was about to argue. Even the All Blacks, if pushed, might have found within this unity of the South African nation some solace for their defeat. This was something that transcended winning and losing a game. Luyt's boastfulness could have undermined it, but the afternoon had already provided the most fitting climax of all.

The 1995 World Cup had begun with two qualifying rounds the previous autumn. There was a European section of round-robin matches to determine the seedings, involving Italy, Romania and Wales, who had emerged from an earlier European round. The Welsh, having failed to make the quarter-finals in 1991, were the first of the original International Rugby Board countries to have to take this route.

The Asian Rugby Football tournament was used as the Asian zone qualifying competition to determine the 16th and final place

for the World Cup. In Kuala Lumpur, Japan emerged as the winners against Korea. They joined Wales in Pool C.

For the first time, the World Cup would be held in just one country. The tournament opened at Newlands, Cape Town, on May 25. It was only five years since white South Africa had condemned the National Party's Minister for Foreign Affairs, Pik Botha, for his "irresponsibility" when he admitted openly that one day his country would have a black President. Now 50,000 people – mostly white and Afrikaner – gave a thunderous reception to their first black leader.

After the parade of the 16 participating nations in a colourful and moving opening ceremony – part of the evidence South Africa wished to present in its bid for the 2004 Olympic Games – the new national anthem, *Nkosi Sikelele' I Africa*, was sung as if everyone in the Republic meant it for the first time. The old theme *Die Stem* was also voiced, but not with the same gusto as of yore. "One team, one nation" became the slogan for the period.

The first match was between the host nation and the winners of the previous tournament, Australia, in Pool A. This was a team which had consistently proven its pedigree through the vast experience of its talented component parts. Australia were a force to be reckoned with and were, indeed, seen as favourites not only to win this opening fixture but the competition for the second successive occasion. Michael Lynagh was the world's leading points-scorer, David Campese the leading try-scorer. Bob Dwyer, who had masterminded the success in 1991, remained in charge and, if anything, had enhanced his reputation as the leading light among international coaches. He was an astute and modern thinker. Man for man, there was no better team in the tournament than Australia.

As an extra incentive, the winners of the first match would have much the best route to the Final, with the losers probably having to face the twin leviathans of England and New Zealand.

It was suggested, too, that although the opening ceremony might inspire the Springboks, the celebrations could also be so emotional as to weigh down the home team with the burden of expectation. The "wave of goodwill" was something that the South African manager Morne du Plessis, one of the greatest Springbok captains, had not felt in his country in 25 years of rugby experience. How would his team respond?

In the event, this euphoria worked to South Africa's advantage, whereas Australia seemed overawed by it, and misjudged the mood and tempo of the game. The Wallabies, 13-9 ahead at one stage, looked patiently to be building a platform. Their pack supplied a wealth of possession, particularly from the lineout, where they won 22 to South Africa's five. But the stalwarts of so many tough campaigns were fragile to the point of brittleness. Lynagh erred, Campese hesitated, George Gregan at scrum half was harried out of his stride.

South Africa closed down their opponents in midfield and hunted voraciously for the loose ball. Joel Stransky played an influential role at outside half, as he was to do throughout the tournament, and scored 22 points in the 27-18 victory. The other score came when Pieter Hendriks – replacing the injured Chester Williams on the wing – stepped out of Campese's less than firm tackle.

Not an auspicious start for the favourites, but there could not have been a more thrilling start to the tournament. South Africa, even at this stage, had the Final in their sights.

Set against this formidable contest between two giants was the following day's fixture between the Ivory Coast and Scotland. In this first game of Pool D, the African team were overwhelmed 89-0. Gavin Hastings, Scotland's steely captain, scored 44 points.

Whenever there is a big score, it is followed by a rustling of the pages as the statisticians rush to find what sort of record has been achieved. An international record? A World Cup record, perhaps? In the event, neither of these totals, team or individual, changed anything. The anorak-wearing lovers of sporting minutiae would have picked up that some months earlier, in a World Cup qualifier, Hong Kong had already set what appeared to be an insurmountable figure in beating Singapore by 164-13 and Ashley Billington of that parish

"Our concentration went. We had trained so well, but when we got out on the pitch we forgot all the training. Why we reacted the way we did, we'll never know for sure. By the finish we did well to keep the score as close as we did."

AUSTRALIA COACH BOB DWYER
after the opening match against South Africa

"I think we were a bit more hungry than them. Some of their players faltered when we put pressure on them. We've improved since 1992 and we can improve some more."

SPRINGBOKS CAPTAIN FRANÇOIS PIENAAR
after beating Australia

Kenny Logan thunders through a challenge on the way to Scotland's record victory over the Ivory Coast. Right: Neil Jenkins passes to Anthony Clement as Wales run up a record score against Japan

had scored 50 points, which included 10 tries. They could not beat either of those figures. But digging further into the record books, it was determined that Scotland had established a record for the finals of the World Cup. Hastings' four tries equalled the number scored by an individual in the finals.

But then, facing the emerging rugby nations in the World Cup is an opportunity to set new records. So that Wales, in their match against Japan in Pool C in Bloemfontein, also created a new high for themselves. This was of some considerable comfort for the Welshmen. They had lost their previous five internationals and experienced a whitewash in the Five Nations Championship. In the wake of these failures, the Australian Alex Evans was appointed as coach just weeks before the World Cup began. Prior to this, Wales had only scored three tries in their last nine games. But the 57 points they accumulated were the highest number in the finals for Wales and the seven tries the most scored for them in the finals.

> "Richard Wallace's forlorn example as Jonah Lomu scored the All Blacks' first try was simply a warning to cause others sleepless nights. Would-be tacklers were cast aside as jetsam and flotsam in his wake."

All these talking points, interesting enough in their fashion, were no more than scribblings in the margin. Canada had beaten Romania 34-3 in Pool A in Port Elizabeth and it was no surprise that, after Western Samoa's reputation-making introduction to the World Cup in 1991, they should defeat Italy handsomely 42-18 in Pool B in East London. To'o Vaega was particularly inventive in midfield for the Pacific islanders while Marcello Cuttitta, the marvellous Italian wing, enjoyed the personal distinction of having scored in every World Cup.

The early exchanges of the 1995 Rugby World Cup had

had their moments but there was nothing much to write home about just yet. This was soon to change…

High on the veldt at 5,750 feet above sea level in Ellis Park, Johannesburg, the first signs of a rugby tornado were brewing. Ireland in Pool C were the first to feel its elemental stirrings. On May 27, on the site of what had once been a mine dump and brickworks, Jonah Lomu swept into international view. Weighing in at 18st and 6ft 3ins, the new All Black presented a sight unseen on a rugby field before – not on the left wing, at any rate.

If Richard Wallace of Ireland was the first to feel exposed and slightly embarrassed in his clumsy attempts to manage this force of nature, he would not be the only one to be made to feel inelegant. His forlorn example as Lomu scored the All Blacks' first try was simply a warning to cause others sleepless nights. Would-be tacklers were cast aside as jetsam and flotsam in his wake. Short of tranquillising him, there appeared to be no answer. His opponents might try to hinder him and obstruct his path, but they would be like hapless victims in a Hollywood movie, casting so much plaster-board furniture in the way of a technologically advanced but villainous Robocop. Players would be hurled aside muttering hopeless threats of vengeance. "I will do such things" – you could sense the frustration – "What they are yet I know not, but they shall be the terrors of the Earth."

Lomu set the rugby world a hitherto unknown dilemma. In the second half against Ireland he ran 80 metres, swatting four players out of his path, to pave the way for Josh

'AS A NATION WE NEED VICTORY'

Chester Williams, the black Springbok who had to pull out due to injury, on rugby's struggle for equality

'Everyone knows it's not going to happen overnight. We, the coloureds and blacks, have to prove our worth, not just in soccer and athletics but in rugby, to prove that we're good enough. The development is strongest in the Cape, where coloureds have always played rugby, but it is further behind among the blacks. Everybody has been supporting me – blacks, whites, coloureds. I could have stayed in the squad and chanced it (the hamstring injury), but more than anything I want South Africa to win the World Cup, and that's why I had to withdraw. The whole country is behind the team, because as a nation we need victory.'

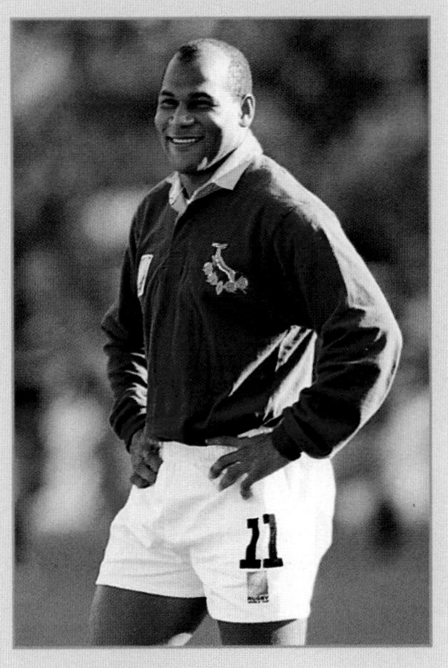

"You can compare us to kamikaze pilots. The players will give their all."

VLADIMIR VLAD
team liaison officer for Romania, before playing South Africa

Eric Elwood of Ireland discovers how hard it is to flag down the Lomu Express

"We would get a shotgun for him."

IRELAND CAPTAIN TERRY KINGSTON
when asked what Ireland would do if they had to face Jonah Lomu again

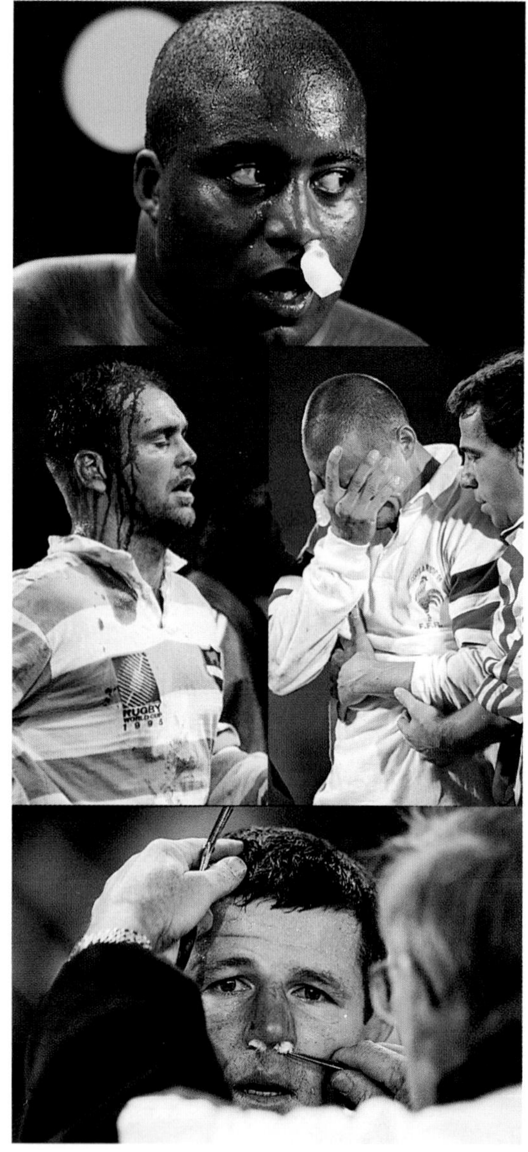

Kronfeld to score. Still only 20 and playing in his third game for New Zealand, Lomu scored two tries and made another. The force, to mix the Hollywood allusion, was undoubtedly with him.

Yet, for all this, Ireland battled bravely and unsettled the All Blacks to begin with. In fact, even though they lost 43-19, Ireland probably put up the best performance against New Zealand by anyone apart from South Africa.

Ouch! England's Steve Ojomoh, Christian Viel of Argentina, France's Guy Accoceberry, who broke his arm, and All Black Sean Fitzpatrick. Right: Three Romanians give Canada's Winston Stanley a nice welcome

The Irish even went into an early lead after Gary Halpin scored a try. Later Denis McBride also crossed after Simon Geoghegan's brilliant break. Geoghegan was a fine player and a match-winner but he was allowed to languish too long as a spectator and not given opportunities enough to participate. In full stride, strong and determined, he was difficult to stop. He was the kind of player to get the crowd on its feet. Ireland did not use his talents enough.

New Zealand had no such qualms. They unleashed Lomu on an unsuspecting and astonished rugby world. He was a sensation because he was allowed to be.

England, if the time came, would have every chance to prepare to be the immovable object to meet this irresistible force. But, on the back of a Grand Slam in the Five Nations Championship, England – under the same captain, Will Carling, but with a new manager in Jack Rowell – had not given many grounds for confidence in the first match. They were expected to dent the reputations and expectations of the southern hemisphere nations. But against Argentina, in King's Park, Durban, England had to rely on the right foot of Rob Andrew to kick all the points in a 24-18 victory. Argentina scored the game's two tries, courtesy of Patricio Noriega and Lisandro Arbizu.

France in the meantime were far from pleased with their

opening win against Tonga, by 38-10, in Pool D. Their coach Pierre Berbizier complained that "there were too many vain egotists among the players who are too much in love with themselves and the TV cameras". This was a new angle on a coach's review of a team's performance.

Despite a 54-18 victory against the Ivory Coast, France were not to distinguish themselves in their early matches. They did enough to keep ahead of the pack. But, just as they had done in the first World Cup, they would ensure that their natural flamboyance would emerge to embellish the tournament. France would ultimately give very good reason why the television cameras should be in love with them; why their own vanity would insist they would not let themselves down. But that was to come…

On the day of the last two fixtures in Pool D, the 1995

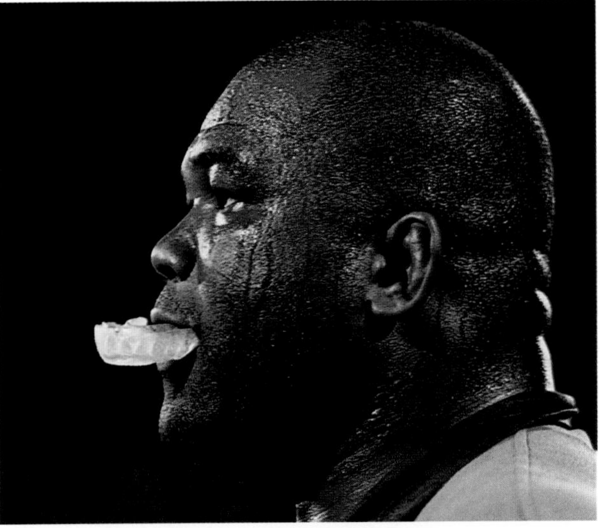

"Time I got these dentures fixed…" Toussaint Djehi of the Ivory Coast chews a mean mouthguard. Left: A posse of Ivory Coasters try to fell France's man mountain Abdelatif Benazzi

"There are too many vain egotists in the French side who fancy themselves. They are too interested in the TV cameras and the photographers. They just want to look good, as if they are thinking, 'Take my photo, bring the camera to me'. They love themselves a bit too much....In the end we just showed a whole lack of respect for the event itself."

FRENCH COACH PIERRE BERBIZIER after France beat Tonga 38-10 but played a disappointing game

"I would not have thought this was possible. If someone before the match said we would break 100 points, I would have laughed."

NEW ZEALAND COACH LAURIE MAINS on his team's 145-17 win over Japan

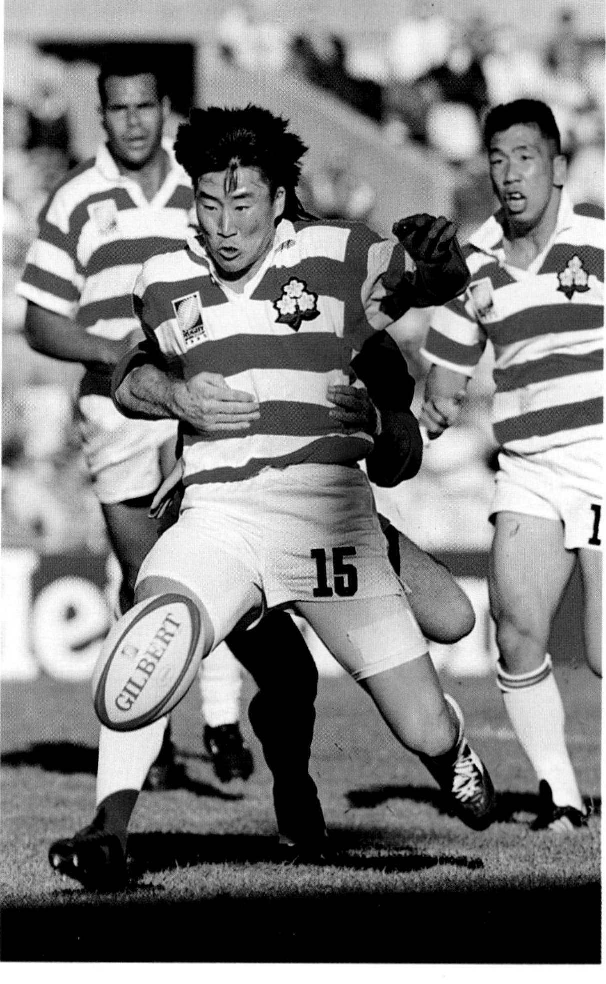

David Campese of Australia takes flight against Canada while Tsutomu Matsuda of Japan kicks ahead against Ireland

World Cup would encompass great glory as well as profound tragedy. These elements are ever present in rugby. Amid the drama of sport we can be uplifted one moment with the joy of triumph, only to give way the next to the tears of the vanquished. For all the memories sport creates – the sweetness of laughter as much as the pangs of despair – sport is ultimately ephemeral.

"Sadly, we are forced most compellingly to consider the frivolity at the heart of sport when tragedy strikes. Tragedy struck Max Brito, the Ivory Coast winger, in the sixth minute of the game against Tonga, when a tackle left him paralysed."

Sadly, we are forced most compellingly to consider the frivolity at the heart of sport when tragedy strikes. Tragedy struck Max Brito, the Ivory Coast winger, in the sixth minute of the game against Tonga, when a tackle left him paralysed. For all the urgency with which the tournament was being pursued, this heart-rending incident obliged everyone to pause for a time: to ponder the little acts of heroism, and to wonder. To admire enterprising, sometime inexplicable, talent and be charmed, but never forget the non-negotiable moment of danger.

This was the occasion, too, to recognise the imbalances that exist between teams, in fitness, in size and in strength. Standards vary considerably so that rugby, with its new expansionist ambitions, finds gulfs of difference between nations. We were further reminded of this in the Ireland-Japan game. Given the chance, Japan, with their speed and ingenuity, could run Ireland – or anyone else, for that matter – ragged. But Ireland showed them, by forcing their scrum to collapse twice and thereby gaining two penalty tries, that you cannot get very far in rugby without some big men. They had imported some players from the South Sea islands but it was not enough. Japan were scintillating; Ireland were dogged. Ireland won 50-28.

New Zealand, as ever, were happy to expose the underdogs to a more ruthless examination. In doing so, they rewrote the record books for the Rugby World Cup finals. They demolished Japan by scoring 145 points, scoring 21 tries. Only six of these All Blacks had played against Ireland, making it New Zealand's second-string team. Simon Culhane recorded the most points (45) for an individual player as well as kicking the most conversions (20). In addition he broke the record set by his colleague Andrew Mehrtens for a player on his international debut. Marc Ellis recorded the most tries in one game (six), so that the only record left for Gavin Hastings to share with Thierry Lacroix was for the most penalty goals (eight).

The biggest cheers, naturally, were for the two tries Hiroyuki Kajihara scored for Japan.

Five days earlier, the All

"Ieuan Evans has proved himself to be one of the world's great wings. Let Lomu worry about him."

WALES MANAGER GEOFF EVANS

Above: "C'mon, Jonah boy, you don't scare me! Uh oh, he heard me..." Ieuan Evans lays down the Welsh challenge. Left: It's that Lomu Express again, leaving Wales beached

Blacks had given Wales the treatment. Wales, who had to look back 42 years to the last time they had defeated New Zealand, had attempted to talk a good game, but they were no match for Sean Fitzpatrick's men. Mehrtens was in fine form with his kicking, Walter Little and Frank Bunce were superb creators in midfield, but the man who most caught the eye was Josh Kronfeld, the flanker. With his skull-cap, you could hardly miss him, but his speed and anticipation were something to behold. He scored the third try to give his team a 34-9 victory. Neil Jenkins kicked two penalties and a drop goal.

With Japan knocked out, the dogfight – and it turned out to be little more than that – for second position to join the All Blacks in the quarter-finals was between Ireland and Wales. It was an eminently forgettable contest. Ireland scored two

Emile Ntamack and Laurent Cabannes celebrate France's win over Scotland, while Gavin Hastings and Philippe Saint-André practise their synchronised diving. Thierry Lacroix kicked 17 points in France's 22-19 victory

"I cannot believe that we have lost the game. I am shell-shocked."

GAVIN HASTINGS
after Scotland lost to France 19-22, having been 13-3 up at half-time

"Our ball retention was deplorable at times. There was sheer dislocation throughout. If Argentina had had a Rob Andrew, that would have been it. If we do not improve we will go home faster than we came out."

ENGLAND MANAGER JACK ROWELL

"Go, Victor!" England scrum half Dewi Morris gives Ubogu a rocket against Western Samoa

tries, by Nick Popplewell and Denis McBride, early in the match, then held on to win by the skin of their teeth, 24-23. Eddie Halvey, who had replaced McBride, scored the third. Jonathan Humphries and Hemi Taylor scored tries for Wales but for the second time in a row, their team failed to make the cut for the quarter-finals.

This match was as poor an advertisement for European rugby as the France-Scotland was good. On a warm evening at Loftus Versfeld, France and Scotland met to resume where they left off at Christchurch in 1987. If that game was a wonderful contest, this one was to prove even better.

France's performance cast our minds back to that year in another way, too. They managed to steal the spoils from under Scottish noses in extra time, as they had done against Australia in the great semi-final in the first World Cup. If Serge Blanco was Australia's nemesis in 1987, here it was Emile Ntamack who broke Scottish hearts.

The big prize for the winner of this match was to finish top of Pool D – and so avoid meeting New Zealand in the quarter-final. Scotland got their noses in front, with a 13-3 lead at half-time. With 16 minutes to go they were still seven points ahead. With four minutes remaining they were four ahead. For 84 minutes, Scotland had held sway – but then a grand sweep of a movement, to left and right and left again, ended with Ntamack scoring in the corner. Thierry Lacroix's conversion from near the touchline to add to his quarter-final penalties secured a 22-19 victory and a quarter-final date with Ireland.

In Pool B, England's play had lacked conviction against Argentina, whose renowned immovability in the scrum had

Rees's pieces

BY

GARETH REES

The only man to play in all four Rugby World Cups

Canada had to go into the 'pool of death' against Australia and South Africa in the 1995 World Cup. As captain, I was furious because, having been quarter-finalists in 1991, we felt that finally we were in the top eight in the world and so we were hoping to get a seeding. But because South Africa hadn't been in the previous World Cups, they weren't seeeded. So we found ourselves in a group with the 1991 World Champions and the team who became the 1995 World Champions.

We had been beaten heavily in New Zealand only a month before the tournament, which made us wonder, what are we here for? There was still a very condescending attitude, from the British in particular – "You actually play rugby in Canada?" But it's always been part of Canadian rugby culture to try and prove those people wrong, and I think that was the most rewarding campaign of my rugby career.

On arrival in South Africa we were given six bodyguards – three black, three white (including Pierre Coetzer, the boxer!). There was a black minstrel band waiting to greet us, and as I got to the door of the plane, one of the security men looked at this band and said, "Wait a minute!" – and he got out his gun and cocked it. It was a severe case of over-reaction, but it did show that the problems weren't all sorted out.

We stayed in Port Elizabeth, and every day the local women who worked in the hotel would come out and sing us on to the bus in their traditional gear. So many teams had gone into the townships for a brief training session with the kids that it had almost begun to seem like a photocall. The first time we went there, we all piled back on to our bus to go back to our comfortable air-conditioned hotel, and one of the guys summed up everybody's feelings when he said: "That's not good enough." So we set up a trust with the local township, and I got to meet some of the ANC politicians there. That's the sort of experience only rugby can bring you.

"I thought the referee was calling me over as captain. When he told me I was sent off, I was absolutely shocked."

We started the tournament well, by beating Romania 34-3. Then we went out against Australia and gave up 17 points in the first quarter of an hour. We had a big hole in our side in the second row department in terms of height, and there was no lifting then. We realised that the set-piece game wasn't going to work for us, so we started to keep the ball on the field and let our athleticism take over. We had talented athletes who had played a high level of American football, basketball, ice hockey and handball, and I think we won the last 60 minutes of that game. We took the World Champions to the limit, and it finished 27-11.

The game against South Africa was one of those evenings that you'll tell your grandchildren about. We were very confident in a quiet kind of a way. We warmed up, then went out and sang our anthem and then we came into a circle to do our traditional cheer and suddenly the lights went out. We assumed it was some kind of protest. I said to the guys, "Even their own people don't want them to play. We'll stay here and sit this out together until the lights go on" – and as I said that, you could hear the footsteps crunching behind us as the South African team sprinted off the field. A helicopter rose over the field with a spotlight shining down, and our security guards came racing out to us and said, "What the hell are you doing? Get inside, it could be a bomb threat!" So our guys said: "Bugger you, Rees, forget all about sticking together through thick and thin, we're getting inside" – which is what we all did.

Then we had one of the weirdest 40-minute periods I can ever remember, sitting there waiting for the lights to come on. When the match finally started, we played some great rugby, but there was some niggle throughout the game. Pieter Hendriks twice tackled our young winger, Winston Stanley, late, into the advertising boards – or Stanley felt it was late. There were boots and punches going in on both sides. The final straw was when our full back Scott Stewart went up for a high ball and was pulled down by his collar and slammed on his head. As captain I probably should have asked that he went off, but the game continued with about 20 minutes to go. In hindsight, after that incident there was a sentiment from our team that referee McHugh, who had failed yet again to warn the offending Springbok, was not going to protect our players and we would have to look after ourselves.

We tapped a penalty and ran it out of our own end. Winston Stanley was knocked into touch again, Scott Stewart took exception, and all hell broke loose. It has become famous, or infamous, now. I'm handbags at dawn at the best of times, but I was just jogging into the mêlée when I saw Scott Stewart being held by two South Africans and punched by a third. So I reacted to that and that's what I eventually got thrown out for. Referee McHugh called me over, and I thought he was calling me over as captain. When he told me that I was sent off, I was absolutely shocked. He also sent off Rod Snow and James Dalton; I couldn't believe that two of our players had gone and only one of theirs. I think my mum sums it up best when she says it was character-building!

Gareth Rees makes the long walk after his dismissal in Canada's battle against South Africa

There were guys on our side who were at fault, but he completely missed the real culprits. I didn't make any excuses at the time and this is probably the first time I've commented about the referee since that tournament. Naturally it's a sad day to be sent off while playing for your country, so in a way I was pleased that I was sent off along with Rod Snow, because there is no prouder Canadian. I remember standing with him in the tunnel, watching the last 15 minutes unfold, when some bureaucrat came and told us that we were't allowed to be there. I refused to move because we had made a banner thanking the people of Port Elizabeth for being so supportive, which we intended to show at the end during a lap of honour at Boet Erasmus, our host for all three matches.

For once I was glad to be captain, and have a chance to speak at the post-match reception, responding to François Pienaar. I said I knew there were those who said I had disgraced my country, but Canadians aren't dirty players. By the same token, we don't back down and accept things against our team-mates. I had asked my players to stick up for each other all tournament. We're not proud that the incident happened, but we're proud of each other and of playing for Canada. It was one of those times when the right words came out.

A few of us stayed on and drove down the garden route to Cape Town. I walked into Joel Stransky's bar, The Green Man – and when I was spotted, everyone started chanting "Off! Off! Off!" I'm disappointed that we are remembered for that brawl, when we played some good rugby. The home team beat us 20-0 but had we decided to kick some of our penalties instead of running the ball, I dare say we would have lost 20-12 against the eventual champions.

Now that professional rugby has arrived, the World Cup will be the test of whether a team like ours, in which half the players are still amateurs, can manage to keep up. They keep telling me that I will be the only person to have played in all four World Cups, but I'm not trying to break a record. It's a little bit sad that I haven't been replaced at 31, but I'm also very proud. I got a chance really young and I took it. As ever, we're going into it to upset people and to try and gain a little bit more respect for rugby in our country.

"We're not a particularly good side but in the physical confrontation we're just hoping to set up a battle, and to win it. Nothing illegal. Just good old confrontational rugby in which the game can be won or lost."
CANADA CAPTAIN GARETH REES
before playing South Africa

On the run, from left: Ilie Tabua of Australia in the 42-3 win against Romania, Ezequiel Jurado of Argentina, in the 25-31 defeat by Italy, and Akuila Mafi of Tonga, in their 29-11 win over Ivory Coast. Opposite: Gareth Rees and Rod Snow of Canada watch from the sidelines after being sent off, and Scottish fans celebrate their team's 41-5 victory against Tonga

given them a few problems. Nor were the Englishmen any better against Italy, where the match only occasionally achieved any structure and the 27-20 scoresheet was dominated by Andrew's five penalties. England were too wary, strangely lacking in confidence for a team which had so dominated the European stage; they needed to cut loose.

Collectively, their opponents had scored more tries than them (four tries to two). England were in danger of entering the knockout stage still unclear as to the best way to play.

Meanwhile, Argentina and Western Samoa produced the best match of the Pool with a score of 32-26 to the Samoans. England might have learnt a lesson from this, because when they came to play Western Samoa in the fixture between the two unbeaten teams, they gave their best performance to date, scoring four tries in a 44-22 victory.

England, by coming top of their Pool, had ensured that the quarter-finals would witness a reprise of the 1991 Final, with another showdown against Australia.

The Aussies had not had a comfortable time themselves. Canada had dispatched Romania 34-3 in Pool A. Now they gave Australia a stirring contest. One unflinching tackle by Winston Stanley on Campese, when the maestro on the wing was in his stride, epitomised their wholehearted spirit. The final score was 27-11 to the Wallabies.

This fighting spirit was not always going to keep Canada in good opinion. Four days later, in the Boet Erasmus Stadium in Port Elizabeth, they encountered unbeaten South Africa, who had overcome a much-improved Romania (21-8). This was the final match of Pool A, and the signs were not encouraging from the start. The game was delayed for 45 minutes because of power failure. There was failure elsewhere, too. Failure of discipline.

This proved to be the most shameful episode of the tournament. Three players – the Canadians Gareth Rees and Rod Snow, and Springbok hooker James Dalton – were sent off the field. Two others who had been prominent in the brawl – Pieter Hendriks of South Africa and Scott Stewart of Canada – were later cited and banned.

South Africa won 20-0, giving themselves the prospect of a quarter-final with Western Samoa. It now emerged that Chester Williams had recovered from the hamstring injury which caused his withdrawal from the World Cup before the start of the tournament. Williams's replacement was Hendriks. Now the banning of Hendriks created a

debatable loop-hole through which Williams might be able to return to the Springbok squad.

But should a player suspended because of ill-discipline be replaced? Surely the team should forfeit a player, otherwise the misdeed goes unpunished. Now it looked as if the Springboks would actually benefit from Hendriks' suspension. The regulations did allow a replacement to be brought in – but this was on safety grounds, to prevent a physical imbalance in a squad, such as when a player from the front row is suspended.

But no one, in the circumstances which prevailed in South Africa in 1995, was going to be so mean of spirit as to dissect the detail of this case. There was an element of sentiment attached to Williams, and everyone had been saddened by his withdrawal.

Not only was Chester Williams a better player than Hendriks, but he had come to be the living embodiment of what most people wished Mandela's South Africa to be: free of racial inequalities. No longer cosmetic, no longer a token, Chester Williams was a black man who had earned his rightful place in the Springbok squad. The pieces were fitting into place.

POOL A FINAL TABLE

	P	W	D	L	F	A	Pts
South Africa	3	3	0	0	68	26	9
Australia	3	2	0	1	87	41	7
Canada	3	1	0	2	45	50	5
Romania	3	0	0	3	14	97	3

POOL B FINAL TABLE

	P	W	D	L	F	A	Pts
England	3	3	0	0	95	60	9
W Samoa	3	2	0	1	96	88	7
Italy	3	1	0	2	69	94	5
Argentina	3	0	0	3	69	87	3

POOL C FINAL TABLE

	P	W	D	L	F	A	Pts
New Zealand	3	3	0	0	222	45	9
Ireland	3	2	0	1	93	94	7
Wales	3	1	0	2	89	68	5
Japan	3	0	0	3	55	252	3

POOL D FINAL TABLE

	P	W	D	L	F	A	Pts
France	3	3	0	0	114	47	9
Scotland	3	2	0	1	149	27	7
Tonga	3	1	0	2	44	90	5
Ivory Coast	3	0	0	3	29	172	3

"The press cuttings come trickling out of the faxes from London. The press reaction is critical but one paper annoys me more than intensely by calling us 'gutless'. It really is a contemptible over-reaction considering we have qualified for the quarter-finals. I really would like that sports editor to come along and call me gutless to my face."

ENGLAND HOOKER BRIAN MOORE

Canada scrum half John Graf fires a pass towards Gareth Rees during their 27-11 defeat by Australia while, below, Australia and Romania battle for lineout possession in the scenic surrounds of the Coetzenburg Stadium, Stellenbosch

· POOL A RESULTS ·

SOUTH AFRICA 27 AUSTRALIA 18
25 May • Cape Town
SOUTH AFRICA: Joubert; Small, Mulder, H Le Roux, Hendriks; Stransky, Van der Westhuizen; Du Randt, Dalton, Swart (Pagel 65), Andrews, Strydom, *Pienaar, Straeuli, Kruger.
SCORERS: *Tries:* Hendriks, Stransky. *Con:* Stransky. *Pens:* Stransky (4). *DG:* Stransky.
AUSTRALIA: Pini; Campese, Herbert, Little, Smith; *Lynagh, Gregan; Crowley, Kearns, McKenzie, McCall, Eales, Ofahengaue, Gavin, Wilson.
SCORERS: *Tries:* Lynagh, Kearns. *Con:* Lynagh. *Pens:* Lynagh (2)
Referee: Derek Bevan (Wales)

CANADA 34 ROMANIA 3
26 May • Port Elizabeth
CANADA: D Stewart; Stanley, C Stewart, Gray, Lougheed; *Rees, Graf: Evans, Cardinal, Snow, Ennis, James, Charron, McKenzie, Gordon.
SCORERS: *Tries:* Snow, Charron, McKenzie. *Cons:* Rees (2). *Pens:* Rees (4). *DG:* Rees.
ROMANIA: Solomie; Colceriu, Racean, Gontineac, Rotaru; Nichitean (Ivanciuc 66), Neaga (Flutur 53); Leonte, Negreci, Vlad, *Ciorascu, Cojocariu, Oroian, Slusariuc, Gealapu.
SCORER: *Pen:* Nichitean.
Referee: C J Hawke (New Zealand)

SOUTH AFRICA 21 ROMANIA 8
30 May • Cape Town
SOUTH AFRICA: Johnson; Small, Scholtz, Venter, Hendriks; H P Le Roux, J P Roux; Pagel, Rossouw, Hurter, Wiese, Otto, Kruger, *Richter, Brink.
SCORERS: *Tries:* Richter (2). *Con:* Johnson. *Pens:* Johnson (3).
ROMANIA: Brici; Colceriu, Racean, Gontineac, Solomie; Ivanciuc, Flutur; Leonte, Negreci (Tufa 62), Vlad, Ciorascu, Cojocariu, Guranescu, *Brinza, Gealapu.
SCORERS: *Try:* Guranescu. *Pen:* Ivanciuc.
Referee: K W McCartney (Scotland)

AUSTRALIA 27 CANADA 11
31 May • Port Elizabeth
AUSTRALIA: Burke; Campese, Little, Horan, Roff; *Lynagh, Slattery (Gregan 80); Daly, Kearns (Foley 70), Hartill (McKenzie 56), Waugh, Eales, Ofahengaue, Gavin, Tabua.
SCORERS: *Tries:* Tabua, Roff, Lynagh. *Cons:* Lynagh (3). *Pens:* Lynagh (2)
CANADA: D Stewart; Stanley, C Stewart, Gray, Lougheed; *Rees, Graf: Evans, Svoboda, Snow, James, Rowlands (Ennis 70), Hutchinson, Charron, MacKinnon.
SCORERS: *Try:* Charron. *Pens:* Rees (2).
Referee: P Robin (France)

AUSTRALIA 42 ROMANIA 3
3 June • Stellenbosch
AUSTRALIA: Burke; Smith, Herbert, Horan, Roff; Bowen, Gregan (Slattery 71); Daly, Foley, McKenzie, *McCall, Eales, Tabua, Gavin, Wilson.
SCORERS: *Tries:* Roff (2), Foley, Burke, Smith, Wilson. *Cons:* Burke (2), Eales (4).
ROMANIA: Brici; Colceriu, Racean, Gontineac (Lungu 56), Solomie; Ivanciuc, Flutur; Leonte, Negreci (Tufa 73), Vlad, Ciorascu, Cojocariu, Guranescu, *Brinza, Gealapu.
SCORER: *DG:* Ivanciuc.
Referee: N Saito (Japan)

SOUTH AFRICA 20 CANADA 0
3 June • Port Elizabeth
SOUTH AFRICA: Joubert; Johnson (Van der Westhuizen 17), Scholtz, Venter, Hendriks; Stransky (H Le Roux 59), J Roux, Pagel, Dalton, Hurter, Wiese, Strydom (Otto 73), *Pienaar, Richter, Brink.
Sent off: Dalton.
SCORERS: *Tries:* Richter (2). *Cons:* Stransky (2). *Pens:* Stransky (2).
CANADA: D Stewart; Stanley, C Stewart, Gray, Lougheed; *Rees, Graf: Evans, Cardinal, Snow, Charron, Ennis (Hutchinson 65), Gordon, McKenzie (Michaluk 80), MacKinnon.
Sent off: Rees, Snow.
Referee: David McHugh (Ireland)

· POOL B RESULTS ·

WESTERN SAMOA 42 ITALY 18
27 May • East London
WESTERN SAMOA: Umaga; Lima, Vaega, Fa'amasino, Harder; Kellett, Nu'uli'itia; Mika, Leiasamaivao, *Fatialofa, Falaniko (Leavasa 57), Williams, Vaifale, Tatupu, Paramore.
SCORERS: *Tries:* Lima (2), Harder (2), Tatupu, Kellett. *Cons:* Kellett (3). *Pens:* Kellett (2).
ITALY: Vaccari; Ravazzolo, Francescato, Bonomi, Marcello Cuttitta; Dominguez, Troncon; *Massimo Cuttitta, Orlandi, Properzi Curti, Pedroni, Favaro, Arancio, Checchinato, Gardner.
SCORERS: *Tries:* Marcello Cuttitta, Vaccari. *Con:* Dominguez. *Pen:* Dominguez. *DG:* Dominguez.
Referee: J Dume (France)

ENGLAND 24 ARGENTINA 18
27 May • Durban
ENGLAND: Catt; T Underwood, *Carling (De Glanville 79), Guscott, R Underwood; Andrew, Morris; Leonard, Moore, Ubogu, Johnson, Bayfield, Rodber, Ojomoh, Clarke.
SCORERS: *Pens:* Andrew (6). *DG:* Andrew (2).
ARGENTINA: Jurado; Teran, Cuesta Silva, *Salvat, Albanese; Arbizu, Crexell; Corral, Mendez, Noriega, Llanes, Sporleder, Martin, Sanatamarina, Viel (Irazoqui 70).
SCORERS: *Tries:* Noriega, Arbizu. *Con:* Arbizu. *Pens:* Arbizu (2).
Referee: Jim Fleming (Scotland)

WESTERN SAMOA 32 ARGENTINA 26
30 May • East London
WESTERN SAMOA: Umaga; Lima, Vaega, Fa'amasino, Harder (Leaupepe 51); Kellett (Sini 80), Nu'ali'itia; Mika, Leiasamaivao, Latu (Fatialofa 45), Leavasa, Falaniko, Tatupu, *Lam, Paramore.
SCORERS: *Tries:* Harder, Leaupepe, Lam. *Con:* Kellett. *Pens:* Kellett (5).
ARGENTINA: Jurado; Cuesta Silva, Arbizu, *Salvat, Teran; Cilley, Crexell; Corral, Mendez, Noriega, Llanes, Sporleder, Martin, Sanatamarina, Viel (Irazoqui 70).
SCORERS: *Tries:* PT, Crexell. *Cons:* Cilley (2). *Pens:* Cilley (4).
Referee: D Bishop (New Zealand)

ENGLAND 27 ITALY 20
31 May • Durban
ENGLAND: Catt; T Underwood, De Glanville, Guscott, R Underwood; *Andrew, Bracken; Rowntree, Moore, Leonard, Johnson, Bayfield, Rodber, Clarke, Back.
SCORERS: *Tries:* R Underwood, T Underwood. *Con:* Andrew. *Pens:* Andrew (5).
ITALY: Troiani; Vaccari, Bordon, Francescato, Gerosa; Dominguez, Troncon; *Massimo Cuttitta, Orlandi, Properzi Curti, Pedroni, Giacheri, Arancio, Gardner, Sgorlon.
SCORERS: *Tries:* Vaccari, Massimo Cuttitta. *Cons:* Dominguez (2). *Pens:* Dominguez (2).
Referee: Stephen Hilditch (Ireland)

ITALY 31 ARGENTINA 25
4 June • East London
ITALY: Troiani; Vaccari, Francescato, Bordon, Gerosa; Dominguez, Troncon; *Massimo Cuttitta, Orlandi, Properzi Curti, Pedroni, Giacheri, Arancio, Gardner, Sgorlon.
SCORERS: *Tries:* Vaccari, Gerosa, Dominguez. *Cons:* Dominguez (2). *Pens:* Dominguez (4).
ARGENTINA: Jurado: Cuesta Silva, Arbizu, *Salvat, Teran; Cilley, Crexell; Corral, Mendez, Noriega, Llanes, Sporleder, Martin, Santamarina, Viel.
SCORERS: *Tries:* Martin, Corral, Cilley, PT. *Con:* Cilley. *Pen:* Cilley.
Referee: C Thomas (Wales)

ENGLAND 44 WESTERN SAMOA 22
4 June • Durban
ENGLAND: Callard; Hunter, *Carling (Hopley 70), De Glanville, R Underwood; Catt, Morris; Rowntree (Mallett 25), Dawe, Ubogu, Johnson, West, Ojomoh, Richards (Moore 73), Back (Rodber 33).
SCORERS: *Tries:* Back, R Underwood (2), PT. *Cons:* Callard (3). *Pens:* Callard (5). *DG:* Catt.
WESTERN SAMOA: Umaga; Lima, Vaega, Fa'amasino, Leaupepe; Puleitu (Sini 40), Nu'ali'itia; Mika, Leiasamaivao, Latu (Fatialofa 74), Williams, Falaniko, Leavasa (Tatupu 29, Lemamea 67), *Lam, Iupeli.
SCORERS: *Tries:* Sini (2), Umaga. *Cons:* Fa'amasino (2). *Pen:* Fa'amasino.
Referee: P Robin (France)

Rob Andrew was England's top scorer in the group games, with all 24 points against Argentina – where his two drop goals equalled the World Cup record – and 17 points out of 27 against Italy. He did not play against Western Samoa

· POOL C RESULTS ·

WALES 57 JAPAN 10
27 May • Bloemfontein
WALES: Clement; I Evans, *Hall, N Jenkins, Thomas; A Davies (D Evans 57), Moore; Griffiths, G Jenkins, J D Davies, Jones (Roy 72), Llewellyn, S Davies, Lewis, Taylor.
SCORERS: *Tries:* I Evans (2), Thomas (3), Taylor, Moore. Cons: N Jenkins (5). *Pens:* N Jenkins (4).
JAPAN: Matsuda; Oto, A Yoshida, Motoki, Masuho; Hirao, Horikoshi; Ota, *Kunda, Takahashi, Sakuraba, Ferguson, Kajihara, Sione Latu, Sinali Latu.
SCORERS: *Tries:* Oto (2).
Referee: E J Sklar (Argentina)

NEW ZEALAND 43 IRELAND 19
27 May • Johannesburg
NEW ZEALAND: Osborne; Wilson (Ellis 32), Bunce, Little, Lomu; Mehrtens, Bachop; Dowd, *Fitzpatrick, Brown, Jones, Larsen, Joseph, Brewer (Schuler 78), Kronfeld.
SCORERS: *Tries:* Lomu (2), Bunce, Kronfeld, Osborne. *Cons:* Mehrtens (3). *Pens:* Mehrtens (4).
IRELAND: Staples (Field 36); Wallace, Mullin, Bell, Geoghegan; Elwood, Bradley; Popplewell, *Kingston, Halpin, Fulcher, Francis, Corkery, Johns, McBride.
SCORERS: *Tries:* Halpin, McBride, Corkery. *Cons:* Elwood (2).
Referee: W J Erickson (Australia)

IRELAND 50 JAPAN 28
31 May • Bloemfontein
IRELAND: O'Shea; R Wallace, Mullin, Field, Geoghegan; Burke, Hogan; *Popplewell, Wood (Kingston 9), P Wallace, Tweed (Foley 73), Francis, Corkery, Johns, Halvey.
Scorers: Tries: PT (2), Corkery, Francis, Geoghegan, Halvey, Hogan. Cons: Burke (6). Pen: Burke.
JAPAN: Matsuda; Oto, A Yoshida, Motoki, Y Yoshida; Hirao, Horikoshi; Ota, *Kunda, Takura, Sakuraba, Ferguson, Kajihara, Sione Latu (Izawa 20), Sinali Latu.
SCORERS: *Tries:* Sinali Latu, Izawa, Hirao, Takuru. *Cons:* Y Yoshida (4).
Referee: S Neethling (South Africa)

NEW ZEALAND 34 WALES 9
31 May • Johannesburg
NEW ZEALAND: Osborne; Lomu (Rush 71), Bunce, Little, Ellis; Mehrtens, Bachop; Dowd, *Fitzpatrick, Brown, Jones, Larsen, Joseph, Brewer, Kronfeld.
SCORERES: *Tries:* Little, Ellis, Kronfeld. *Cons:* Mehrtens (2). *Pens:* Mehrtens (4). *DG:* Mehrtens.
WALES: Clement; I Evans, *Hall, G Thomas, Proctor; N Jenkins, R Jones; R Evans, J Humphreys, J D Davies, D Jones, Prosser, Llewellyn, Taylor, Bennett.
SCORERS: *Pens:* N Jenkins (2). *DG:* N Jenkins.
Referee: Ed Morrison (England)

NEW ZEALAND 145 JAPAN 17
4 June • Bloemfontein
NEW ZEALAND: Osborne; Wilson, Ellis, Ieremia, Rush; Culhane, Strachan; Dowd, Hewitt, Loe, R Brooke, Larsen (Joseph 16), Schuler, Z Brooke, *Henderson.
SCORERS: *Tries:* Ellis (6), Rush (3), Wilson (3), Osborne (2), R Brooke (2), Loe, Ieremia, Culhane, Dowd, Henderson. *Cons:* Culhane (20).
JAPAN: Matsuda; Oto, A Yoshida, Motoki, Y Yoshida; Hirose, Murata; Ota, *Kunda, Takahashi, Sakuraba, Ferguson, Kajihara, Sinali Latu (Akatsuka 56), Izawa.
SCORERS: *Tries:* Kajihara (2). *Cons:* Hirose (2). *Pen:* Hirose.
Referee: G Gadjovich (Canada)

IRELAND 24 WALES 23
4 June • Johannesburg
IRELAND: O'Shea; R Wallace, Mullin, Bell, Geoghegan; Elwood, Hogan; Popplewell, *Kingston, Halpin, Fulcher, Francis, Corkery, Johns, McBride (Halvey, temp).
SCORERS: *Tries:* Popplewell, McBride, Halvey. *Cons:* Elwood (3). *Pen:* Elwood.
WALES: Clement; I Evans, *Hall, N Jenkins, G Thomas; A Davies, R Jones; Griffiths, J Humphreys, J D Davies (R Evans 84), D Jones, Llewellyn, S Davies, E Lewis, Taylor.
SCORERS: *Tries:* Humphreys, Taylor. *Cons:* N Jenkins (2). *Pens:* N Jenkins (2). *DG:* A Davies.
Referee: I Rogers (South Africa)

Welsh captain Mike Hall breaks through the Japanese defence in the 57-10 victory in Bloemfontein while, below, Nick Popplewell hands off Walter Little during Ireland's stunning 43-19 defeat by the All Blacks in Johannesburg

Gavin Hastings kicked 16 points against France. Below: Referee Reordan talks to Thierry Kouame and Djakaria Sanoko of the Ivory Coast in the match against Tonga in which Kouame came on as substitute for the unfortunate Max Brito

· POOL D RESULTS ·

SCOTLAND 89 IVORY COAST 0
26 May • Rustenburg
SCOTLAND: *G Hastings; Joiner, Stanger, Shiel, Logan; Chalmers, Redpath; Burnell, McKenzie, Wright, Weir, Campbell, Walton, Wainwright, Smith.
SCORERS: *Tries:* G Hastings (4), Walton (2), Logan (2), Chalmers, Stanger, Burnell, Wright, Shiel. *Cons:* G Hastings (9). *Pens:* G Hastings (2).
IVORY COAST: Kouassi; Bouazo, Sathicq, Niakou, N'Gbala (Brito 40); *Dali (Camara 28), Dupont; Bley, Angoran, Djehi, Bado (Okou 71), Kone, Pere, Sanoko, Lassissi.
Referee: F Vito (Western Samoa)

FRANCE 38 TONGA 10
26 May • Pretoria
FRANCE: Sardourny; Ntamack, Sella, Lacroix, *Saint-André; Delaigue, Hueber; Armary, Gonzalez, Gallart, Merle, Brouzet, Benetton, Cecillon (Cabannes 58), Benazzi.
SCORERS: *Tries:* Lacroix (2), Hueber, Saint-André. *Cons:* Lacroix (3). *Pens:* Lacroix (3). *DG:* Delaigue.
TONGA: Tu'ipulotu; Taufa, U Va'enuku, Latu, T Va'enuku; E Vunipola, M Vunipola; Fe'ao, Masila (F Vunipola 9), Fukofuka, Lose, Mafi (Afeaki 76), Mahoni, *Otai, Fenukitau.
SCORERS: *Try:* T Va'enuku. *Con:* Tu'ipulotu. *Pen:* Tu'ipulotu.
Referee: Steve Lander (England)

FRANCE 54 IVORY COAST 18
30 May • Rustenburg
FRANCE: Viars; Techoueyres, Mesnal, Lacroix, *Saint-André; Delaigue (Deylaud 40), Accoceberry; Benezech, De Rougemont, Califano, Brouzet, Roumat, Costes, Benazzi (Benetton 71), Cabannes.
SCORERS: *Tries:* Lacroix (2), Benazzi, Accoceberry, Viars, Costes, Techoueyres, Saint-André. *Cons:* Lacroix (2), Deylaud (2). *Pens:* Lacroix (2).
IVORY COAST: Kouassi; Soulama (Bouazo 79), *Sathicq, Niakou, Brito; Camara, Dupont; Ezoua (Bley 47), Niamien, Djehi (Angoran 74), Aka, Sanoko (Kone 56), Pere, Lassissi, Okou.
SCORERS: *Tries:* Camara, Soulama. *Con:* Kouassi. *Pens:* Kouassi (2).
Referee: H Moon-Soo (South Korea)

SCOTLAND 41 TONGA 5
30 May • Pretoria
SCOTLAND: *G Hastings; Joiner, S Hastings, Jardine, Logan; Chalmers, Patterson; Hilton, Milne, Wright (Burnell 76), Cronin, Weir, Wainwright, Peters, Morrison.
SCORERS: *Tries:* Peters, G Hastings, S Hastings. *Con:* G Hastings. *Pens:* G Hastings (8).
TONGA: Tu'ipulotu; Taufa, U Va'enuku, Latu, T Va'enuku; E Vunipola, M Vunipola (Tufui 57); Fe'ao (Talakai 75), F Vunipola, Fukofuka, Lose, Latukefu, Afeaki, *Otai, Fenukitau.
SCORER: *Try:* Fenukitau.
Referee: B Leask (Australia)

TONGA 29 IVORY COAST 11
3 June • Rustenburg
TONGA: Tu'ipulotu; Latu, Mafile'o, U Va'enuku (Isitolo 68), T Va'enuku; E Vunipola, Tufui; Fukofuka (Lutua 51), F Vunipola, Talakai, Latukefu, Mafi, Afeaki (Fakaongo 64), *Otai, Lose.
SCORER: *Tries:* Tu'ipulotu, Latukefu, Otai, PT. *Cons:* Tu'ipulotu (3). *Pen:* Tu'ipulotu.
IVORY COAST: Kouassi; Soulama, *Sathicq, Niakou, Brito (Kouame 6); Camara (Dali 39), Dupont; Bley (Quansah 50), Angoran, Djehi, Bado, Kone (Sanoko 40), Pere, Lassissi, Okou.
SCORERS: *Try:* Okou. *Pens:* Dali (2).
Referee: D Reordan (USA)

FRANCE 22 SCOTLAND 19
3 June • Pretoria
FRANCE: Sardourny; Ntamack, Sella, Lacroix, *Saint-André; Deylaud, Accoceberry (Hueber 33); Benezech, Gonzalez, Califano. Merle, Roumat, Benazzi, Benetton (Cecillon 19), Cabannes.
SCORERS: *Try:* Ntamack. *Con:* Lacroix. *Pens:* Lacroix (5).
SCOTLAND: *G Hastings; Joiner, S Hastings, Shiel (Jardine 44), Logan; Chalmers, Redpath; Hilton, Milne, Wright (Burnell 70), Cronin, Weir, Wainwright, Peters, Morrison.
SCORERS: *Try:* Wainwright. *Con:* G Hastings. *Pens:* G Hastings (4).
Referee: W J Erickson (Australia)

THE 1995 ·QUARTER-FINALS·

French fans cheer as Emile Ntamack, right, runs in to score a late try, for a flattering 36-12 win over Ireland

"There are moments when I think, my God, why am I doing this? The pressure is huge. Yet I accept the situation. I won't be doing it in a year's time and I'm not sad or worried about that."

SCOTLAND CAPTAIN GAVIN HASTINGS after announcing that if Scotland are knocked out by New Zealand, he will retire

Of the four matches constituting this stage of the tournament, three were expected to run a fairly predictable course. It would be a turn-up for the books if South Africa, New Zealand and France did not move on to the semi-finals. The conundrum was the match which brought the finalists of 1991 together: Australia and England.

From the start, the hopes of the home unions, indeed of Europe, had rested with England. Indeed, it was the Grand Slam winners that all the other teams, including the three from the southern hemisphere, feared most. Brian Lochore, the New Zealand manager, said as much. So did Morne du Plessis of South Africa.

England's powerful forwards, their beefy content and talent for not only winning the ball but denying it to others, could suffocate the life out of an opponent. England were universally respected; worldly forwards trembled at the prospect of Dean Richards and his stampeding gang. England determined the metronomic pulse of a game. It was disciplined, efficient and so successfully muscular that they gave many a tremulous adversary an agitated midnight contemplating the following day's events. Without the ball, what could the others do?

But England were being caught in two minds. With the agile guile of Jeremy Guscott, the thrusting Will Carling, the speed of the Underwoods and the potentially inventive Mike Catt, and conscious of what outsiders – their own supporters and the media – were wishing of them, England began thinking they ought to consider some other way of playing. By the second week of June and after so much hesitation and, at times, impotence in the early rounds, they lacked conviction. More importantly, if they continued to play to the same tempo, would they survive the six matches needed to win the World Cup? Would somebody else, given time to observe their strengths, scupper them?

The England-Australia game proved to be the highlight of the quarter-final round. It was the third to be played, the first two – France and Ireland, South Africa and Western Samoa – having taken place on Saturday. In Durban, Ireland put up an obstinate resistance against a wavering French team hampered by their timidity at facing the unpredictable Irish and, on occasions, paralysed by the thought of not progressing further. This nervousness was characterised by their outside half Christophe Deylaud, whose misjudgements disrupted any hope of fluid play. That he should have attempted four drops at goal, thus denying opportunities to others, was further testament of their edginess.

The French played the Irish in those areas where the Irish might feel content. It was a set-piece game, which, territorially, the French dominated, particularly through the contributions of Laurent Cabannes and Abdelatif Benazzi. In this way Thierry Lacroix was within kicking

"I would be honest and say it's strange that we're allowed a replacement. I am personally a bit surprised."

SOUTH AFRICA COACH MORNE DU PLESSIS on hearing that Chester Williams will be allowed to replace Pieter Hendriks, who was suspended after the brawl with Canada

distance for all his eight penalties. Eric Elwood, with four kicks at goal, kept Ireland in touch. As if exasperation got the better of the French towards the end, or they realised belatedly that there might be an easier route to the next round, *les Bleus* cut loose in the final quarter when their two wingers, Philippe Saint-André and Emile Ntamack, scored a couple of tries to give them a 36-12 win.

In Johannesburg, the Springboks got past Western Samoa but not without worrying moments, some of which were manifest to the eye while others, it was said afterwards, were more furtive. The tackles inflicted by the South Sea islanders, particularly by full back Mike Umaga, were dangerously high or late. The Springboks, after the rumpus against Canada, had to check their instinct to respond.

The victory was not achieved without cost. They had to use all four of their replacements because of injuries. More worrying was the accusation that Joost van der Westhuizen, who had been a target of the reckless tackles, had made racist comments on the field. This was denied. On a happier note, Chester Williams made his return on the left wing – and celebrated in style by scoring four tries, two in each half. A South African Airways advertisement with Williams' face had announced: "The waiting's over", but he could not have expected to wait quite so long to grace the World Cup stage. His four tries were a record for his country. For the image of the rainbow nation to approach a reality, the World Cup required an exhibition of brilliance from such a player at such a time. In its way, it was a triumphal moment.

Late tries for Western Samoa came from Tu Nu'uali'itia and Shem Tatupu which, with Tupo Fa'amasino's two conversions, gave them 14 points against South Africa's 42.

It would be a shock if there was a similar scoreline with a hatful of tries at Newlands in Cape Town. Bob Dwyer, the percipient Wallaby coach, thought his team's game with England could be the match of the tournament, but added: "I do not necessarily equate 'good' with 'open'." He expected

Chester Williams made his World Cup debut with four tries against Western Samoa. Above left: George Harder escapes the clutches of Joost van der Westhuizen

"Both teams will be well briefed on the need for discipline, but one also hopes, for the good of the game, that they remember who the trophy they are playing for was named after. William Webb Ellis grew frustrated with only being allowed to kick the ball and so picked it up and ran with it."

NICK FARR-JONES commenting that with two great defensive teams and so much at stake, the match between England and Australia could deteriorate into a Lynagh versus Andrew kicking duel

Right: Will Carling leads the English charge against Australia, while Dean Richards battles on with a head wound

a tough contest of high quality rugby. They were two very well-matched teams. Carling and Guscott would renew the challenge with Tim Horan, only recently recovered after 13 months from a serious left-knee injury, and Jason Little. We should anticipate the duel of accurate kicking in and out of hand of Rob Andrew and Michael Lynagh; the finely-tuned expressions of wing play between Rory Underwood and David Campese; the locking of horns of two mighty packs of forwards and the battle for back-row supremacy.

Nine Australians survived from the 1991 Final as against six of England. Neither country had played as well as

had been expected in their first three matches of the 1995 tournament. Yet the game was relished in the anticipation and, the losers' disappointment notwithstanding, fulfilling in the accomplishment. It was a great encounter.

There were only two tries, one apiece, but it was no less enthralling for that. To say that it was no more than a shoot-out between Andrew and Lynagh would be misleading, such was the vibrancy of the spectacle and the sheer hardness of the combat. England, against the wind, were the dominant team in the first half. Counter-attacking from Lynagh's dropped pass on England's own 22, Andrew began the move which led to Tony Underwood's try. At one point England held a 10-point lead but by the interval this had been reduced to 13-6.

'HE'S A VERY DIFFICULT BOY TO STOP'

Ireland wing Simon Geoghegan on a momentous World Cup – and his first sight of Jonah Lomu

'Playing New Zealand in the opening game was the highlight of the 1995 World Cup for me. We started very well. Flanker Gary Halpin scored a good try – then gave the All Blacks the finger, which I don't think went down too well with the governors of the school where he was a teacher. Probably didn't please the All Blacks too much, either...

Once New Zealand got on top, they just ran away with it, mainly thanks to Jonah Lomu, who scored two tries and made another in a 43-19 win. That was the first time anyone had really seen him. I would have liked to have played against him, but I was on the other wing. Whether it would have been a good or bad thing, I don't know. Probably bad! He's a very difficult boy to stop when he gets into his stride. After that he got better each game.

After reaching the quarter-finals we went up to Sun City for a few days of golf, gambling and watersports, then it was down to Durban, where we met France at King's Park. Like all the stadiums over there, it was incredible. It had an indoor kicking area, so you didn't even have to go out on the ground to warm up. Not that I was in a state to notice. I picked up a virus two days before the match and was bedridden for 36 hours. I managed to play the game but I was really weak, and I don't remember much about it. I thought I was going to die.

We were well beaten 36-12 by a good French side who ran away with it at the end. They had a great team spirit: they had all shaved their heads before they came away because they had been to a training camp where they felt they had been treated as convicts.

I would have liked to have stayed on to see the Final, but I had to go back to work."

The Lomu Express – once seen, never forgotten

Within a minute of the start of the second half, the two teams were level. Damian Smith, in reaching high, Australian rules-style, from a Lynagh high kick, scored for Australia. With the two outside halves trading kicks, Lynagh, during the course of this duel, became the first player to score more than 900 international points.

England had to come from behind twice to bring the score level at 22-22. With the contest reaching the closing stages, tension rising, England were awarded a penalty. Full back Mike Catt dispatched the ball down to the Wallabies' 22-metre line. At the lineout, Martin Bayfield caught the

"We don't want to be going home just yet."

ROB ANDREW
before the quarter-final against Australia

Australia full back Matthew Burke eludes England's Rob Andrew

'Suddenly there was pandemonium...'

THE 1995 WORLD CUP QUARTER-FINAL • AUSTRALIA v ENGLAND

It was the 80th minute of a battle of the giants. England 22 Australia 22. Martin Bayfield won a lineout and the ball was fired out to the waiting fly half... Rob Andrew recalls the most famous kick in English rugby history

BY ROB ANDREW

I cannot recall a game more emotionally draining than the 1995 World Cup quarter-final. It was not the hardest one physically in which I had played but the mental effort was huge: to lead by ten points, to have that clawed back, then suffer the nip and tuck of penalty kicks by each side.

Many people might have thought the game was drifting away from us, but we knew we had to dig in and just keep in touch. We had lost our way after such a wonderful start when we were so hungry; so precise in all we did. But we kept making our tackles and we stayed calm and all the time we had the immense encouragement of seeing the Australians making mistakes too, because of the pressure they were under. The crowd was important for us, too: the support at Newlands made it seem like Twickenham.

From the moment that Mike Catt struck such a beautiful penalty kick to touch on Australia's 22-metre line, I knew that a dropped goal was the best option. I think we all knew that when David Bishop, the referee, awarded the penalty in our own half; the scores were level, time was running out and it was an obvious opportunity.

As Dean Richards passed me running up to the lineout he said: "What do you need for the dropped goal?" I told him we needed to catch the ball and drive it, then see what the position was.

The idea was to make a bit more ground, perhaps move a little way into midfield, tie in the Australian back row then keep the head down, hit and hope. It worked, and it earned England a place in the World Cup semi-finals.

'Martin made a wonderful leap. The forwards piled in behind, produced the ball – and all I could hope was that the kick would go over'

But for it to work, so many others had to play their part. Catt, for instance. I thought he was outstanding and a couple of times I had given him the ball to find touch, partly to bring him into the game and partly because all week he had been kicking so well in training.

It was a wonderful touch he found. If he had missed, it would have been awful because Australia would have had the chance to run the ball back at us; if he had found a shorter touch it would have made the dropped goal that much more difficult. But he hit a pearler, all of 50 metres, which brought Brian Moore and Martin Bayfield into the picture.

Martin made a wonderful leap at the lineout. The forwards piled in behind, produced the ball – and all I could hope was that the kick would go over. It did, and suddenly there was pandemonium.

No one knew whether it was the end of the game, there were people on the pitch, the security people too, some of our boys were starting a lap of honour and the Australians were kicking off in a last-ditch attempt to retrieve the position.

That it was the goal which knocked out the world champions made it all the sweeter. Had we lost, it would have been no disgrace: Australia were a great side and this was a wonderful game of rugby.

• *Originally published in The Times, London, on June 12, 1995*

Coca-Cola
Coca-Cola

Right: Jonah Lomu of New Zealand leaves Scotland centre Scott Hastings in his wake. Lomu and Hastings both scored tries

ball. England drove. Three minutes into injury time, scrum half Dewi Morris delivered to Andrew. The outside half struck for a drop goal.

It was one of those sporting moments when the world seems to stop and for a second no one breathes. In the mind's eye, those figures in that particular landscape are always standing still, an eternal, unchanging tableau. Waiting and looking. At that instant it is best to keep your eyes on the kicker; in this case, Andrew. He knows sooner than anyone whether the kick is good. He is in the best position to judge, and he knows how the strike felt. He is always the first to raise his arms in salute or drop his head in misery.

Andrew did not have to shed any tears. He turned and raised his hands in the air; smiling the smile of fulfilment. It was one of the greatest of drop goals, coming as it did when it did and to win such a prize.

· QUARTER FINALS ·

FRANCE 36 IRELAND 12
10 June • Durban
FRANCE: Sadourny; Ntamack, Sella, Lacroix, *Saint-André; Deylaud, Hueber; Armany, Gonzalez, Califano, Merle, Roumat, Benazzi, Cecillon, Cabannes.
SCORERS: *Tries:* Saint-André, Ntamack. *Con:* Lacroix. *Pens:* Lacroix (8).
IRELAND: O'Shea; Mahony, Mullin, Bell, Geoghegan; Elwood, Hogan; Popplewell, *Kingston, Halpin, Fulcher (Halvey 61), Francis, Corkery, Johns, McBride.
SCORER: *Pens:* Elwood (4).
Referee: Ed Morrison (England)

SOUTH AFRICA 42 WESTERN SAMOA 14
10 June • Johannesburg
SOUTH AFRICA: Joubert (Venter 18); Johnson, Scholtz, Mulder, Williams; H Le Roux, Van der Westhuizen; Du Randt, Rossouw, Swart, Weise (Drotske 78), Andrews (Otto 71), *Pienaar, Straeuli, Kruger (Richter 48).
SCORERS: *Tries:* Williams (4), Rossouw, Andrews. *Cons:* Johnson (3). *Pens:* Johnson (2).
WESTERN SAMOA: Umaga; Lima, Vaega, Fa'amasino, Harder; F Sini, Nu'uali'itia; Mika (Reidy 71), Leiasamaivao, Latu (Fatialofa 65), Falaniko, Lemamea, Tatupu (Vaifale 75), *Lam, Paramore.
SCORERS: *Tries:* Nu'uali'itia, Tatupu. *Cons:* Fa'amasino (2).
Referee: Jim Fleming (Scotland)

ENGLAND 25 AUSTRALIA 22
11 June • Cape Town
ENGLAND: Catt; T Underwood, *Carling, Guscott, R Underwood; Andrew, Morris; Leonard, Moore, Ubogu, Johnson, Bayfield, Rodber, Richards, Clarke.
SCORERS: *Try:* T Underwood. *Con:* Andrew. *Pens:* Andrew (5). *DG:* Andrew (2).
AUSTRALIA: Burke; Campese, Little, Horan, Smith; *Lynagh, Gregan; Crowley, Kearns, McKenzie, McCall, Eales, Ofahengaue, Gavin, Wilson.
SCORERS: *Try:* Smith. *Con:* Lynagh. *Pens:* Lynagh (5).
Referee: D J Bishop (New Zealand)

NEW ZEALAND 48 SCOTLAND 30
11 June • Pretoria
NEW ZEALAND: Wilson; Ellis, Bunce, Little, Lomu; Mehrtens, Bachop; Loe, *Fitzpatrick, Brown, Jones, R Brooke, Joseph, Z Brooke, Kronfeld.
SCORERS: *Tries:* Little (2), Lomu, Mehrtens, Bunce, Fitzpatrick. *Cons:* Mehrtens (6). *Pens:* Mehrtens (2).
SCOTLAND: *G Hastings; Joiner, S Hastings, Shiel, Logan; Chalmers (Jardine 40), Redpath; Hilton, Milne, Wright, Cronin (Campbell 63), Weir, Wainwright, Peters, Morrison.
SCORERS: *Tries:* Weir (2), S Hastings. *Cons:* G Hastings (3). *Pens:* G Hastings (3).
Referee: Derek Bevan (Wales)

> "I've never felt so caught up in an atmosphere so close to a game. I'm sure the whole of South Africa and everyone at home will be behind us. I'm going to sing Flower of Scotland like I've never sung it before and then crawl off that pitch at the end."
>
> SCOTT HASTINGS
> before the quarter-final against New Zealand

In a tumult of emotions, the world had changed: to the victor the joy, to the vanquished the despair. England 25, Australia 22. Australia were on the next plane home, England off to Cape Town to await the All Blacks or the Scots.

It was not long before they knew who their semi-final opponents would be. When the pipes call, very rarely are the Scots found wanting. They gave more than a good account of themselves at Loftus Versfeld against New Zealand. The All Blacks were expected to swamp them. But in the event, Scotland gave almost as good as they received. They crossed their opponents' line three times. They disrupted the All Blacks into uncharacteristic errors.

The All Blacks were in a cynical mood. Derek Bevan, the referee, penalised them three times early on for rash tackles. But what was clear was that these were not the All Blacks of old. They were playing a different game: a high-risk game designed to score tries. If the rampant Lomu, running for

"It's a knockout competition and whether we win by one point or ten, we don't care. We are best when we are the underdogs.We have got to concentrate for 80 minutes. We cannot afford a single lapse, for that is when they put the knife in. Everything we do has got to be precision. We don't want this to be Gavin's last game."

CRAIG CHALMERS
Scottish stand-off half before the quarter-final against the All Blacks which was, indeed, Gavin's last game

60 metres, had fashioned a try for Walter Little after four minutes, the winger himself scored the next. Gavin Hastings kept his side in touch with three penalties. But even though Scotland lock Doddie Weir scored two tries, and Scott Hastings one, the All Blacks were not to be denied, and finished with six tries in a free-scoring 48-30 victory.

The two captains both created personal memories. In his 100th appearance in an All Blacks jersey, Sean Fitzpatrick scored at the end of the most sustained movement of the evening, while in converting his brother's try Gavin Hastings collected his last points in his country's colours.

Above left: Doddie Weir and Rob Wainwright carry Gavin Hastings from the pitch as he ends a record-breaking career. Left: His victorious opposite number, All Blacks skipper Sean Fitzpatrick, in his 100th Test match

1995 THE · SEMI-FINALS ·

"He told me about Robben Island and asked me about rugby, of which he knows a lot. I never thought I would be a Springbok because we were so isolated for so long. Mr Mandela and Mr de Klerk brought South Africa back into the world hand in hand."
FRANÇOIS PIENAAR
on meeting Nelson Mandela

In the semi-finals – the first in King's Park, Durban, on Saturday, the other the following day in Newlands, Cape Town – we were to witness two remarkable, almost preternatural, events. If they were utterly different in essence, they both nonetheless contained rare elemental forces, defiantly out of proportion with what we naturally expect.

To the province of KwaZulu Natal on Saturday June 17 there came a deluge on a Biblical scale. Durban's pride in its water sports took on a different hue that day. The rains turned King's Park into a lake and put an end to the chit-chat, the bare masculine knees and the sound of coughing around the smoky *braaivleis* in the extensive car parks. The heavens opened to make you vow never to complain again at the pitter-patter rainfall of home.

Black women – not a white face in sight to begin with – came on in a line to brush away the surface water. Old habits, it was illustrated, die hard. Word got about that if South Africa was truly to be a rainbow nation, perhaps a white person or two should be called into service. In the end, they were. The kick-off was postponed for an hour and a half. There were suggestions that the fixture should be delayed for 24 hours. But that would create logistical problems: hotel accommodation, aircraft flights, broadcasting timings, bookings of all sorts would need to be changed. In the end it was left to the referee, Derek Bevan, and the two captains – all of whom elected to play. The conditions would have been unacceptable even for Michael Green's fictional *Art of Coarse Rugby* club, the Old Rottinghamians RFC, let alone a World Cup semi-final.

What followed was a jerky scenario riddled with mistakes which Green himself might well have proudly imagined. The ball would skim over the water one moment, stop still the next. Players might over-run the ball or slip while in hot pursuit. Worse, they might tread gingerly as if they feared drowning on a day which could only find its parallel in a New Zealand-Scotland match in Auckland in 1975 when to be caught at the bottom of a ruck presented hazards which put life at risk. The world's best rugby players might not have been able parade their talent, but they did show their courage and indomitable spirit.

South Africa made five changes from their quarter-final team. Joel Stransky returned to outside half, Mark Andrews was moved from lock to No 8 and James Small came back on the wing. Most notably, full back André Joubert, who had broken a bone in his hand against Western Samoa, was declared fit – and went on to play an important role.

France made one change, with Fabien Galthié, who played in all the 1991 games, returning to scrum half instead of Aubin Hueber.

But, in truth, none of these personalities would have much chance to impose himself on the events of the afternoon – soon to turn into early evening. Rather, it was the weather that took centre-stage. South Africa adopted the more direct tactics. The French on critical occasions tried to turn their hand to more fancy stuff, only to come a cropper. Christophe Deylaud was partly the culprit. It was the outside half's miskick that led to the solitary try in a game dominated by the penalty kicks of Stransky (four) and Thierry Lacroix who, remarkably in such atrocious conditions, missed only one in six attempts at goal.

Stransky had already kicked one penalty. Then France

At least one supporter came well prepared! Left: South Africa's François Pienaar makes a splash while, opposite, mopping-up operations begin

took the heel against the head at a scrum in their own half. Their forwards' joy was shortlived when, on getting up, they saw Deylaud's kick, instead of gaining an invaluable 50 metres for them, fall into the hands of Joubert. The full back took the ball back into France's territory, from where the Springboks took control. Driving irresistibly for the line, Ruben Kruger was forced over for a try. Stransky converted, breaking the exchange of penalty kicks which was always likely to ensue in such limiting conditions. Furthermore, this try ensured that Derek Bevan, the referee, would not have to invoke a controversial regulation. Since the storm had not gone away altogether, there was always a chance that the match would be abandoned. In the event of this happening before half-time, if no tries had been scored, the winner would be the team with the best disciplinary record. After the game against Canada, and the sending-off of James Dalton and the banning of Pieter Hendriks, South

> "One person has to slow him down, a second has to knock him over. He's young, naive, and we'll put pressure on him. It's something to work on."
>
> WILL CARLING
> looking forward to tackling Lomu in the semi-final

Mark Andrews wins a lineout as the South Africans show France how to keep it simple

Africa would be declared the losers. The furore this would have precipitated could only be imagined. Kruger's try, fortunately, invalidated this regulation.

With time running out, France forced South Africa on the defensive. Twice they seemed to cross the line for a score. Emile Ntamack did so first, but was recalled for an earlier knock-on. Then Abdelatif Benazzi went over, only for the try to be disallowed. Despite this late French rally, South Africa were believed overall to have been the better team in the bizarre conditions, justifying the 19-15 scoreline.

"Not a lot of people gave us a chance of being in the Final. We made so many mistakes, basic errors, but it was great defence and the guys kept their cool. It was great discipline."
FRANÇOIS PIENAAR
after the semi-final victory against France

South Africa had reached the Final on their first appearance in the World Cup. Their estimable captain, François Pienaar, and his team exhaled a collective sigh of relief in having now delivered the least that a patriotic and passionate rugby nation expected. But did the Springboks have it within them to go one step further and actually win the Cup?

It would take some doing, for by this time New Zealand had established themselves as favourites to win the tournament. They had managed to create their own momentum during the first two weeks and were playing a brand of rugby which was manifestly different to all the other countries. Quite simply, they were expanding the boundaries of the game's possibilities.

At the start of the tournament, New Zealand had been the last of the nations to arrive in South Africa, stepping off their aircraft almost invisibly. In contrast to the attention paid to the much-fancied South Africa, Australia, England and France, the All Blacks had crept into Johannesburg virtually under cover of darkness, so underwhelming was their reception.

Rarely in their long and distinguished history had they been placed in such a subordinate role. This was a strange situation for them but one with which their captain, Sean Fitzpatrick, was content. "We don't mind being tagged the underdogs," he said. "It means we have a point to prove." The All Blacks? Underdogs? Surely no New Zealand captain had ever had to admit as much. They had had an indifferent season in 1994. Philippe Saint-André's France had been to New Zealand and won the two-match Test series for the first time. The All Blacks had then beaten South Africa in a three-match series before Australia took the Bledisloe Cup back with them across the Tasman Sea. And in 1993 they had also lost to England. Laurie Mains, the coach, had begun refashioning the team with disturbing selections; players were swapped and changed. Not only that, but there was a sullen disharmony between the New Zealand management and the media.

The appointment of Colin Meads as team manager and Brian Lochore as campaign manager put two of the most respected former All Blacks in charge – but where was the team going? Rumour had it that the All Blacks were trying to break with their rugby past. They were playing the handling game in the open spaces. Could this be true?

Yet suddenly, in the World Cup, the All Blacks were leading the pack. After just two games, they had made their point. Their transformation was swift and clinical. Writing from South Africa, I reported in *The Times*:

"What has elevated the All Blacks from the rest is the clarity with which they have demonstrated their potency. While others still talk of their team's potential, New Zealand are giving proof of theirs. They have been impressive. There are those who point out that the two teams they have encountered so far have lacked the necessary skills and power to put them to the test. But Ireland and Wales have reputations that are at least recognisable at this level in a way that some countries in the tournament have not. Neither of these two Five Nations Championship teams is as formidable as in times past, but New Zealand are likely to be more wary and respectful of them than they would be of, say, Italy, Romania and Canada, against whom England, South Africa and Australia have recently played and been less than convincing."

New Zealand came to South Africa with the intention

Guess who won the lottery? Despair for Olivier Roumat and joy for the Springboks

"Jonah Lomu was the difference. Without being funny, if New Zealand didn't have him, then the game could have been very different. We tried to stop him, but we couldn't and that's very sad for us but the man is unbelievable."
WILL CARLING

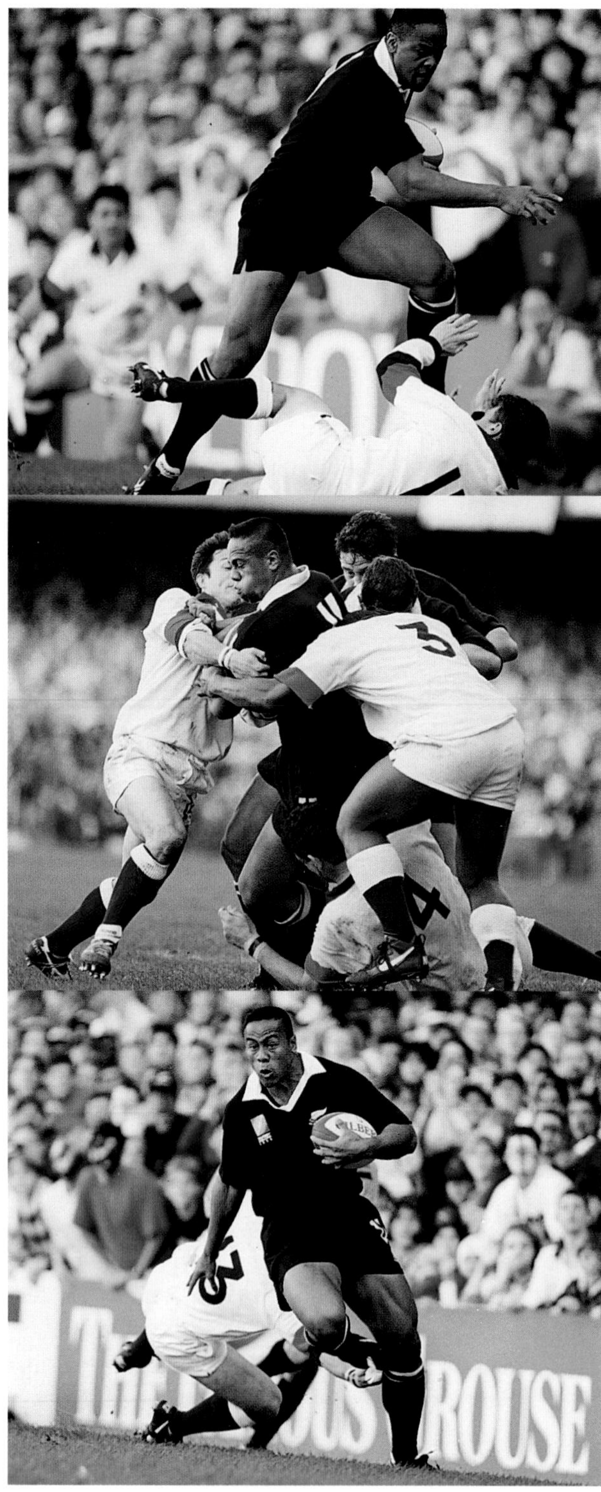

Congratulations! You've just been Lomu'd. Jonah puts out the Catt, requires three England players to stop him, and gives Will Carling something to grouse about

of playing high-speed handling rugby of the kind they had shown in their last match against Australia and in their trial matches at home. But would they have the conviction to do so throughout the pressurised cauldron of the World Cup?

Before their arrival, the world was aware of the high standards of Glenn Osborne at full back, Jeff Wilson on the wing, Walter Little and Frank Bunce in the centre. They had a new and exciting pair at half-back in Andrew Mehrtens and Graeme Bachop.

This much was already known. But as for Jonah Lomu, the young 20-year-old, well, he was not properly in the frame at all. None of the New Zealand pundits had included him in their prospective World Cup teams. In fact, he had

"Someone from rugby league should have bought him before the World Cup started!"
ENGLAND MANAGER JACK ROWELL

almost been left out of the party on a disciplinary matter. Now he was the talk of the town, painting it in the boldest red. He seemed unstoppable. Only the late-night talkers had a good game against Lomu.

In the semi-final, the All Blacks were to play the team they feared most. They feared their power, their height and their forward command. England, they knew from their 1993 experience at Twickenham, were formidable. Where, asked Brian Lochore in the days leading up to the contest, was the weakness? He did not find it among England's players. He found it in England's tactics. They played to a pattern which, on the recent evidence, appeared inflexible.

Lochore wondered what would England's response be if they found themselves behind on the score sheet. Not by a penalty goal or two, but by a converted try – which, in the light of England's dearth of tries, would require the kicking of three penalty goals or, knowing Rob Andrew's acute eye, three drop goals to take the lead. Thus England, to achieve a victory, might have to go in search of different methods. Lochore questioned whether they could.

To upset England's pattern was the key; not to allow Richards, Rodber, Johnson, Moore and the rest to set the steady foot-soldier tempo which, given their often impenetrable vanguard, would be difficult to break. New Zealand, despite perceptions, were not a particularly big side – but they were athletic and skilful. Furthermore, they were fine thinkers. By the time they emerged on Newlands they had done their homework.

However, it is one thing to draw up a strategy; to implement it is quite another…

New Zealand's first-half performance in the semi-final of the 1995 World Cup was one of the most extraordinary and extravagant in the history of rugby football. The All Blacks threw down the gauntlet from their own kick-off to start the match. Instead of kicking normally to that side where the forwards had congregated, Mehrtens kicked it to the open, where Lomu was prowling – and where Carling and Tony Underwood collided. This split the English forwards.

Not at any stage did the All Blacks allow England to settle to their routine of a set-piece game; nor did they relinquish the tactical initiative which this bold first stroke created. In the third minute they scored their first try. Bachop's long pass found Lomu, who dispatched Underwood with a hand-off, then beat Carling for pace, and drove like a runaway train over Catt for the first of his four tries.

From the restart, deep on their own 22-metre line – and stemming from the error of Graeme Bachop's long pass going astray in midfield –

Will Carling puts in a thunderous tackle on New Zealand wing Jeff Wilson

Zinzan Brooke, the New Zealand No 8, took the game into the realms of fantasy with this drop goal from 50 yards out

Walter Little, the brilliant centre who had been ignored in 1991, picked the ball up so eloquently from his toes that he initiated the move which ended at the other end of the field with Josh Kronfeld's try. This was such a blistering start that it unsteadied Rob Andrew, normally so utterly unfazed. He missed a penalty and a drop goal.

> "In the context of this breathless beginning, this was so audacious the crowd looked on open-mouthed, hardly believing what they were seeing"

It seemed that nothing could go wrong for New Zealand. Mehrtens kicked his penalty chance from near the halfway line and then, when Carling tried to relieve the onslaught with a kick out of defence, Zinzan Brooke gathered the high ball and dropped for goal. From some 50 metres and an acute angle, the No 8 succeeded. In the context of this breathless beginning, this was so audacious the crowd looked on open-mouthed, hardly believing what they were seeing.

With Lomu's second try, the All Blacks had scored as many points as the 25 minutes on the clock. The contest was over with almost an hour still to play. By half-time another try by the 19-stone winger, inspired by Little again, gave his team a 30-point lead. Bachop's try early after the interval gave them 35 points.

Everything these men touched was dusted with gold; there was scarcely an error in movements of mesmerising speed and agility. This was rugby at its most expansive. Such rugby, at such pace, had never been seen before.

What's more, all this was happening in a semi-final for rugby's greatest prize, where the received wisdom advised caution and a wary cat-and-mouse game. Instead, New Zealand launched an unstoppable Exocet to destroy England's most cherished hopes. It was a devastating display. When they had finished, the stadium stood in stunned silence, unable to take in fully what they had just seen.

There were many who felt that the difference between the two teams was Jonah Lomu. Admittedly, he was a major influence – but this would be to seriously underestimate the quality of the play of the others, which was unmatched by any of the other nations. Jack Rowell, England's coach, recognised immediately that New Zealand were aspiring to a different style of rugby, exploring the game to its limits. Having arrived in South Africa with such high expectations, the manner of England's exit must have unnerved him. New Zealand had dared to play a game often talked about, wistfully and wishfully, in imaginary schoolyard scenarios of the 'what if…' kind – a game which, in the cold light of dawn, and in serious and fearful adulthood, was unthinkable to play. The All Blacks dared and won. By any standards, it was an extraordinary display.

If England had not reached the heights of which they were capable in the pool games, apart from the Western Samoa match, they had shown when the crunch came against Australia that they could generate a style of such tenacious and unforgiving pressure, played to their own tempo, that hardly anyone could match them. To overcome this needed an unorthodox response. New Zealand provided a kind of rugby, particularly in the first half, that had not been contemplated at this level before.

England recovered during the second half. Rory Underwood and Carling, in a fine captain's rearguard-action performance, scored two tries each and with Andrew – who had been awarded the MBE in the Queen's Birthday Honours List – recovering from his early yips to convert three and kick a penalty, a tinge of respectability was given to the final score of 45-29.

No England team had conceded 45 points before. The last player to score four tries against them in one match was the Welshman Maurice Richards in Cardiff in 1969.

It was generally felt that the closeness of the score, with only 16 points separating the teams, was due to the All Blacks taking their foot off the accelerator rather than any kind of English revival.

The All Blacks on Sunday June 18, 1995 were playing rugby of a different power and speed.

"They were very fast, dynamic, direct. We were in shock. It was not until the second half that we got even with the pace. Many sides would have laid down in front of such awesome attack."
WILL CARLING

Will Carling led a defiant second-half fightback, but England's hopes were already shattered

· SEMI-FINALS ·

SOUTH AFRICA 19 FRANCE 15
17 June • Durban
SOUTH AFRICA: Joubert; Small, Mulder, H Le Roux, Williams; Stransky, Van der Westhuizen (J Le Roux 52); Du Randt, Rossouw, Swart, Weise, Strydom, *Pienaar, Andrews, Kruger.
SCORERS: *Try:* Kruger. *Con:* Stransky. *Pens:* Stransky (4).
FRANCE: Sadourny; Ntamack, Sella, Lacroix, *Saint-André; Deylaud, Galthié; Armany, Gonzalez, Califano, Merle, Roumat, Benazzi, Cecillon, Cabannes.
SCORER: *Pens:* Lacroix (5).
Referee: Derek Bevan (Wales)

NEW ZEALAND 45 ENGLAND 29
18 June • Cape Town
NEW ZEALAND: Osborne; Wilson, Bunce, Little, Lomu; Mehrtens, Bachop; Dowd, *Fitzpatrick, Brown, Jones, R Brooke, Brewer, Z Brooke (Larsen 64), Kronfeld.
SCORERS: *Tries:* Lomu (4), Kronfeld, Bachop. *Cons:* Mehrtens (3). *Pen:* Mehrtens. *DGs:* Mehrtens, Z Brooke.
ENGLAND: Catt; T Underwood, *Carling, Guscott, R Underwood; Andrew, Morris; Leonard, Moore, Ubogu, Johnson, Bayfield, Rodber, Richards, Clarke.
SCORERS: *Tries:* R Underwood (2), Carling (2). *Cons:* Andrew (3). *Pen:* Andrew.
Referee: Stephen Hilditch (Ireland)

'To lose in those conditions was terrible'

THE 1995 WORLD CUP SEMI-FINAL • SOUTH AFRICA v FRANCE

Philippe Saint-André is probably the most unfortunate captain in World Cup history. France knew how to beat South Africa – but not how to beat the weather. Four years après le déluge, the pain still won't go away

BY PHILIPPE SAINT-ANDRÉ

France had had mixed fortunes on our way to the World Cup in South Africa. We had won a Test series in New Zealand but then we did not play well in the Five Nations. We knew we had a lot of work to do, and for three months we worked with a lot of passion, like commandos. We were all one family. Pierre Berbizier was a very hard coach. By the time of the World Cup all the players were full of confidence.

Having the Rugby World Cup in South Africa is like holding the soccer World Cup in Italy, because rugby is a religion. The event was wonderful. When South Africa won the Final it transcended rugby. It was the resurrection of a country, with the black and white people all on the same side.

We knew the most important pool game would be against Scotland, because they had beaten us four months previously at Parc des Princes – and the team which lost would have to play New Zealand in the quarter-finals. It was a good game which we won in injury time with a try by Emile Ntamack. With five minutes to go, Scotland had an eight-point lead – and we were awarded a penalty. Pierre Berbizier said we must play with the hands, but I asked the referee how much time was left and when he said three minutes plus four minutes' injury time, I said: "Thierry Lacroix must kick."

So we took the penalty and scored the three points and then we came back into Scotland's 22 metres and got another penalty. This time we didn't kick it, but ran it through the hands in a move we had worked on in training, with the forwards, nine and 10, then into the forwards again and then there was a miss-pass and Emile Ntamack came over from the right wing to the left side with Jean-Luc Sadourny and me. Ntamack came into the line, played a dummy and scored in the left-hand corner. It was an incredible moment, because we scored a try in injury time and we won the game.

'Twice we went out to play and twice the weather was too bad. It was very difficult, I had to make my pre-match speech three times!'

The quarter-final against Ireland was not an open game. It was a very hard game but because we had been training for three months, we were very fit. Our forwards were very strong and so against Ireland we played a game lacking in French flair. We played a powerful game with a lot of kicks, and our two tries didn't come until the last five minutes. In the Five Nations we have more problems against Ireland, but I think that by the time they reached the quarter-final they were knackered, whereas we were very fit.

So we were due to meet South Africa in the semi-final. We had played them four or five times in the previous couple of years and they had all been very close games. We knew the way we wanted to play them. We were very confident and wanted to play more open rugby, because although South Africa were very strong, we thought we could beat them by playing it wide.

All week we worked on our game plan, with lots of moves involving loops outside Philippe Sella, the outside centre, and we worked on lots of ways to counter-attack. We intended to play at speed.

But then everything changed. All the way through the World Cup, the weather in South Africa had been wonderful – and then on the day of the semi-final it was awful. It was just amazing weather. There was thunder and lightning and a torrential downpour. Twice we went out to play the game and the referee said no, we must wait because it is not possible, so we stopped our preparation.

To keep stopping and starting like that made it very difficult for me as captain because we were stuck in the changing room for two hours. It was very difficult for the French mentality and the Mediterranean mentality. Now that I am a coach in England, I can see that English people don't prepare in the same way. It's more relaxed and more quiet. But in France we have a lot of speeches and a lot of mental preparation – and each time we got ready to start, the game was delayed for 10 or 15 minutes more. It was not easy, because we built the pressure up and when the pressure was ready, the game was cancelled! The pressure goes down, we build it up again, the game was cancelled ... but that's life. I think I made my speech three times – and I had to change it every time in order to get the team's attention!

Philippe Saint-André and his fellow razorhead Jean-Luc Sadourny tangle with the Tongans

After that it was very hard, because we lost. South Africa went on to win the World Cup, and I am very happy for South Africa. But for me it was very frustrating because it was the end of an adventure that had lasted four years. After the 1991 World Cup, we worked for four years together towards the 1995 World Cup. We weren't professionals, so over that four-year period there was a lot of hardship and a lot of effort. You spend a lot of time away from your wife and your family and your job. You take your holidays to go training together.

To lose in a semi-final is frustrating. To lose in a semi-final in such terrible conditions is worse still. If it's a nice day, you can play your best rugby, and then if you lose, you can say: "Well, it's because the other team was better." But we lost because the ball was too slippery to play the sort of game we wanted to play. Towards the end of the game we spent 15 minutes in the South African 22. But when the weather is so bad, it becomes much more of a game of luck.

After South Africa beat us, they became the champions of the world. That is the reality and we can't come back.

It was awful in the changing room after the game because it was the end of the adventure for half the guys in that team. It was terrible because we had played everywhere in the world; we had played a lot of games together. We didn't only lose the semi-final of the World Cup, we lost a complete generation of players. It was the end of that team. It felt like the sky had fallen in on our heads. Throughout the four years' preparation we were dedicated to winning the World Cup because we wanted to kill the French mentality that says it's OK if you reach the quarter-final or semi-final. So when we lost in the semi-final, we were not ready to lose.

Sometimes if you reach the semi-final you are happy because you have achieved your objective, but that was not our objective.

After the semi-final, we beat England in the third-place play-off. Then we went to the Final. It was a wonderful atmosphere and the President of South Africa, Nelson Mandela, wore Pienaar's jersey. But when you are sitting there in the stadium, having narrowly lost the semi-final, it's terrible. It's so frustrating because you say, it's an incredible day but here am I sitting with my jacket on when I should be on the pitch.

1995

THE PLAY-OFF FOR · THIRD PLACE ·

The prime motive for the two teams contemplating the least appetising of fixtures was that the result would allow the winner automatic qualification to the 1999 tournament. For England there was the additional aim of avoiding two consecutive defeats – an ignominy they had not suffered since 1991. France could seek motivation in their quarter-final defeat in 1991 and the recent confrontational encounter when they lost to England at Parc des Princes.

Everyone tried their damnedest to talk up the match. But their body language told a different story. The players went shopping for gifts to take home or wandered aimlessly about. For them, like us, the only question remaining and the one that mattered would be answered at Ellis Park on Saturday. There was no glory to be found at Loftus Versveld on Thursday.

As Gavin Hastings had put it when he experienced this strange third place play-off situation four years earlier: "It's the hardest game to play, because no one wants to be there". Sean Fitzpatrick, the New Zealand captain, had added: "If you've played in one play-off match, you don't want to play in another."

The third place match is essentially for losers. If the game in Rotorua in 1987 between Australia and Wales was tense and of high excitement, the play-off in 1991 was of indifferent quality. Sadly, the 1995 encounter fell into the latter category. England or France, accustomed as they rightly were to being top of the bill, were nowhere near their shoe-shuffling best.

After an hour's play, members of the press will have

"With a hint of daring so lacking overall, the winger ran once more from his own half, swaying in and out on the touchline to leave Dewi Morris, Rory Underwood and Mike Catt in his wake. Andrew's despairing tackle was not quite good enough to deny Emile Ntamack a brilliant score."

Dewi Morris can only watch as Ntamack brings some joie de vivre to Pretoria

looked at their writing pads and noted the less than enthralling legend that in the first half Thierry Lacroix and Rob Andrew had kicked a penalty each, which carried the latter's total to over 400 points in international rugby.

Ten minutes into the second half they repeated these manoeuvres, only for Lacroix to steal a march a few minutes later by kicking one more. It wasn't riveting watching.

> "So on Saturday, New Zealand and South Africa will play for the World Cup. Today, France and England play for the European Cup."
>
> PIERRE ALBALADEJO
> Former France fly half, on the harsh facts of the third place play-off

But then something happened! Striking a note for the beleaguered spectator, Ntamack ran from deep within his own 22 metres. He linked up with Laurent Cabannes. The flanker, who had had a great tournament and managed to shine even in splashing Durban, made the decisive drive in midfield. The scintillating movement ended with Philippe Saint-André being tackled into touch short of England's line. But the momentum was not entirely lost. From the ensuing lineout, Olivier Roumat drove over for the try

Christian Califano and Philippe Sella celebrate victory over the old foe, England

With so little firm possession, England did not look like scoring a try and it was left to Ntamack to have the final say. With a hint of daring so lacking overall, the winger ran once more from his own half, swaying in and out on the touchline to leave Dewi Morris, Rory Underwood and Mike Catt in his wake. Andrew's despairing tackle was not quite good enough to deny Ntamack a brilliant score.

The French winger had a special tournament. While he did not get on the score card in the early, easy rounds, he scored crucial tries against Scotland and Ireland and one to marvel at against England as well as creating the position for the first try in that match. He was tantalising to watch.

With both outside halves kicking three penalties, these two tries made the difference in the final scoreline of 19-9. Saint-André was happy to be on the winning side for the first time in six outings against England. He could now join his colleagues Philippe Sella and Franck Mesnel, who up to this moment had been the only players in the French squad to have enjoyed this experience.

· 3RD PLACE PLAY-OFF ·

FRANCE 19 ENGLAND 9
22 June • Pretoria
FRANCE: Sadourny; Ntamack, Sella, Lacroix, *Saint-André; Mesnel, Galthié; Benezech, Gonzalez, Califano, Merle, Roumat, Benazzi, Cigagna, Cabannes.
SCORERS: *Tries:* Roumat, Ntamack. *Pens:* Lacroix (3).
ENGLAND: Catt; Hunter, *Carling, Guscott, R Underwood; Andrew, Morris; Leonard, Moore, Ubogu, Johnson, Bayfield, Rodber, Ojomoh, Clarke.
SCORER: *Pens:* Andrew (3).
Referee: D J Bishop (New Zealand)

1995 THE · FINAL ·

"There has never been a match of this magnitude in this country. I wonder how long it will take before there is a match like it. The earliest we could expect to host it again would be around 2011, and even then we would have to reach the Final again."
SPRINGBOKS MANAGER MORNE DU PLESSIS

This was the moment when South Africa truly felt that they were back in the international rugby fold. They had spent the previous three years in many a skirmish as they emerged tentatively from their sporting isolation. With their laager mentality, South Africans still believed that their play was superior to anything that might exist beyond their boundaries. They grow up understanding their pre-eminence in the oval ball game but in the short time they had returned, they had found the world not quite as it was when they left.

In 1992, England had beaten them twice. In 1992 and 1993 France had won two of their four games, with a loss and a draw. Australia had won three of their last four outings in 1992 and 1993, and New Zealand between 1992 and 1994 had won three of their four games with, significantly, a draw in their final fixture which gave a hint that the Springboks might at last be stretching themselves out of the dormant state. This had been a hectic and punishing schedule to reacquaint themselves with international standards. It had been an intense course against the world's best rugby nations but it was a road they chose to travel with an unerring eye fixed on 1995.

This journey had not been without its casualties. After the New Zealand tour, coach Ian McIntosh was jettisoned. The new coach was Kitch Christie, who coached Transvaal and whose captain was François Pienaar. The partnership had less than 12 months to put things right. The visit to Scotland and Wales helped them along the way, but by the end of it Jannie Engelbrecht, the manager, was also to lose his role. Morne du Plessis became the manager.

Thus, in the footsteps of New Zealand in 1987 and England in 1991, the host nation had reached the Final of the World Cup. But this achievement would always mean more to South Africa. There were other, broader dimensions: nothing less than an oppressive and persecuting regime giving way to the hope of a more benevolent society honouring the dignity of all men. The grandeur of this vision was manifest on a balmy afternoon on a rugby pitch in a somewhat down-at-heel suburb in Johannesburg.

The significant difference was that whereas in the past the Springboks had stood for the white supremacists – a victory for the men wearing the gold and the green was a victory for apartheid – the Springboks of June 1995 came to represent reconciliation in a unified South Africa. The old national anthem of the Afrikaners, *Die Stem* ('The Voice'), and the new one which belonged to the rainbow nation, *Nkosi Sikelel'i Afrika* ('God Bless Africa'), had both been rung out wherever the Springboks played.

"I have a dream," intoned the Reverend Martin Luther King, in another country far away. "I have a dream." The sense of touching on that dream had grown during the weeks of the World Cup tournament and, finally, in Ellis Park, of that dream being given the substance of truth. We all wished that this was not an illusion inspired by the momentary, uplifting joy of a simple but great sporting festival. Would it really prove to be something more?

If South Africa had time to ponder who they would want as their opponents, they would unequivocally have called out the name of their historical rugby foe, New Zealand. Other nations have had their glorious golden afternoons in the sun but for most of this century, since

New Zealand scrum half Graeme Bachop clears up from a ruck

"We are not a one-man band, though people watching Jonah Lomu try to make us one. We are happy he has played as well as he has, but he is only one of 26. Other people make him a star."

BRIAN LOCHORE
New Zealand campaign manager, before the Final

battle was first joined in 1921 in Dunedin, the All Blacks and the Springboks have fought for world supremacy. The sheer will, drawn from some primitive source, to triumph against another, toe to toe, eyeball to eyeball, sometimes brutally, cannot find a parallel expression in sport outside a boxing ring.

Both New Zealand and South Africa kept their teams unchanged after the semi-finals. Joost van der Westhuizen, a stubbornly competitive scrum half who had an athlete's talent for running, had come off the field 51 minutes into the game in Durban because of a trapped nerve in his ribs. He was declared fit enough to play.

The game provided a stern and unbending contest which, while full of feverish excitement, fell short of being an epic encounter. It was magnificently emotive. And, ultimately, it gave us the gripping drama of a deliriously nail-biting climax. There were no tries but the match was no less vivid for that. That it failed to touch the pinnacle was the result of too many errors.

There was the contrasting style. South Africa had to hold their opponents in check, for they knew on the evidence already that, given a hint of daylight, Little, Osborne and Wilson, orchestrated by the precocious Mehrtens, would take to the open spaces. Kruger and Pienaar, giving a captain's performance, and Van der Westhuizen, acting as a fourth back-row forward, closed them down. Mulder in midfield was also a tower of strength. The Springboks' strategy was largely a defensive one for the attacking initiative belonged to the All Blacks.

Ian Jones in the lineout had, in the truest sense, a great game. Impressively and conspicuously he rose time and again in a salmon's leap to claim the ball as his own. With total control, as if suspended in the air, he gave Bachop and the rest a stream of fine possession. But try as they might,

"We just couldn't get the ball to him as often as we had planned."

SEAN FITZPATRICK
after the Final

· 1995 STATISTICS ·

INDIVIDUAL SCORING RECORDS

Most points in tournament
112 **Lacroix** (France)
104 **G Hastings** (Scotland)
84 **Mehrtens** (New Zealand)

Most tries in tournament
7 **Ellis** (New Zealand)
7 **Lomu** (New Zealand)

Most points in a match
45 **Culhane** (for New Zealand v Japan)
44 **G Hastings** (for Scotland v Ivory Coast)
31 **G Hastings** (for Scotland v Tonga
30 **Ellis** (for New Zealand v Japan)

Most tries in a match
6 **Ellis** (for New Zealand v Japan)
4 **G Hastings** (for Scotland v Ivory Coast)
4 **Lomu** (for New Zealand v England)
4 **Williams** (for South Africa v W Samoa)

"With energy wilting and bodies weakening in the unrelenting physical struggle, it was, more than ever, a trial of will. Who, when all else had been laid bare, had the real unyielding iron left in his soul? Mehrtens kicked a long penalty goal in the first period of extra time. The All Blacks were in the lead and time ticking away…"

New Zealand could not find the untrammelled rhythm of their previous matches. There was too much hurry to their game.

There was too much urgency, in particular, in wanting to get the ball to Jonah Lomu. There was to be no repetition of the mixture of power and flamboyance of the other games. Sure he was well-marked by his opposite number, James Small, but Lomu's colleagues kept shifting the ball his way, without too much thought or accuracy. Losing their flanker, Mike Brewer, at half-time did not help the New Zealand cause. There was a feeling that they had lost their way.

Meanwhile South Africa pursued a carefully structured, though limited, game using their power and force either side of their pack of forwards. Joel Stransky, at outside half, was the architect. Almost third choice before the tournament behind Brendan Venter and Hennie le Roux, Stransky very nearly did not help take part in the Cup at all. Yet he was always in charge, as he had shown from the beginning against Australia. He knew his team's strengths and played to them. He knew his team's limitations, and sheltered them. This is as it should be for an outside half, the team's fulcrum. The broad style was not theirs.

Stransky had kicked two penalty goals and a drop goal to give his side the lead at half-time against Mehrtens' two penalty goals. Halfway through the second period

Right: François Pienaar and Hennie Le Roux bring down All Black centre Walter Little

Mehrtens brought the scores equal with a drop goal. But, trying again, he failed with an easier chance – if ever a chance can be thought as such in a sporting cauldron – just before Ed Morrison blew his whistle for full time. How that moment with the score frozen eternally at 9-9 might come back to visit the 22-year-old outside half who himself had enjoyed such a brilliant time in South Africa.

With energy wilting and bodies weakening in the unrelenting physical struggle, it was, more than ever, a trial of will. Who, when all else had been laid bare, had the real unyielding iron left in his soul? Mehrtens kicked a long penalty goal in the first period of extra time. The All Blacks were in the lead and time ticking away... Feelings were

> "They are your boys, your pride."
>
> NELSON MANDELA
> at Ellis Park on South Africa's World Cup Final win

The moment the World Cup was won: Joel Stransky strikes a stunning drop goal to clinch South Africa's dream and start a celebration which went beyond the players to encompass an entire new nation

mixed. Was this what the neutral observer really wanted? That the team with the dashing rugby who had charmed us all along the way should win? Or should there be, on an occasion of such uniqueness, a more charitable outcome whose meaning would be interpreted beyond the sphere of mere sport?

Stransky levelled. For all the wit and endeavour, and the creeping tiredness, the defences remained as tight as they had been all windless afternoon. In this titanic struggle there was no give; no surrender. Neither line was breached, even if Kruger and du Randt thought they had; no try was scored.

With seven minutes left, Stransky from 30 metres and with Mehrtens close enough to charge down the ball, struck his second drop goal to win the 1995 World Cup, 15-12.

On a beautiful Transvaal day the match ended with the right score – even if justice was not done to New Zealand, who had performed, unlike an often ponderous South Africa, with exhilarating clarity throughout the tournament. This is quibbling. Sport is rarely about fairness. The moment exalted and blessed the Rugby World Cup 1995 as an iconic 20th-century moment. One team, one nation.

· THE FINAL ·

SOUTH AFRICA 15 NEW ZEALAND 12 (AFTER EXTRA TIME)
24 June • Johannesburg
SOUTH AFRICA: Joubert; Small (Venter 97), Mulder, H Le Roux, Williams; Stransky, Van der Westhuizen; Du Randt, Rossouw, Swart (Pagel 68), Weise, Strydom, *Pienaar, Andrews (Straeuli 90), Kruger.
SCORERS: *Pens:* Stransky (3). *DGs:* Stransky (2).
NEW ZEALAND: Osborne; Wilson (Ellis 55), Bunce, Little, Lomu; Mehrtens, Bachop; Dowd (Loe 83), *Fitzpatrick, Brown, Jones, R Brooke, Brewer (Joseph 40), Z Brooke (Larsen 64), Kronfeld.
SCORERS: *Pens:* Mehrtens (3). *DG:* Mehrtens.
Referee: Ed Morrison (England)
Attendance: 55,000

The drop goal that won the World Cup

THE 1995 WORLD CUP FINAL • SOUTH AFRICA v NEW ZEALAND

Before the tournament, Springboks fly half Joel Stransky wasn't even sure he would play a part in the World Cup. Little did he realise that, deep into extra time in the very last game, he would get the chance to win it for his country

BY JOEL STRANSKY

The whole of South Africa was excited about the World Cup and, with the tournament being held there, a lot was expected of us. We had tea with Nelson Mandela – he flew in to one of our training sessions in an air force helicopter, landed on the field and wished us all luck – and then we went to the welcome dinner before the World Cup. But it wasn't until I sat back a month after the World Cup and reflected on it all that I realised we had missed the opening ceremony, and the closing ceremony, and the jumbo jet flying over Ellis Park. We'd missed all the razzamatazz. Mind you, it was worth it.

Although I had played seven Tests in three years, I hadn't established myself in the team. But Kitch Christie selected me for a warm-up match against Western Province and I kicked a drop goal in injury time to win it for the South African XV. From then on in he tended to pick me – which was great.

We were in a tough pool with Australia, Canada and Romania, and we knew that if we lost to Australia in the first game we would probably have to face England and New Zealand on consecutive weekends to make it to the final. Whoever finished top of the pool definitely had an easier route. There was no second chance.

From January, when we sat down and looked at the whole thing, we trained for five months to beat Australia in that opening game. We led nearly all the way through the match and once we scored our second try it made it very difficult for Australia to come back. I scored the try, but that was the easy part. It came from a set move which we had used before and scored with every time. It was really tough to defend against, particularly with Joost van der Westhuizen at scrum half, because he's got so much gas off the mark and he gets wide and draws flankers to him. The forwards had a good scrum, Joost drew the defence and I went over almost unopposed. We beat them 27-18.

'We had a scrum on their 22, about 15 metres in. Joost van der Westhuizen fed the ball out to me and I went for the drop…'

It was great to win the first game in my home city. I owned a pub/restaurant in Cape Town, and after the match I went down there with my friends, my family and my partner – and about a million other people. It was so packed I couldn't get in. I had to go round the back and unlock the delivery gate. It was a great evening, but I just had two beers and then went back to the hotel. We were very disciplined.

I was on the bench for the victory against Romania, and then got injured in the 20-0 win over Canada – but not during the famous brawl. The mood of the game was not helped by the fact that the lights went out during the national anthems, giving us a frustrating 45-minute wait. I think all that tension boiled over. The Canadians are a very robust team – as are the South Africans when the going gets tough – and it did boil over in one or two nasty incidents which ended with three players sent off.

I got injured in a completely innocent moment. I took a big bang and had a scratch on my eye, so I missed the quarter-final against Western Samoa because I couldn't see anything. But while I was sitting that match out, Chester Williams came in on the wing and really made his mark. He hadn't been in the World Cup squad at all at first, because he had pulled a hamstring. Then when Pieter Hendriks was suspended after being cited by the Canadians, Chester was called in and scored four very good tries. It was a fantastic day for him.

On the day of the semi-final we were more worried about the weather than the French were, because we had had a player sent off and if the game didn't go ahead, we would have lost by default. Being the home team, I suppose we had a bit more knowledge of what was going on. We knew of the delays well in advance, so we just chilled out and waited for play to start.

The conditions were atrocious: wet, miserable, windy and rainy, and very difficult. I had played a lot of my rugby in Cape Town, so I was used to kicking in the wet there. King's Park is a very hard field and the water sits on top, so it was never really a mud bath. I think France lost that game by about four centimetres when Benazzi got held up just short of the try line. It was so close, I thought he had scored. It was a bit of a lottery and we were lucky to come through.

Before the Final Kitch Christie and Morne du Plessis took us to Sun City to get away from the hype with a bit of golf and prepare for the game. The one thing we really prided ourselves on was our defence. In any competition, the winners are usually the team with the best defensive record. Jonah Lomu had destroyed England the week before the Final, but we worked out a defence pattern that we thought could stop him, and fortunately it did.

Joel Stransky celebrates the greatest moment in his rugby career – "just absolute joy"

Maybe it's a shame there weren't any tries; we had one disallowed, but we weren't moaning about that. And then in extra time James Small put me through with a pass that was marginally forward – I probably over-ran it a little bit, James probably slowed down a little, and we were just lucky it didn't count at the death.

The game was won by a drop goal in extra time, and although we had never thought about the possibility of extra time, Kitch Christie had always said that the fittest team would win the World Cup, so we had trained extremely hard. He also had me working on drop goals, because he said it was the easiest form of points – and how right he was. I like to think that you only go for the drop goal when there's nothing else on. Having said that, I did get one in the first half, and Andrew Mehrtens scored one in the second half. He also had a drop goal chance two minutes from the end of normal time to win it, but he missed.

It was 9-9 at full-time, then 12-12 at half-time in extra time. With seven minutes to go, we had a scrum on their 22 about 15 metres in. François called a back row move, but I shouted "Cancel" to cancel the move. Joost shouted "Cancel" and fortunately Rudolph Straeuli, who had just come on at No 8, went with that call. Joost fed the ball out to me and I went for the drop and it went over. I was ecstatic. At that point in the game, any points would do.

When the final whistle went there was just absolute joy. There's no other way to describe it. We were so elated. We had worked so hard for such a long time, striving for the ultimate goal in rugby, and we had achieved it. As you go through your career you have many special moments and that was certainly one of mine. I remember standing under the podium watching François Pienaar receive the trophy from Nelson Mandela, and then taking it round the stadium with all our friends, family and supporters there. To do a lap of honour as world champions was fantastic.

Afterwards there was the official dinner, and then we all went out for a few drinks. That night François Pienaar and Gary Pagel and I got the bus to drop us and our wives at a really good night spot in Johannesburg called the Rattlesnake Diner. We had our sports bags with us, with our medals inside, but when we tried to get in it was so packed that we ended up standing outside on the stairs. People absolutely mobbed us, buying us drinks and congratulating us. We were stuck on the stairs for half an hour and eventually decided we would never get in, so we left. There was no chance of getting a taxi, so we actually hitched back to the hotel carrying our bags, medals and all!

PREVIEW

WELCOME TO WALES

Gerald Davies believes his fellow countrymen will host a very special World Cup, and their hopes of a host nation victory may be more than idle daydreams

"After six successive wins, there is, suddenly, a sense that this is no longer a false dawn for Wales. There is, suddenly, a wink of a chance."

The fourth Rugby World Cup kicks off on Friday, October 1, 1999 when Wales play Argentina at Cardiff Arms Park or, as the less imaginative are prone to call it without a modicum of vision or a hint of a soul, the Millennium Stadium. Faceless men enjoy their anonymity, I assume, and that of all they touch.

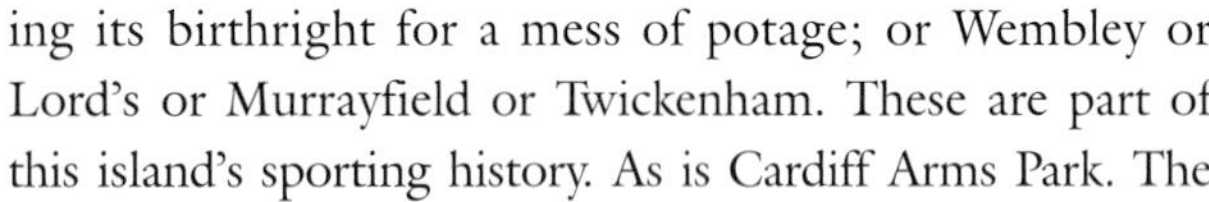

The stadium has cost more than £120 million. Half of this sum derives from the Millennium Fund and in consequence, it would appear, the funders have stipulated that their name should be attached to Cardiff's great sporting arena. Doffing their collective caps, the members of the Millennium Stadium plc acceded deferentially. With one servile nod, and blind to the great deeds of a glorious past, they were casting aside a century's inspiring tradition. We cannot imagine Wimbledon changing its name and sacrificing its birthright for a mess of potage; or Wembley or Lord's or Murrayfield or Twickenham. These are part of this island's sporting history. As is Cardiff Arms Park. The world recognises and immediately understands its eminence. It belongs to Wales and is rugby's grand theatre.

This small Celtic nation, as host, will embrace the world of rugby for five weeks. During that time, however, fixtures will be spread, as in England's tournament in 1991, throughout five European countries, culminating in the return to Cardiff for the Final on Saturday, November 6. There are 20 teams, not 16 as before. With four teams in each of five pools, and with quarter-final play-offs in addition, there will be 41 matches altogether, making the last tournament of the millennium the biggest so far. It is possible, too, because of the play-offs, that a team may win the competition having played seven fixtures instead of the customary six. For some the whole Rugby World Cup experience is new. Namibia, Spain and Uruguay make their first appearances. It would take a leap of the imagination to see any of those three going beyond the first round. But they, and we, are glad they are there. So to whom should we look as the tournament front runners ?

In each of the three competitions so far, the host nation has reached the Final. Only England in 1991 failed to lift the trophy. In each of those years, too, it is fair to say that the host nation was counted beforehand to be among the favourites, if not the first choice. With the tournament this time in Wales, can the same expectation apply? Until the remarkable turn of events over the last couple months of the 1998-99 season, it would have required a boyhood fantasy, nourished on an inexhaustible diet of the marvels of Roy of the Rovers, to imagine Wales among the tournament's high fliers. The comic-strip hero always managed against all the odds to pull the game out of the fire in the dying moments and so, in a reverie, win the match for Melchester Rovers. Dream on, Wales, the wilder, the better.

Since the early Eighties Welsh rugby has been, maddeningly, a tale of unceasing woe, an inexorable downward drift of playing failure and administrative incompetence. Players have come and gone, as, indeed, have the national coaches. Domestically, rugby has been in a state of disarray. This is epitomised by the panic which prevailed in the preparations for the last two World Cups. Only months before the 1991 competition Ron Waldron, the coach, resigned. Alan Davies replaced him and was meant to take Wales beyond the '95 tournament. Yet with barely weeks to go before the Welsh departed for South Africa, he was replaced by Alex Evans, an Australian who had rejuvenated the Cardiff club. He did not last long either, and a permanent coach, Kevin Bowring, was appointed.

By the end of the 1997-98 season, Bowring had also departed and a caretaker in the shape of Dennis John, the successful Pontypridd coach, was found. With Wales humiliated 96-3 by South Africa in the summer of 1998, a desperate situation needed a desperate action. By late autumn Graham Henry, a New Zealander from Auckland, was appointed coach, with a £1.25m five-year contract. There was less than a year to go before World Cup 1999.

In eight months, Henry has transformed Wales. On his first outing his team came close to beating South Africa, the world champions, at Wembley (Wales's home over the two years while the new stadium was built). They did beat Argentina at home and Italy away. In the Five Nations they lost to Scotland and Ireland, but overcame France in Paris and England. In June they returned from Argentina having won both Tests and the series, something no other team from these islands had done before. It was Wales's first overseas series success.

As if this was not enough, on June 26, in the first game in the new stadium, the Welsh beat South Africa for the first time in 93 years of trying. Thus Wales, under Henry, had achieved six consecutive victories. There is, suddenly, a sense that this is no longer a false dawn. There is, suddenly, a wink of a chance. Wales can look forward to the World Cup with, if not confidence, at least with a generous heart and a belief that they are capable of springing a surprise.

Yet, whatever else Europe might thrust to the forefront, it is the three countries of the southern hemisphere against

Wales on fire in 1999 – Chris Wyatt and Ben Evans celebrate a Five Nations win over England while, left, try-scorer Mark Taylor runs through the Springboks' front row during the historic victory that opened the new Cardiff Arms Park, opposite

"The World Cup in South Africa was incredible – the atmosphere, all the stadiums – and I am a little sad that the 1999 World Cup is split between several countries. One day I hope France will organise the World Cup on its own."

PHILIPPE SAINT-ANDRÉ
Captain of France in the 1995 World Cup

whom everyone entering the tournament will wish to be measured. Consistently New Zealand, South Africa and, lately, Australia set the standards in a way that the five major countries in the northern hemisphere fail to do.

The Springboks, since the advent of Nick Mallett as their national coach, have returned to world prominence in a way they had not quite managed in 1995, despite winning the Cup. They were not convincing then and, in consequence, in pure rugby terms, were overshadowed by New Zealand's more stirring accomplishments.

Suited and booted – New Zealand's metronomic Andrew Merhtens, South Africa's powerful Percy Montgomery and England wonder boy Jonny Wilkinson

Mallett changed that. For a period, he made them into an unbeatable force. From August 1997, when they defeated Australia 61-22 in Pretoria, to November 1998, when they beat Ireland 27-13 in Dublin, the Springboks, under the captaincy of No 8 Gary Teichmann, won 17 successive internationals, equalling the record set by the All Blacks between 1965 and 1969. They did so playing brilliantly inventive rugby, but the question remains whether they peaked too soon. There were signs, in losing to Wales (29-19) and to New Zealand (28-0) in a dreadful start to the Tri-Nations, that their armour was not without its flaws, and Teichmann suffered the axe. The loss by a record score against their historical rivals, the All Blacks, was particularly difficult to swallow. Their inherent toughness and deep-rooted pride will ensure they emerge renewed for the autumn's challenge. But there has been discord among the players: between those from the coast and those from the high veldt, as well as the pressure to choose teams which acknowledge a level of political correctness. There is only a short time left to restore the Springbok prestige and injuries have contrived to compound their difficulties, with new skipper Joost van der Westhuizen and Bobby Skinstad returning less than two months before the Cup.

New Zealand have gone a different route. In 1997 under the shrewd John Hart, they travelled the globe and won all their 11 fixtures until the 26-26 draw with England at Twickenham in November. Since Hart took over they had lost only one of 22 matches, against South

Africa (22-32) in Johannesburg in August 1996. They twice won the Tri-Nations with clean sweeps, but forfeited everything in '98. For the first time in their long and distinguished history the All Blacks lost five games in succession.

Yet nothing can be more dangerous than a wounded All Black. They had a year to regroup. Despite their setback they still had wonderful players such as Jeff Wilson and captain Taine Randell, and before the summer was out, the All Blacks had reinstated themselves as World Cup favourites with a powerful Tri-Nations display.

The third of the southern hemisphere countries, Australia, whose centenary year this is, are, like the other two nations, imbued with that sharpened steel of which champions are made. Nowadays they have the consistency, too. They may have enjoyed 100 years of rugby in Australia but their success at the game is only a recent phenomenon. Their coming of age was signalled when they first won the Grand Slam on their 1984 tour of Britain and Ireland.

If their scrummage is an area about which coach Rod Macqueen is worried, there is vast skill among their backs. In wings Joe Roff and Ben Tune they have a pair of classic finishers, while John Eales at lock and Tim Horan at centre – and latterly fly half – and George Gregan at scrum half are players with immense experience. Stephen Larkham and Matt Burke can create and finish.

What marks these three teams from the rest is their bottomless will to win and competitive confidence. There is no soft underbelly.

Neither the consistency nor the same confidence which we readily identify with the teams from below the equator can be said to belong to the European nations. Scotland, England and Ireland will face the might of South Africa, New Zealand and Australia in Pools A, B and E respectively. They need to win their groups to avoid the extra quarter-final play-off fixture, and the home advantage each country will enjoy is the spur they need to upset the odds. However, nothing in the pre-tournament build-up suggests that the form book can be ripped up. England and Ireland failed in Australia in the summer. Scotland had mixed fortunes in their games against the provinces in South Africa. France lost 54-7 to New Zealand, though, of all the teams, France have what might be thought of as the easiest route to the last eight.

Elevation to a higher level – Carlo Caione and Italy hope to prove their worth before joining the 2000 Six Nations

England find themselves in a condition not dissimilar to that which they have experienced in both the last two tournaments. They have a formidable pack of forwards in which Darren Garforth, Richard Cockerill and Jason Leonard will form the cornerstone of their scrum. It is doubtful whether any other nation will have a better pair of locks than Martin Johnson and Tim Rodber. As ever they will have a muscular back row, whoever they choose. Their defence will be comprehensive in its cover.

All this we, and they, know. But niggling at the back of their minds is their bogey of a question: have they got more than this? Matt Perry is a fine attacker, Dan Luger a powerful runner, Jonny Wilkinson a young talent ready to be unleashed. Jeremy Guscott remains a subtly deadly presence. But will we get to see them? Will they be seen, collectively, as a primary attacking force?

The threequarter line is not as yet in the same league as the one which Will Carling and Rob Andrew controlled. In the seasons leading up to the 1999 World Cup we can hardly be said to be familiar with England's back division in an attacking capacity apart from the hints they gave in their match against Wales last season. Given the chances in

Opposite: Sixteen men who may star in 1999 – clockwise from top left: Taine Randell (New Zealand); Keith Wood (Ireland); Dan Luger (England); Jeff Wilson (New Zealand) and Rob Howley (Wales); John Graf (Canada); Jeremy Guscott (England); Federico Mendez (Argentina); Gragos Niculae (Romania); Thomas Castaignède (France); Jason Little (Australia); Neil Jenkins (Wales); Keiji Hirose (Japan); Eric Elwood (Ireland); Jose Ignacio Zaperterq (Spain); Pat Lam (Western Samoa)

that game, they failed to capitalise. Instead of winning the Grand Slam, they stumbled at the final hurdle and allowed in Scotland for the title. Will England be thought of, as in previous years, as potential unrealised?

That Scotland, very much the unfancied team at the start of the 1999 Five Nations, should clinch the championship indicates not only their resilience but their bottomless capacity to surprise us with their swank and verve. Their success against France in 1999 was dashing and brave. In fact, a glittering display of positive running rugby. With Ian McGeechan back in harness with Jim Telfer and John Rutherford, Scotland will prove a handful to any nation. In each of the previous World Cups, Scotland have enjoyed a style of play which seemed beyond their means before the competition began. For this they have achieved a certain popularity, too.

Studying Ireland's progress in Pool E will be interesting. Recent form is hardly an issue – they have been bottom of the championship for three of the last four seasons. History has far more bearing. The critical fixture will be against Australia. Memories of Dublin 1991, and Australia's daring late push to take the cup of celebration from Irish lips, will come flooding back. If the avenging angels preside, Ireland might come top of the pool. This could give them a game against Wales in the quarter-finals in Cardiff, where they have not lost since 1983.

But suppose Ireland were runner-ups in their pool, which includes Romania and the USA. They could come up against Western Samoa in Lens in the quarter-final play-offs. Success there would mean they would return to Dublin to face probably France in the quarter-finals. With such a draw it is not inconceivable to see Ireland making the semi-finals. All is supposition. Interesting, nonetheless.

At any rate, the competition, we must hope, will not be as predictable as any of the form might suggest. As in 1991, when Western Samoa changed people's preconceptions, so we must wish in 1999 – for the general development of rugby, as well as to wake us from our complacency – that Canada and the USA, for instance, will find the extra ingredient to make their mark. Or that Fiji and Tonga will fulfil that which they have so long promised. And isn't it about time Italy and Romania started questioning the old order in Europe? And that the enthusiasm and dedication of Argentina and Japan should be rewarded? Rugby, even if this tournament is only the fourth, needs to break the mould.

> "We must hope Canada and the USA will find the extra ingredient to make their mark, or that Fiji and Tonga will fulfil that which they have so long promised. And isn't it about time that Italy and Romania started questioning the old order in Europe, or that the enthusiasm and dedication of Argentina and Japan should be rewarded? Rugby, even if this tournament is only the fourth, needs to break the mould."

As we contemplate the great rugby jamboree that lies ahead, I recall words from a book written a long time ago, *Report on Rugby* (Heinemann), by two men I came to know well, the late Geoffrey Nicholson and John Morgan, the latter a near neighbour who became, in his word, a "chum" whose judgments I valued.

"It really is astonishing," they wrote, "how complex the apparently simple can grow. A game starts with young men wanting exercise, excited by competitive spirit, and kicking a ball around for fun; and in no time at all a vast structure is erected. Stadiums must be built, an intricate administrative organisation created and, around the art of kicking and running the ball, recondite strategies plotted. And because the young men are human and grow old, inevitable feelings of nostalgia attach themselves. Not just pleasure at the time, or disappointment, but the remembrance of games past. The romantic spirit burns steadily about the game."

And so it is that I look back at my good fortune of having been in New Zealand at the birth of a new-fangled idea – a structure erected – called the Rugby World Cup. I was there, too, when the carnival happily moved on for the next two tournaments. It is with joy and unparalleled pride that I look forward to the World Cup coming to Wales, where I hope, with a passion, that "the romantic spirit will burn steadily about the game".

CROESO I GYMRU. YMLAEN CWPAN Y BYD.

Cellnet
Cellnet

· OVERALL STATISTICS ·

World Cup winning captains

David Kirk: New Zealand 1987
Nick Farr-Jones: Australia 1991
François Pienaar: South Africa 1995

Fastest try:

1 min: Zinzan Brooke for New Zealand v Italy at Leicester

Biggest scores in Rugby World Cup Finals

145 New Zealand v Japan 145-17 (1995)
89 Scotland v Ivory Coast 89-0 (1995)
74 New Zealand v Fiji 74-13 (1987)
70 New Zealand v Italy 70-6 (1987)
France v Zimbabwe 70-12 (1987)

Leading scorers in the Finals

126 Grant Fox (New Zealand) 1987
112 Thierry Lacroix (France) 1995
104 Gavin Hastings (Scotland) 1995
84 Andrew Mehrtens (New Zealand) 1995
82 Michael Lynagh (Australia) 1987

Overall leading scorers

227 Gavin Hastings (Scotland) 1995/1991/1987
195 Michael Lynagh (Australia) 1995/1991/1987
170 Grant Fox (New Zealand) 1991/1987
124 Thierry Lacroix (France) 1995/1991
99 Jonathan Webb (England) 1991/1987
85 Didier Cambérabéro (France) 1991/1987
Rob Andrew (England) 1995/1991
84 Andrew Mehrtens (New Zealand) 1995
71 Gareth Rees (Canada) 1995/1991/1987
68 Ralph Keyes (Ireland) 1991
Diego Dominguez (Italy) 1995/1991

Gavin Hastings, the top World Cup scorer

Individual appearances

17 Sean Fitzpatrick (New Zealand)
15 David Campese (Australia)
Michael Lynagh (Australia)
Rory Underwood (England)
14 Brian Moore (England)
Philippe Sella (France)
13 Gavin Hastings (Scotland)
Rob Andrew (England)
12 Gary Whetton (New Zealand)

Leading try scorers in finals

11 Rory Underwood (England) 1995/1991/1987
10 David Campese (Australia) 1991/1987
9 Gavin Hastings (Scotland) 1995/1991/1987
7 Iwan Tukalo (Scotland) 1991/1987
Jonah Lomu (New Zealand) 1995
Marc Ellis (New zealand) 1995
Ieuan Evans (Wales) 1995/1991/1987
6 Jean-Baptiste Lafond (France) 1991
Craig Green (New Zealand) 1987
John Jeffrey (Scotland) 1991/1987

Leading penalty kickers

36 Gavin Hastings (Scotland) 1995/1991/1987
33 Michael Lynagh (Australia) 1995/1991/1987
31 Grant Fox (New Zealand) 1991/1987
30 Thierry Lacroix (France) 1995/1991
21 Jonathan Webb (England) 1991/1987
17 Gareth Rees (Canada) 1995/1991/1987
16 Ralph Keyes (Ireland) 1991
14 Andrew Mehrtens (New Zealand) 1995
13 Diego Dominguez (Italy) 1995/1991
Joel Stransky (South Africa) 1995

Biggest scores in Rugby World Cup qualifying

164 Hong Kong v Singapore 164-13 (1995)
134 Japan v Chinese Taipei 134-6 (1998)
110 England v Netherlands 110-0 (1998)
104 Italy v Czech Republic 104-8 (1995)
102 Italy v Denmark 102-3 (1999)
Wales v Portugal 102-11 (1995)
97 Japan v Malaysia 97-9 (1995)
93 Hong Kong v Thailand 93-0 (1995)
92 Papua New Guinea v Tahiti 92-6 (1999)
90 Korea v Singapore 90-3 (1995)
89 Latvia v Bulgaria 89-0 (1999)
85 Scotland v Spain 85-3 (1998)
Scotland v Portugal 85-11 (1998)
84 Sweden v Latvia 84-17 (1999)
83 Romania v Belgium 83-13 (1997)
82 Tonga v Korea 82-15 (1999)
81 Korea v Chinese Taipei 81-21 (1998)
80 Hong Kong v Chinese Taipei 80-26 (1995)
78 Korea v Netherlands 78-14 (1999)
74 Australia v Tonga 74-0 (1999)
Western Samoa v Korea 74-7 (1991)
Romania v Poland 74-13 (1998)
70 Argentina v Chile 70-7 (1995)

Most tries in a match

(Q for qualifying)

26 Hong Kong v Singapore (Q, 1994)
21 New Zealand v Japan (1995)
20 Japan v Chinese Taipei (Q, 1998)
16 Italy v Czech Republic (Q, 1994)
Papua New Guinea v Tahiti (Q,1997)
Wales v Portugal (Q, 1994)
England v Netherlands (Q, 1998)
15 Western Samoa v Korea (Q, 1998)
Japan v Malaysia (Q, 1994)

Most points in a match by a player

(Q for qualifying)

50 Ashley Billington (10 tries)
for Hong Kong v Singapore (Q, 1995)
45 Simon Culhane (1 try, 20 cons)
for New Zealand v Japan (1995)
44 Gavin Hastings (4 tries, 9 cons, 2 pens) for Scotland v Ivory Coast (1995)
34 Jamie McKee (17 cons)
for Hong Kong v Singapore (Q, 1995)
31 Gavin Hastings (1 try, 1 con, 9 pens)
for Scotland v Tonga (1995)
30 Marc Ellis (6 tries)
for New Zealand v Japan (1995)
Didier Cambérabéro (3 tries, 9 cons)
for France v Zimbabwe (1987)
Pierpaolo Rotillo (6 tries)
for Italy v Denmark (Q, 1999)
Paul Grayson (15 cons)
for England v Netherlands (Q, 1998)
Jaco Coetzee (3 tries, 6 cons, 1 pen)
for Namibia v Kenya (Q, 1993)

STATISTICS BY COUNTRY

Statistics by country of all teams that have participated in the finals

Argentina

Best: Pool stages 1987, 1991, 1995.
Best win: 25-16 v Italy (1987)
Worst defeat: 15-46 New Zealand (1987)

All-time record

	P	*W*	*D*	*L*	*F*	*A*
	9	1	0	8	156	260
1995	3	0	0	3	69	87
1991	3	0	0	3	38	83
1987	3	1	0	2	49	90

Qualifying Rounds:
Best win: 70-7 v Chile (1995)
Worst defeat: 9-15 v Canada

Australia

Best: Winners 1991
Best win: 47-12 v USA (1987)
Worst defeat: 24-30 v France (1987)

All-time record

	P	*W*	*D*	*L*	*F*	*A*
	16	12	0	4	421	229
1995	4	2	0	2	109	66
1991	6	6	0	0	126	55
1987	6	4	0	2	186	108

Qualifying Rounds – 1999 only:
Best win: 74-0 v Tonga (1999)

Canada

Best: Quarter-finals 1991
Best win: 37-4 v Tonga (1987)
Worst defeat: 19-46 v Ireland (1987)

All-time record

	P	*W*	*D*	*L*	*F*	*A*
	10	4	0	6	168	202
1995	3	1	0	2	45	50
1991	4	2	0	2	58	62
1987	3	1	0	2	65	90

Qualifying Rounds:
Best win: 38-15 v Uruguay (1999)
Worst defeat: 28-54 v Argentina (1999)

Ivory Coast

Best: Pool stage 1995
Best win: None.
Worst defeat: 0-89 v Scotland (1995)

All-time record

	P	*W*	*D*	*L*	*F*	*A*
	3	0	0	3	29	172
1995	3	0	0	3	29	172

Qualifying Rounds:
Best win: 17-10 v Zimbabwe (1995)
Worst defeat: 0-32 v Zimbabwe (1999)

England

Best: Losing finalists 1991
Best win: 60-7 v Japan (1987)
Worst defeat: 29-45 v New Zealand (1995)

All-time record

	P	*W*	*D*	*L*	*F*	*A*
	16	10	0	6	384	254
1995	6	4	0	2	162	146
1991	6	4	0	2	119	61
1987	4	2	0	2	103	48

Qualifying Rounds – 1999 only:
Best win: 110-0 Netherlands (1998)

Fiji

Best: Quarter final 1987
Best win: 28-9 v Argentina (1987)
Worst defeat: 13-74 v New Zealand (1987)

All-time record

	P	*W*	*D*	*L*	*F*	*A*
	7	1	0	6	99	195
1991	3	0	0	3	27	63
1987	4	1	0	3	72	132

Qualifying Rounds:
Best win: 53-7 v Cook Islands (1999)
Worst defeat: 20-66 v Australia (1999)

France

Best: Losing finalists 1987
Best win: 70-12 v Zimbabwe (1987)
Worst defeat: 9-29 v New Zealand (1987)

All-time record

	P	*W*	*D*	*L*	*F*	*A*
	16	12	1	3	491	244
1995	6	5	0	1	184	87
1991	4	3	0	1	92	44
1987	6	4	1	1	215	110

Ireland

Best: Quarter-finals 1987, 1991, 1995
Best win: 55-11 v Zimbabwe (1991)
Worst defeat: 12-32 v France (1995)

All-time record

	P	*W*	*D*	*L*	*F*	*A*
	12	6	0	6	324	274
1995	4	2	0	2	105	130
1991	4	2	0	2	120	70
1987	4	2	0	2	99	74

Qualifying Rounds – 1999 only:
Best win: 70-0 v Georgia (1998)

Italy

Best: Pool stages 1987, 1991, 1995
Best win: 30-9 v USA (1991)
Worst defeat: 6-70 v New Zealand (1987)

All-time record

	P	*W*	*D*	*L*	*F*	*A*
	9	3	0	6	166	280
1995	3	1	0	2	69	94
1991	3	1	0	2	57	76
1987	3	1	0	2	40	110

Qualifying Rounds:
Best win: 104-8 v Czech Republic (1995)
Worst defeat: 19-29 v Wales (1995)

Japan

Best: Pool stages 1987, 1991, 1995
Best win: 52-8 v Zimbabwe (1991)
Worst defeat: 17-145 v New Zealand (1995)

All-time record

	P	*W*	*D*	*L*	*F*	*A*
	9	1	0	8	177	462
1995	3	0	0	3	55	252
1991	3	1	0	2	77	87
1987	3	0	0	3	48	123

Qualifying Rounds:
Best win: 134-6 v Chinese Taipei (1998)
Worst defeat: 11-37 v Western Samoa (1991)

Namibia

Debut in World Cup Finals

All-time record
Qualifying Rounds:
Best win: 64-20 v Arabian Gulf (1995)
Worst defeat: 17-20 v Tunisia (1999)

New Zealand

Best: Winners 1987
Best win: 145 -17v Japan (1995)
Worst defeat: 6-16 v Australia (1991)

All-time record

	P	*W*	*D*	*L*	*F*	*A*
	18	16	0	2	768	245
1995	6	5	0	1	327	119
1991	6	5	0	1	143	74
1987	6	6	0	0	298	52

Romania

Best: Pool stages 1987, 1991, 1995
Best win: 21-20 v Zimbabwe (1987)
Worst defeat: 12-55 v France (1987)

All-time record

	P	*W*	*D*	*L*	*F*	*A*
	9	1	0	8	106	264
1995	3	0	0	3	14	97
1995	3	0	0	3	31	64
1987	3	1	0	2	61	103

Qualifying Rounds:
Best win: 83-13 v Belgium (1999)
Worst defeat: 35-53 v Ireland (1998)

Scotland

Best: Semi-final 1991
Best win: 89-0 v Cote d'Ivoire (1995)
Worst defeat: 30-48 v New Zealand (1995)

All-time record

	P	W	D	L	F	A
	14	8	1	5	479	338
1995	4	2	0	2	179	75
1991	6	4	0	2	162	64
1987	4	2	1	1	138	99

Qualifying Rounds – 1999 only:
Best win: 85-3 v Spain (1998)

South Africa

Best: winners 1995
Best win: 42-14 v Western Samoa (1995)
Worst defeat: unbeaten

All-time record 1995 only
(barred from previous tournaments over apartheid)

	P	W	D	L	F	A
1995	6	6	0	0	144	67

Joel Stransky – 13 penalty kicks in 1995

Spain

Debut in World Cup Finals

All-time record
Qualifying Rounds:
Best win: 67-3 v Belgium (1995)
Worst defeat: 3-85 v Scotland (1999)

Tonga

Best: Pool stages 1991, 1995.
Best win: 29-11 v Cote d'Ivoire (1995)
Worst defeat: 5-41 v Scotland (1995)

All-time record

	P	W	D	L	F	A
	6	1	0	5	73	188
1995	3	1	0	2	44	90
1987	3	0	0	3	29	98

Qualifying Rounds:
Best win:82-15 v Korea (1999)
Worst defeat: 0-74 v Australia (1999)

Uruguay

Best: Debut in World Cup finals

All-time record
Qualifying Rounds:
Best win: 67-3 v Paraguay (1995)
Worst defeat: 0-55 v Argentina (1999)

USA

Best: Pools stages 1987, 1991
Best win: 21-18 v Japan (1987)
Worst defeat: 12-47 v Australia (1987)

All-time record

	P	W	D	L	F	A
	6	1	0	5	63	212
1991	3	0	0	3	24	113
1987	3	1	0	2	39	99

Qualifying Rounds:
Best win: 60-3 v Bermuda (1995)
Worst defeat: 24-52 v Argentina (1999)

Wales

Best: Semi-final 1987
Best win: 57-10 v Japan (1995)
Worst defeat: 6-49 v New Zealand (1987)

All-time record

	P	W	D	L	F	A
	12	7	0	5	244	236
1995	3	1	0	2	89	68
1991	3	1	0	2	32	64
1987	6	5	0	1	126	104

Qualifying Rounds – 1995 only:
Best win: 102-11 v Portugal (1995)
Worst defeat: none

Western Samoa

Best: Quarter-final 1991, 1995
Best win: 42-18 v Italy (1995)
Worst defeat: 14-42 v South Africa (1995)

All-time record

	P	W	D	L	F	A
	8	4	0	4	170	192
1995	4	2	0	2	110	130
1991	4	2	0	2	60	62

Qualifying Rounds:
Best win: 74-7 v South Korea (1991)
Worst defeat: 13-25 v Australia (1999)

Zimbabwe

Best: Pool stage 1991
Best win: none
Worst defeat: 12-70 v France (1987)

All-time record

	P	W	D	L	F	A
	6	0	0	0	84	309
1991	3	0	0	0	31	158
1987	3	0	0	0	53	151

Qualifying Rounds:
Best win: 43-9 v Tunisia (1999)
Worst defeat: 14-39 v Namibia (1999)

- Photographic Acknowledgements -

All photographs except where specified below are by Allsport.
Many thanks to Justin Davies and Neil Loft
for their tireless work in supplying these cracking images

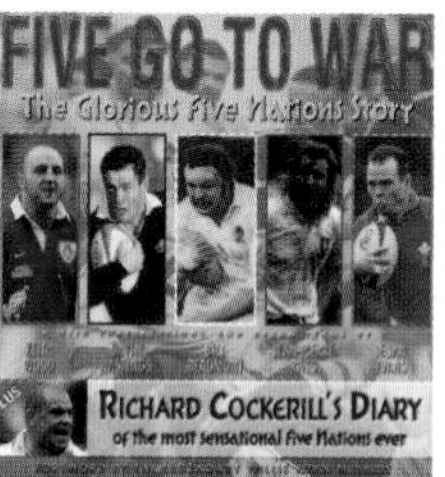